D0908593

BRIDGES TO
LITERATURE

McDougal Littell

Evanston, Illinois • Boston • Dallas

READING • FLUENCY • LITERATURE • VOCABULARY

Author

Jane Greene Literacy Intervention Specialist; Reading, Writing, Language, Evaluation Consultant to schools nationwide; author of *LANGUAGE! A Literacy Intervention Curriculum.* Dr. Greene established the underlying goals and philosophy, advised on the tables of contents, reviewed prototypes, and supervised the development of the assessment strand.

English Language Advisor

Judy Lewis Director, State and Federal Programs for reading proficiency and high-risk populations, Folsom, California; Editor, *Context,* a newsletter for teachers with English learners in their classes. Ms. Lewis reviewed selections for the program and provided special guidance on the development of EL notes.

Consultant

Olga Bautista Reading Facilitator, Will C. Wood Middle School, Sacramento, California. Ms. Bautista provided advice on reading, pacing, and EL instruction during the development phase and reviewed final prototypes of both the Pupil Edition and Teacher's Edition.

ISBN 13: 978-0-618-90583-6   ISBN 10: 0-618-90583-9

Printed in the United States of America.

10 11 12 13 14 15 0914 20 19 18 17 16 15 14 13
4500417586

Teacher Panel

Katherine S. Barg, Teacher
Central Middle School
San Carlos, California

Annie Muchnick, Literacy Coach
Garvey School
Rosemead, California

Claudette Burk, English Department Chairperson
Tetzlaff Middle School
Cerritus, California

Joanne Nash, English Teacher
Sunnyvale Middle School
Sunnyvale, California

Susan Busenius, Core Teacher
Valley View School
Pleasanthill, California

Patricia Radotich, Teacher
Woodbridge Middle School
Woodbridge, California

Deborah Dei Rossi, Teacher
Cunha Intermediate School
Half Moon Bay, California

Frances Rubin, English Teacher
Emerson Middle School
Los Angeles, California

Lana Fenech, Teacher, Technology Coordinator,
Borel Middle School
San Mateo, California

Sue Sermeno, Grade Level Coordinator
North Park Middle School
Pico Rivera, California

Joy Martineau, Language Arts Teacher
Warner Middle School
Westminster, California

Margaret Williams, English Language Arts
   Chairperson
Carmenita Middle School
Cerritus, California

Teacher Reviewers

Lillie Alfred, Teacher
Altgeld School
Chicago, Illinois

Stephanie Gates, Teacher
Miriam G. Canter Middle School
Chicago, Illinois

Tracy Arrington, Teacher
George W. Curtis School
Chicago, Illinois

Regina Gooden-Hampton, Teacher
Kipling Elementary School
Chicago, Illinois

Student Reviewers

Aunyetta Crosby, Detroit, Michigan

Phimy Danh, Long Beach, California

Julie Daniels, Sacramento, California

Maria Fraga, Sacramento, California

Eduardo Obeso, Detroit, Michigan

Erik Quirk, Encinitas, California

Michael Roett, Tallahassee, Florida

Michelle Schmitt, Tallahassee, Florida

Barbara Schwenk, Weston, Massachusetts

Renee Sevier, Long Beach, California

Shane, Lincoln, Massachusetts

BRIDGES TO
LITERATURE

Level I

12 Reader's Choice LONGER SELECTIONS FOR INDEPENDENT READING

Student Resources

 Some selections available on the Reading Coach CD-ROM

We All Make Mistakes

Fiction

A story that is made up is **fiction.** Short stories, novels, and myths are examples of fiction.

Some stories seem real. The characters act like real people and have problems like real people. In other stories, the characters are talking animals or people with unusual powers. All fiction has these four things:

- **Characters:** the people or animals in the story
- **Plot:** what happens in the story
- **Setting:** where and when the story happens
- **Theme:** the writer's message about life or human nature

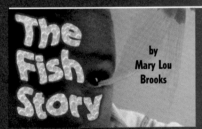

MIDAS
AND THE
GOLDEN TOUCH

retold by Tana Reiff

Will one wish solve all of your problems? Or will it create more problems?

Reading Coach
CD-ROM selection

Connect to Your Life

Have you ever wanted something badly? What happened when you finally got it? Was it all that you hoped it would be, or were you disappointed?

Key to the Myth

A **myth** is a story about how things work or how something came to be. It often teaches a lesson about life. Myths have been told for hundreds of years. "Midas and the Golden Touch" is a Greek myth. Greek myths often tell about characters who are greedy or disobedient. Because of their actions, bad things happen to them.

Midas was a greedy man who happened to be a king. He ruled over the Land of the Roses. It was called that because so many roses grew there.

One day, King Midas found a man under a rose bush. "Where did you come from?" Midas asked the man.

"I was at a party with Bacchus, the god of wine," answered the man. "I must be lost."

King Midas led the man inside. He took care of him for 10 days. Then he sent him back to Bacchus.

10 The wine god was always happy to get people back. "Thank you!" he told Midas. "For your trouble, you may make a wish. Wish for anything you want!"

"I want everything I touch to turn to gold," King Midas said.

"It shall be done!" said Bacchus.

King Midas couldn't believe his good luck. How wonderful! All he had to do was touch something and it would turn to gold! Midas looked forward to 20 becoming very rich.

REREAD
Do you think Midas will be happy?

He sat down to eat his dinner. He picked up his fork. As soon as his fingers touched it, it turned to gold. "Who needs silver forks when I can have gold?" Midas laughed.

Then he picked up a piece of bread. It, too, turned to gold. Midas started to put the bread in his mouth. But it was gold. He couldn't eat gold!

He picked up his glass to take a drink. The glass turned to gold. And as soon as the water touched his 30 mouth, it also turned to gold.

"Daughter! Daughter!" he called to his dear child. "Help me! Everything I touch turns to gold!"

He reached out to the young girl. Sure enough, she turned to gold. She froze in place. She couldn't move. It was as if she were dead.

"Oh, dear!" cried Midas. "Now I've really done it." He looked up to the sky. "Please, oh please, Bacchus! Take my wish away! I am hungry and thirsty! I have lost my daughter! I don't want 40 everything to turn to gold!"

THINK IT THROUGH
What is the problem with the wish?

Bacchus heard Midas crying. "Go down to the river," said Bacchus. "Wash yourself in the clear water. Your wish will wash away. Then pour the water of the river on your daughter. You will have her back."

Midas did as Bacchus told him. When he touched the grass by the river, it did not turn to gold. It stayed as green as grass should be. The terrible wish was gone! But for years after, people found gold along the river where Midas had washed.

THINK IT THROUGH

1. How does Midas solve his problem?
2. The **theme** of a story is its message or lesson about life. What is the theme of this story?
3. Why is this story still meaningful today?

THE GREEN RIBBON

retold by Alvin Schwartz

COULD A GREEN RIBBON BE THE MOST IMPORTANT THING IN YOUR LIFE? MEET ONE PERSON WHO THINKS IT IS.

Connect to Your Life

Have you ever been sorry that you asked someone a question? Was the answer to the question something you would rather not have known?

Key to the Folk Tale

"The Green Ribbon" is a folk tale. A **folk tale** is a short story that is told for fun. You may have heard this folk tale at camp. It is often told to campers as they sit around a campfire. Sometimes the person who tells the story changes the setting or the characters. As you read, decide how you might tell this story to someone else.

 Reading Coach CD-ROM selection

Once there was a girl named Jenny. She was like all the other girls, except for one thing. She always wore a green ribbon around her neck.

There was a boy named Alfred in her class. Alfred liked Jenny, and Jenny liked Alfred.

One day he asked her, "Why do you wear that ribbon all the time?"

"I cannot tell you," said Jenny.

But Alfred kept asking, "Why *do* you

10 wear it?"

And Jenny would say, "It is not important."

REREAD
Do you think the reason is important?

THINK IT THROUGH
What is different about Jenny?

Jenny and Alfred grew up and fell in love. One day they got married.

After their wedding, Alfred said, "Now that we are married, you must tell me about the green ribbon."

"You still must wait," said Jenny. "I will tell you when the right time comes."

Years passed. Alfred and Jenny grew old. One day

20 Jenny became very sick.

The doctor told her she was dying. Jenny called Alfred to her side. "Alfred," she said, "now I can tell you about the green ribbon. Untie it, and you will see why I could not tell you before." Slowly and carefully, Alfred untied the ribbon, and Jenny's head fell off.

1. Did the ending surprise you? Why or why not?
2. Do you think Jenny should have told her husband the truth? Why or why not?
3. What do you think of this story?

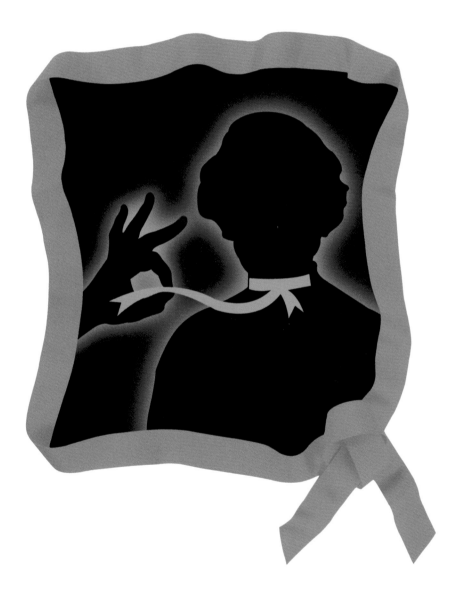

The Fish Story

by Mary Lou Brooks

How can you mess up a job you haven't started yet?

Connect to Your Life

Have you ever had a job that you messed up? What happened? What lesson did you learn?

Key to the Short Story

"The Fish Story" is an example of **realistic fiction.** The story is made up. But the characters act like real people. They have problems just like real people in modern life.

Often a story has a problem that a character has to solve. This problem is called the **conflict.** As you read "The Fish Story," pay attention to the conflict and what the character does about it.

Vocabulary Preview

Words to Know

unemployed	dreading
glared	responsible

 Reading Coach CD-ROM selection

I know what I'm going to be when I grow up—unemployed. "Face it, Ernie," my dad always says. "The way you mess up every job, you have a great future—as a bum."

> **unemployed**
> (ŭn' ĕm ploid')
> *adj.* without a job

He's probably right. My first summer job was cutting the neighbor's lawn. The mower got away from me and ate ten tomato plants. Another time, I forgot to close the windows when I
10   washed Mr. Hammer's car. The weeds I pulled out of Mrs. Miller's garden turned out to be flowers.

> **REREAD**
> How did Ernie mess up each summer job?

So I was really surprised when the Bensons asked me to look after their house while they were away on vacation. The Bensons are new on the block. I guess they hadn't heard about me yet.

"We're leaving on Monday," explained Mrs. Benson. "You'll start on Tuesday. Just bring in the newspapers and the mail." That didn't sound too hard. Even *I*
20   could probably handle this job.

"And feed Jaws once a day," Mrs. Benson added.

"*Jaws?*" I gulped. Did they have a pet shark or something?

Mrs. Benson laughed. "That's what the twins named their goldfish."

THINK IT THROUGH
Why is Ernie surprised to get this job?

On Tuesday, I had baseball practice. So I was late getting to the Bensons'. I put the mail and the newspaper on the hall table. Then I headed for the fishbowl. Jaws was floating on top of the water.

30 I moaned. My first day on the job, and I killed the dumb fish! Not even the Army would want me now. That's what my dad would say—after he stopped yelling.

Now wait a minute, Ernie, I said to myself. This little fellow *could* still be alive. His eyes are open. He could be in a coma . I bent down very close to the water.

> **coma**
> (kō' mə)
> state of being totally unaware of one's surroundings because of illness or injury. A person in a coma seems to be sleeping.

"Jaws!" I yelled. "It's me, Ernie, your babysitter. If you can hear me, blink once."
40 He didn't.

I touched him with my finger. He was cold, stiff, and very slimy. "Face it, Ernie," I said out loud. "This is one dead fish you have here."

That night, I lay awake a long time trying to figure out why that dumb fish died. I didn't overfeed him. I never had a chance to feed him at all.

When I finally fell asleep, I had a nightmare. The shark from *Jaws* was chasing me. He was
50 wearing a six-shooter. "You bumped off my kinfolk," he yelled. "Draw!"

> **REREAD**
> Picture this scene in your mind.

FOCUS ——————————————————————

Read to find out what Ernie does about Jaws.

I didn't tell my parents about Jaws. Every day, I went over to the Bensons' as though nothing was wrong. I had until Sunday. That's when the Bensons were coming home. Why rush things?

On Saturday, I remembered that Jaws was still in the fishbowl. I was about to toss him into the garbage. Suddenly, I had a great idea. I slipped Jaws into a baggie and ran to the nearest pet store.

60 "I'd like another goldfish exactly like this one," I told the owner. Then I held up the baggie.

The owner glared at me. Half an hour later, he was still glaring. That's how long it took to find a perfect match. I paid the owner and headed back to the Bensons' house.

> **glared**
> (glârd)
> v. looked in an angry way; past tense of *glare*

When I got there, I cleaned the fishbowl and added fresh water. Soon, Jaws II was in his new home. But instead of swimming around, he just stared at me.

70 "What you did was wrong," those tiny black eyes seemed to say.

THINK IT THROUGH

Do you think Ernie's solution is a good one? Why or why not?

FOCUS ——————————————————————

Read to find out what happens when the Bensons come home.

The Bensons arrived home at 1:55 Sunday afternoon. I watched from my bedroom window as they piled out of their car. At 2:13, my mom called up the stairs.

"Ernie," she said, "Mrs. Benson is here." Caught! I trudged down the stairs to face the music.

Mrs. Benson was sitting at the kitchen table with my parents. "Here's the boy behind the Great Goldfish Switch," she said.

REREAD

What does Mrs. Benson know?

I felt like running. But Mrs. Benson put her arm around my shoulder.

"That was very thoughtful, Ernie," she said. "Monday was so crazy I didn't have time to pick up another fish. I've been dreading telling the twins that Jaws died. Thanks to you, I won't have to."

dreading
(drĕd' ĭng)
v. afraid of

She handed me money in an envelope.

"This is for house-sitting," she said. "There's something extra for the new Jaws. You hear so many wild stories about kids these days. It's nice to know one who is responsible."

responsible
(rĭ spŏn' sə bəl)
adj. able to be trusted to do the right thing

Mom looked so proud I thought she might cry. But Dad had a funny look on his face. I think he was trying not to laugh.

THINK IT THROUGH

1. Why does Mrs. Benson think Ernie did a good job?
2. Where in the story do you think the conflict begins? Use sentences from the story to support your answer.
3. Should Ernie feel guilty about taking the extra money? Why or why not?

Sometimes, not following the plan can have bad results.

The Turtle and the Swans

retold by
Robert Scott

Connect to Your Life

Do plans that you make always work out?
What do you do when they don't work?

Key to the Fable

"The Turtle and the Swans" is a fable. A
fable is a brief story that teaches a
lesson about life. In many fables the
characters are animals that act and talk
like humans. A fable often ends with a
moral. A **moral** states a lesson about life.

Vocabulary Preview

Words to Know

serious   admiration
clamping   irritated
suitable

 Reading Coach CD-ROM selection

The turtle lived in a great lake with a lot of other creatures. He made friends with a pair of swans. They had a lot of interests in common and each evening they would settle down together for a pleasant chat. The swans would tell about the many different places they had visited and the turtle would reveal some of the interesting things he had discovered while exploring the bed of the lake.

Then one year the rains failed and the lake began to
10 dry up. Soon it was little more than dry, cracked mud.

"It's no use," the swans said to the turtle one evening, "we shall have to leave here. We're sorry to say goodbye when we've been such good friends, but there's nothing else for us. How will you manage?"

The turtle shook his head sadly. "I've no idea," he said. "You can fly off somewhere else, but I'm stuck here. Not only that. I *need* the water. I can't live without it. It isn't quite so serious for you."

"I don't see how we can help," one of
20 the swans said. "If only you could fly. We'll try to think of something."

serious
(sîr' ē əs)
adj. important

THINK IT THROUGH
What is the turtle's problem?

FOCUS ——————
What idea do the swans and the turtle have?

"Perhaps you could carry me," said the turtle when they met again the next day.

"You'd be too heavy," said one of the swans.

"You'd fall off," said the other. "Nothing to hold on to."

"I can grip very tight," said the turtle, clamping his mouth around a stick to prove his point.

clamping
(klăm' pĭng)
adj. holding

30   "I'm sure you can," said the first swan, "but it's my neck you'd be holding on to."

"But that's the answer!" the other exclaimed. "He can hold on to the stick and we'll carry him that way."

They began to work out the details. They would find a suitable stick, the turtle would grip the middle firmly in his mouth and the swans would hold the ends. That way they could all go to a lake the swans knew of that never dried up.

suitable
(soo' tə bəl)
adj. right for the purpose

40   "But no talking!" the swans said. "We must all grip the stick tightly and not open our beaks. Or mouth," he added, turning a beady eye on their friend. "If you do, you'll fall off."

"Of course not!" snapped the turtle. "I can keep my mouth shut when I have to. Let's get started."

THINK IT THROUGH
What plan do the turtle and the swans have for helping the turtle leave the lake?

FOCUS
Look for clues that tell you what might happen.

So they carried out their plan and the swans were soon flying strongly out towards their new home.

As they were passing over a small town someone happened to notice them.

50 "Hey, look up there!" he shouted in
admiration. "Look at that! There's a turtle
being carried along on a stick by a couple
of swans. Isn't that clever of it."

admiration
(ăd′ mə rā′ shən)
n. wonder

The three friends looked down but said
nothing. "They're right, though," thought the turtle.
"It's very clever to hold on and be carried like this."

The swans' powerful wings carried them out into the
country across parched fields and hills until once more
they were flying over a town. Again they were seen.

60 "Look at that!"

"What? Where?"

"Up there. Those two swans are carrying a turtle
on a stick."

"So they are. That's very clever of them."

"I'll say! Very clever birds, swans."

The turtle, hearing all this, was becoming
more and more irritated. "Stupid fools!" he
thought. "Don't they realize that I'm the one
that's being clever. The swans are just flying

irritated
(ĭr′ ĭ tā′ tĭd)
adj. angry

70 like they always do but you don't see a flying
turtle every day. Really!" Then he forgot where he was.

"Hey! You down there! Don't you—" but as soon
as he opened his mouth to speak he began to fall. He
never did finish what he wanted to say, but was
dashed to pieces on the ground below.

That night the people had turtle soup for dinner.

**Moral: Keep your mind on the job
in hand.**

REREAD
What does this
sentence mean?

1. Why doesn't the plan work?
2. Why do the people have turtle soup for dinner?
3. What lesson does the fable teach? State it in your own words.

Night Moves

Unit 2

Poetry

Poets use many ideas, images, and feelings. Therefore, poets choose each word carefully to give just the right sound and meaning. In this unit, you will read six poems that use just the right words about things that happen at night.

Some poets wrote their poems in special **forms,** or shapes. Some used **rhyme**—words that end in the same sound—and **rhythm**—a pattern of regular beats. Most used **imagery,** words that appeal to your senses and create pictures in your mind. One poem even tells a story.

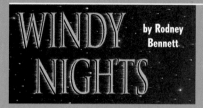

by Pat Mora

RIVER-MOON

A poem can help you see things in a
different way. In this poem, the moon and
a river come to life at night.

| **Connect to Your Life** | **Key to the Poem** | Reading Coach CD-ROM selection |

Connect to Your Life

What is it like to go
boating on a river? What
does the motion of the
boat feel like?

Key to the Poem

The **form** of a poem is its shape. Sometimes a
poem takes on the shape of its subject. This
poem describes the movement of the moon and
a river. Notice how the sentences seem to slide
and glide to the right.

Vocabulary In line 2, *Río* means "river," and
in line 6, *Luna* means "moon" in Spanish.

RIVER-MOON

by Pat Mora

River goes sliding, sliding by.
    Río goes gliding under night black sky.
    River goes hiding in canyons dry.
    Río goes sliding, sliding by.

5 Moon goes sliding, sliding by.
    Luna goes gliding under night black sky.
    Moon goes hiding in canyons dry.
    Luna goes sliding, sliding by,

river-moon sliding, sliding by,
10   *río* and *luna* gliding under night black sky.

THINK IT THROUGH

1. What makes the sentences look as if they are moving?
2. What two words in the poem describe a kind of movement?
3. What do the river and the moon have in common?
4. Why do you think the poet repeated the rhyming words *sliding, gliding,* and *hiding*?

WINDY NIGHTS

by Rodney Bennett

What can you hear but
not see? feel but not touch?
This poem will answer that riddle.

Connect to Your Life

Close your eyes and
picture a night when the
wind was very strong.
What sounds did you hear
that night?

Key to the Poem

 **Reading Coach
CD-ROM selection**

Poems **rhyme** when they contain words that end
in the same sound. Some poems have a strong
rhythm too. The **rhythm** of a poem is like the beat
of a song. Think of the beat in music. Some poems
sound like music because of their strong beat.

Vocabulary In line 6, **raving** means "roaring
or raging."

WINDY NIGHTS

by Rodney Bennett

Rumbling in the chimneys,
   Rattling at the doors,
Round the roofs and round the roads
   The rude wind roars;
5 Raging through the darkness,
   Raving through the trees,
Racing off again across
   The great grey seas.

THINK IT THROUGH

1. Which words **rhyme** in lines 1–4? in lines 5–8?
2. Read the first four lines out loud. Try to clap to the **rhythm** of the poem. Which words or parts of words have a strong beat?
3. What is the poem about?
4. How does the strong beat help you understand what the poem describes?

Winter Dark

by Lilian Moore

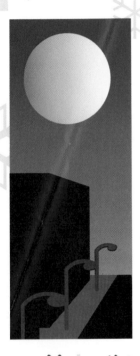

Many things look different at night. Even the moon can look like something else.

Connect to Your Life	Key to the Poem	Reading Coach CD-ROM selection

Connect to Your Life

Have you ever walked home in the dark on a winter afternoon? Did it seem late at night because of the darkness? How did the streets look to you?

Key to the Poem

Poems often use metaphors to describe a subject. A **metaphor** compares one thing to something else, without using the word *like* or *as*. This poem compares the moon to other things in the dark.

Vocabulary In line 13, **punctuates** means "interrupts."

Winter Dark by Lilian Moore

Winter dark comes early
mixing afternoon
and night.
Soon
5   there's a comma of a moon,

and each street light
along the
way
puts its period
10 to the end of day.

Now
a neon sign
punctuates the dark
with a bright
15 blinking
breathless
exclamation mark!

THINK IT THROUGH

1. What punctuation marks are the moon, the street lights, and a neon sign compared to?
2. What does it mean to put a period to the end of day?
3. How is an exclamation mark like a neon sign?

The Falling Star

by Sara Teasdale

Have you ever

seen a falling star?

What do people do when they see one?

THE FALLING STAR by Sara Teasdale

I saw a star slide down the sky,
Blinding the north as it went by,
Too burning and too quick to hold,
Too lovely to be bought or sold,
5 Good only to make wishes on
And then forever to be gone.

THINK IT THROUGH

1. Which words in the poem help you see the star?
2. Which words in the poem tell you how your hand would feel if you touched the star?
3. Describe the falling star in your own words.

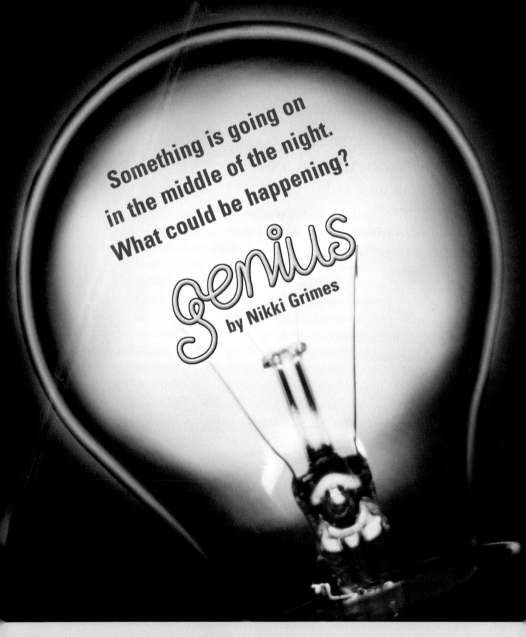

Something is going on
in the middle of the night.
What could be happening?

genius

by Nikki Grimes

Connect to Your Life

Did anyone ever wake
you out of a sound sleep?
What did the person
want? What did you do?

Key to the Poem

**Reading Coach
CD-ROM selection**

This poem tells a story. The story starts in the
middle of the night. What happens when the light
switches on? Read the poem to find out.

Vocabulary In line 3, **urgently** means
"demanding attention." In line 12, **forge** means
"move forward with sudden speed."

 **by Nikki Grimes**

"Sis! Wake up!" I whisper
in the middle of the night.

    Urgently I shake her
    till she switches on the light.

5 The spiral notebook in my hand
provides her quick relief.

    It tells her there's no danger
    of a break-in by a thief.

"Okay," she says, then props herself
10 up vertically in bed.

    She nods for me to read my work.
    I cough, then forge ahead.

The last verse of my poem leaves
her silent as a mouse.

15   I worry till she says, "We have
    a genius in the house."

THINK IT THROUGH

1. What is happening in lines 1–4?
2. How does the speaker's sister know that no thief is in the house?
3. Why does the speaker wake up his or her sister?
4. What does "Sis" think of the poem? How do you know?

DREAMS

by Langston Hughes

Have you ever wanted
a dream to come true? What
would happen if you had no dreams?

Connect to Your Life

What is your favorite dream? It can be a dream that you had while awake. Describe the dream to a partner.

Key to the Poem

Poems often use **metaphors,** or comparisons, in order to describe things. This poem compares life to two things. Those two comparisons are the key to why the writer values dreams.

Vocabulary In line 1, **fast** means "tight."

 Reading Coach CD-ROM selection

DREAMS   by Langston Hughes

Hold fast to dreams
For if dreams die
Life is a broken-winged bird
That cannot fly.

5   Hold fast to dreams
For when dreams go
Life is a barren field
Frozen with snow.

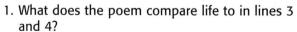

THINK IT THROUGH

1. What does the poem compare life to in lines 3 and 4?
2. In lines 7 and 8, what does the poem compare life to?
3. According to the poem, what will happen if we don't have dreams?
4. Explain why you agree or disagree with the message in question 3.

The Power of Nature

Nonfiction

Did an article in the newspaper tell you about the effects of a heat wave? If so, you were reading nonfiction. **Nonfiction** is writing about real people, places, and events. It is based on facts. So that great comic book in your backpack probably isn't nonfiction. But that book about earthquakes probably is.

In this unit, you'll read a **true account,** an **informative article,** and a **feature article.** You'll meet people who try to escape nature's power and people who race to meet it.

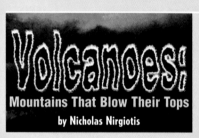

People thought this ship
couldn't sink. But it
sank anyway. Why?

from

The Titanic:
Lost and Found
by Judy Donnelly

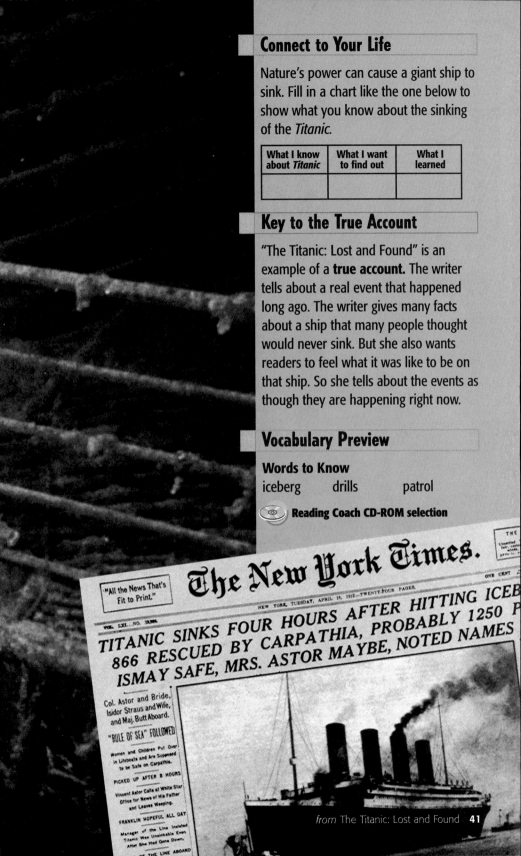

Connect to Your Life

Nature's power can cause a giant ship to sink. Fill in a chart like the one below to show what you know about the sinking of the *Titanic*.

What I know about *Titanic*	What I want to find out	What I learned

Key to the True Account

"The Titanic: Lost and Found" is an example of a **true account.** The writer tells about a real event that happened long ago. The writer gives many facts about a ship that many people thought would never sink. But she also wants readers to feel what it was like to be on that ship. So she tells about the events as though they are happening right now.

Vocabulary Preview

Words to Know

iceberg   drills   patrol

Reading Coach CD-ROM selection

from The Titanic: Lost and Found   **41**

Read to find out what happens to the *Titanic.*

It is April 14, 1912. The *Titanic* is in icy waters off the coast of Canada.

It is almost midnight. The ship is quiet. The sea is smooth as glass. The air is biting cold.

The passengers have had a good dinner. Some of them are still up playing cards. Most are asleep in their rooms.

It is a good night to be inside. But the lookout must watch for danger. He is high above the ship in the crow's-nest. He stares into
10 the darkness.

crow's-nest
(krōz' něst')
place at the top of a ship's mast where a person can keep watch

Suddenly the lookout sees a dark shape. It is a mountain of ice! And the *Titanic* is heading right into it! The lookout rings an alarm. He calls, "Iceberg straight ahead!"

iceberg
(īs' bûrg')
n. large body of floating ice. Most of the ice is below the water.

A seaman is below, steering the ship. He tries to turn the ship away. But it is too late.

The giant iceberg scrapes along the side of the ship.

There is a bump. A grinding noise. It doesn't seem
20 like much. Some people do not even notice.

But the captain hurries from his room. He goes down below. He wants to see if the ship is hurt. Soon he learns the terrible truth.

The iceberg has hurt the ship badly. Water is pouring in. Five of the watertight compartments are already flooded. And that is too many. Nothing can be done now.

watertight
(wô' tər tīt')
built so that water cannot get in or out

It seems impossible. But it is true. The *Titanic* is going to sink!

THINK IT THROUGH
What caused the ship to start sinking?

"All the News That's Fit to Print."

VOL. LXI. NO. 33,88.

TITANIC SINK

30   The captain gives his orders. Wake the passengers! Radio for help! And make the lifeboats ready!

    The captain is afraid. He knows that 2,227 people are on board. And there are only enough lifeboats for 1,100 of them.

    The passengers do not know this. As people come out on deck, they laugh and joke. Some are in evening gowns. Others wear life jackets over pajamas. But they are not worried. They still think they are on a ship that cannot sink.

40   Get in the lifeboats, the sailors tell them. Women and children go first. Men go only if there is room.

    Many do not want to get in. The big ship seems so safe. The little lifeboats do not.

    The sailors are in a hurry. They know there is trouble. They rush people into the lifeboats. Some are only half full, but the sailors lower them anyway.

REREAD
Why aren't the lifeboats full?

    Many passengers are far from the lifeboats. They are the poor ones. Their rooms are down below. They
50 know there is trouble too. But they do not know where to go. A few try to find their way. They go up stairs and down halls. Some are helped by seamen. Most just wait below.

THINK IT THROUGH
What problems kept some people from being saved?

THE WEATHER
Unsettled Tuesday; Wednesday, fair, cooler; moderate southerly winds, becoming variable.

New York Times.

NEW YORK, TUESDAY, APRIL 16, 1912—TWENTY-FOUR PAGES.
ONE CENT

UR HOURS AFTER HITTING ICEBERG;
CARPATHIA, PROBABLY 1250 PERISH;
NOTED NAMES MISSING

Biggest Liner Plunges

In the radio room the operator calls for help. Other ships answer. But they are many, many miles away.

One ship is not far away. Its name is the *Californian*. This ship is only ten miles from the *Titanic*. It could reach the sinking ship in minutes and save everyone.

60   The *Titanic's* operator calls again and again. But the *Californian* does not answer. It is late at night and the ship's radio is turned off. No one on board hears the calls for help.

The *Titanic* tries to signal the *Californian*. It sets off rockets that look like fireworks. Sailors on the *Californian* see the rockets. But they do not understand that the *Titanic* is in trouble. And so they do not come.

REREAD

Why doesn't the *Californian* answer the *Titanic's* calls for help?

70   On the *Titanic* the band is playing. The music is cheerful. But people are afraid now. The deck is slanting under their feet.

The ship tilts more and more. The lower decks are underwater.

Two lifeboats are left, but the sailors cannot get them loose. Hundreds and hundreds of people are still on board. And by now they know the end is near.

An old couple holds hands. The wife will not leave her husband. One man puts on his best clothes. "I
80 will die like a gentleman," he says.

Some people jump into the icy water. A few are lucky. They reach a lifeboat.

The people in the lifeboats row away from the *Titanic*. Everyone is staring at the beautiful ship. Its lights are sparkling. The lively music drifts across the water.

Then the music changes. The band plays a hymn.

One end of the huge ship slides slowly into the ocean. The music stops. There is a great roaring noise. A million sparks fill the air. The other end of the ship 90 swings straight up.

For a moment the *Titanic* stays pointed at the stars. Then it disappears under the black water.

THINK IT THROUGH
Tell three things that happened before the ship sank.

FOCUS ——————
Discover what happens to the people in the lifeboats.

It is 2:20 A.M. on April 15. The *Titanic* is gone. The people in the lifeboats stare into the night. The sky is full of shooting stars. But it is dark. And it is bitter, bitter cold.

Most of the lifeboats have drifted away from each other.

People just wait. And they try to get warm. Some 100 have fur coats. Others are wearing bathrobes and slippers. One man is in nothing but his underwear. Coldest of all are the ones who jumped from the ship and swam to a boat. Their hair and clothes are frosted with ice.

REREAD
Try to picture this scene in your mind. Can you feel the coldness of the people?

One lifeboat is upside down. About thirty men are standing on it. They lean this way and that to keep the boat from sinking. Icy waves splash against their legs.

One lifeboat goes back to try and help. They save 110 one man. He is floating on a wooden door. They do not find many others. No one can last long in the freezing water.

Hours pass. The sky grows lighter. It seems as if help will never come. Then suddenly a light flashes. And another. It is a ship—the *Carpathia*. It has come from fifty-eight miles away.

Everyone waves and cheers. They make torches. They burn paper, handkerchiefs—anything. They want to make the ship see them.

120   The sun begins to rise. There are icebergs all around. The rescue ship almost hits one, but it turns just in time. The ship keeps heading toward the lifeboats.

Help has finally come.

All eyes are on the rescue ship. Boat by boat, the people are taken aboard. The sea is rough and it takes many hours. But at last everyone is safe.

THINK IT THROUGH
| What dangers did the people in the lifeboats face?

FOCUS ————————————————————————————
| What do people learn from this event?

Soon the news flashes all around the world. The unsinkable *Titanic* has sunk. More than 2,200 people set out. Only 705 are rescued.

130   How? Why? No one can understand.

When the rescue ship reaches New York, forty thousand people are waiting. The *Titanic* survivors tell their stories.

The world learns the truth. The safest ship was not safe at all.

It was too late for the *Titanic*. But it was not too late for other ships.

New safety laws were passed. Many changes were made.

Today every ship must have enough lifeboats for
140 every single passenger. And every ship has lifeboat drills so people know what to do if there is an accident.

drills
(drĭlz)
n. practices

Ship radios can never be turned off. Every call for help is heard.

And now there is a special ice patrol. Patrol airplanes keep track of dangerous icebergs. They warn ships. Never again can an iceberg take a ship by surprise.

patrol
(pə trōl′)
n. group assigned to keep watch over an area

The *Titanic* was a terrible loss. But the
150 world learned from it.

THINK IT THROUGH

1. Make a time line of the events in the story. Use it to retell the story in your own words.
2. The lifeboats could hold 1,100 people. Yet only 705 were rescued. Why weren't more people saved?
3. Do you think this event could happen today? Use details from the story to support your opinion.

Volcanoes:

Mountains That Blow Their Tops

by Nicholas Nirgiotis

You don't want to get too close to a mountain when it's having a bad day.

It is a quiet day on an island. Or so it seems.
Suddenly a mountain starts to shake. Clouds of
smoke shoot from the top. The mountain smokes for
days and days. Then it happens! KABOOM! The
mountain blows its top! A red-hot cloud of ash bursts
out. It burns the town in minutes. Just two people get
away. One is a girl. She knows a cave. She used to
play there. She takes a boat to the cave. She is safe.
The other is a man. He is safe in jail underground.
10 This is a true story. It happened in 1902.

Mont Pelee is the name of the mountain. It is on
the island of Martinique in the Atlantic Ocean. Mont
Pelee is a special kind of mountain—it is a
volcano. Long ago, people thought a god of
fire lived inside volcanoes. They thought he
liked to move from one volcano to another.
Every time he moved he stirred things up.

> **stirred**
> (stûrd)
> v. caused
> something to
> happen; past
> tense of *stir*

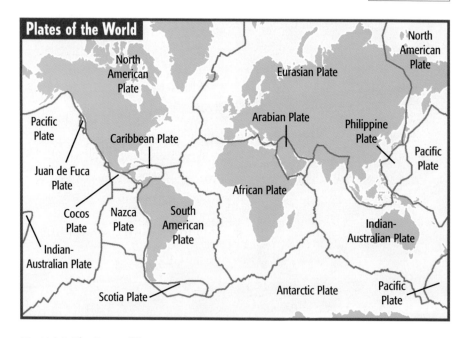

Plates of the World

North American Plate
North American Plate
Eurasian Plate
Pacific Plate
Arabian Plate
Philippine Plate
Caribbean Plate
Pacific Plate
Juan de Fuca Plate
Cocos Plate
Nazca Plate
South American Plate
African Plate
Indian-Australian Plate
Indian-Australian Plate
Scotia Plate
Antarctic Plate
Pacific Plate

Today we know the facts. Volcanoes start deep in the earth. The earth is round—like an orange. It is made of layers of rock.

The top layer is called the crust. It is like the skin of the orange. The layer below is called the mantle. The mantle is very hot. So some of the rock melts. The melted rock is called magma. The top layers of earth are made up of many pieces. These pieces are called plates. The red lines (on page 50) show where the plates meet. This is where most volcanoes happen. The plates are always moving—very, very slowly! Some plates push against each other. Some plates pull away from each other.

The magma is moving too. It pushes up on the plates. Sometimes the magma finds a crack between the plates. Then—SPURT! Out it comes. This is the start of a volcano. The magma bubbles up a tube. The tube is like a long straw. At the top is a hole. The hole is called a crater. The magma spills out of the crater. Now the magma is called lava. (See diagram on page 52.)

REREAD
How does a volcano start?

There are two kinds of lava. One kind is soft and runny—and red hot! It flows in fast, fiery rivers from the volcano. As the lava cools, it turns back into smooth rock. The other kind of lava flows much more slowly. Sometimes it sprays out of the crater into the sky. In the air the lava hardens into sharp rocks and ash. Then black clouds of ash fill the sky. They block out the sun, so it is dark— Even at noon!

fiery
(fīr′ ē)
adj. full of fire

THINK IT THROUGH
Use the facts about the earth's layers to explain what happened to Mont Pelee.

Not many people get to see a volcano being born.
50 But fifty years ago, one boy did. He lived in Mexico.
One day he was helping his father on their farm.
Suddenly the earth split open. Smoke and ash shot
into the air. The boy and his father ran to warn the
people in town. Ash and rock kept shooting up. A hill
started to grow. By the next day, the hill was as tall as
ten houses. The fireworks went on for nine years! The
farm was gone. The town was gone. In their place
was a new volcano.

Some volcanoes start at the bottom of the sea,
60 where no one can see them. The ocean floor splits
open. Hot lava pours out. The lava cools and
hardens. The volcano grows. Slowly it rises above the
water. This is how some islands are made.

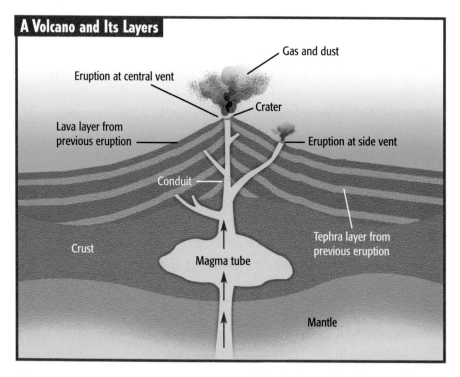

A Volcano and Its Layers

Gas and dust

Eruption at central vent

Crater

Lava layer from
previous eruption

Eruption at side vent

Conduit

Tephra layer from
previous eruption

Crust

Magma tube

Mantle

This is Mount St. Helens as it erupted.

This is Mount St. Helens after it erupted.

Where are the most volcanoes? Around the Pacific Ocean. The volcanoes form a ring. It is called the Ring of Fire. Are there volcanoes in the United States? Yes. Mount St. Helens is in Washington State. In 1980, it erupted.[See above.]

Hawaii has the biggest and busiest
70 volcanoes in the world. Mauna Loa is the biggest. Kilauea is the busiest. Kilauea has been erupting on and off for 100 years. It is called the "drive in" volcano. You can drive or even walk around its giant crater. Who knows? You just might see a lava fire show there!

erupted
(ĭ rŭp′ tĭd)
v. exploded; past tense of *erupt*

THINK IT THROUGH

Hawaii is a state made up of islands. Explain how these islands were probably made.

Read to find out whether volcanoes do any good.

Can volcanoes do any good? Yes. Over time, ash and lava turn into rich soil. The soil is good for farming. Volcanoes also tell us about the past. Two thousand years ago, a volcano erupted in Italy. It

80 buried the city of Pompeii under ash. Now people are digging up Pompeii. The ash preserved everything— even the shapes of the people.

Bodies from the ruins of Pompeii, preserved in the position in which the persons died

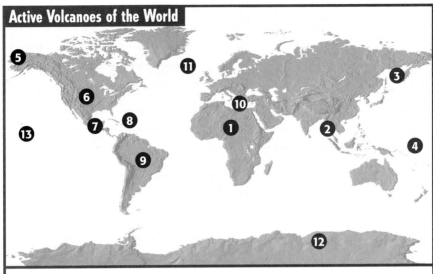

Active Volcanoes of the World

1. Africa and surrounding islands
2. Southwest Pacific, Southeast Asia, and India
3. East Asia
4. Central Pacific, South Pacific, and New Zealand
5. Alaska and North Pacific
6. North America
7. Central America
8. Caribbean
9. South America and surrounding islands
10. Mediterranean
11. North Atlantic, Iceland
12. Antarctica
13. Hawaii

There are about 500 active volcanoes in the world. This map shows where most of them are found. "Active" means the volcano can erupt at any time. Other volcanoes are inactive. They have been dead for thousands of years. And then there are volcanoes that are only sleeping. Now they are quiet. But who knows when they will wake up?

THINK IT THROUGH

1. What good things do volcanoes do? What bad things do they do? Use details from the article to support your answer.
2. Do people in the United States need to be concerned about volcanoes? Why or why not?
3. What are three facts you learned from reading this article?

HUNTING HURRICANES!

by Susan Pilár de la Hoz

For most people, being in a hurricane is a nightmare. For some, it's a dream come true.

Connect to Your Life

Some jobs are more dangerous than others. Do you know someone in a dangerous job? What does that person do? Is the job interesting to you?

Key to the Article

"Hunting Hurricanes!" is a feature article. A **feature article** can appear in a magazine or a newspaper. It usually tells about an interesting person or event.

Before you read the article, read the headings to get an idea of what each section is about. Notice how almost every heading tries to get your attention with a question.

Vocabulary Preview

Words to Know
satellite   parachutes
navigator

 Reading Coach CD-ROM selection

the airplane flies to the eye of the hurricane.

FOCUS ——
| Some people hunt hurricanes. Discover how they do this.

You're flying 5,000 feet above the ocean. Rain is beating against the plane. Powerful winds are shaking it. Every few seconds, lightning flashes through the darkness. You're headed straight into a hurricane!

You look at the other people in the plane. They don't seem scared. In fact, they *want* to be here. The United States Air Force pays them to be here. They are Hurricane Hunters. It's their job to find and study the most powerful storms on earth.

Why Fly into a Hurricane?

10 People need to know when and where these storms will hit. Satellite photos can give people who predict weather a picture of a hurricane. But satellites can't see inside a storm. That's where the Hurricane Hunters come in.

> **satellite**
> (săt' | īt')
> *n.* man-made object that circles the earth

A hurricane has an outer wall. It's made of fast-moving clouds and strong winds. At the center is the "eye," which has no clouds or wind. The Hurricane Hunters fly through the wall and into the eye. Here 20 they can learn more about the storm. They can make up to four trips into the eye on each flight.

Isn't Hurricane Hunting Dangerous?

Safety is always the crew's number one concern. At times, the plane ride can be rough. Near the eye, winds may reach more than 200 miles an hour. The planes are built to withstand the pounding wind and rain. Even in the worst weather, very little scares the crew. One Hurricane Hunter, Michelle Rivera, has been on

crews like to hunt hurricanes

many flights. She says, "I have so much faith in our
30 pilots. I know they know what to do."

   Hurricane Hunters feel that a look inside a storm is
worth the risk. They often see beautiful sights. As
Rivera says, "When we were in the eye, I could see
sunlight up above. . . . There was a solid wall of
white clouds 50,000 feet high."

THINK IT THROUGH
Why do some people fly planes into a hurricane?

The outer wall of a hurricane

crews like hunt hurricanes,
hunters

FOCUS
| Find out how Hurricane Hunters get information.

Who Are the Hurricane Hunters?

Each plane carries six people: a pilot, co-pilot, navigator, flight engineer, and two weather experts. Hurricane Hunters come from all walks of life. Some work for the Air Force
40 full-time. Others work only one weekend a month. The rest of the time they have other jobs, such as doctor, teacher, or cook.

> **navigator**
> (năv′ ĭ gā′ tər)
> *n.* person who plans and records where an airplane flies

Since 1965, the Hurricane Hunters have been flying the WC-130 Hercules. It's a very strong plane. It's built to take bad weather. It's filled with special weather equipment.

The plane has life rafts but no parachutes. The crew has a better chance of surviving if they use the rafts. Jumping
50 out of a plane into a hurricane is not a good idea.

> **parachutes**
> (păr′ ə shoōts′)
> *n.* equipment that slows a person's fall from an airplane

WC-130 Hercules

c hurrican huners use dropsondes to get info.

How Do They Get Information?

Among other equipment, Hurricane Hunters use a dropsonde. This is a small, round tube. It is dropped into the eye of the hurricane. A parachute at the top of the tube opens and slows it down.

The dropsonde falls toward the ocean. It picks up information about the storm. It then radios this information back to the plane. Hurricane Hunters can tell how strong a storm is, how fast it's moving, and where it's going.

Hurricane Hunters radio their information to weather stations. One station is the National Hurricane Center (NHC) in Miami, Florida. Most hurricanes in the United States take place off the coast of Florida. The NHC warns people when to get out of a storm's path. Every year, Hurricane Hunters save thousands of lives on land and at sea.

THINK IT THROUGH

What kind of information do Hurricane Hunters get? How do they use it?

hurrican Hunters work in units.

Who Were the First Hurricane Hunters?

In 1943, a group of British and American pilots were training in Bryan, Texas. A hurricane was coming
70 their way. One of the pilots, Joe Duckworth, said that his plane could fly in any weather. The other pilots dared him to fly into a hurricane.

He did—not just once, but twice! The second time he asked the weather officer to come with him. The officer took notes on the hurricane. The two men became the first Hurricane Hunters.

Soon after, the Air Force created the Hurricane Hunters unit. The unit has its own special decal .

decal
(dē' kăl')
n. decorative sticker or label

Air Force flight symbol

Hurricane symbol

Weather symbol

HURRICANE HUNTERS

Want to Be a Hurricane Hunter?

Does flying into a powerful storm sound like a great job? Here's how to become a Hurricane Hunter:

1. **Take lots of math and science courses. Study for the Air Force Tests. (There are books to help you.)**

2. **Finish high school.**

3. **Get a college degree. All pilots must have a degree.**

4. **Join the Air Force Reserve.**

5. **Choose the job you want—pilot, co-pilot, navigator, flight engineer, or weather expert.**

6. **Get special training in hunting hurricanes. Training can last from four months to over a year.**

7. **Pass the final tests to become a Hurricane Hunter!**

THINK IT THROUGH

1. What does it take to be a Hurricane Hunter?
2. Why do you think a person would want to become a Hurricane Hunter?
3. Do you have what it takes to be a Hurricane Hunter? Why or why not?

The Hurricane

Ashley Bryan

I cried to the wind,
"Don't blow so hard!
You've knocked down my sister
You're shaking
5   And tossing and tilting
The tree!"

And would the wind listen,
Listen to me?

The wind howled,
10   *"Whooree!*
I blow as I wish
I wish
I wish
I crush and
15   I splash and
I rush and
I swish."

I cried to the wind,
"Don't blow so wild!
20   You're chasing the clouds
You're whirling
And swishing and swirling
The sea!"

And would the wind listen,
25 Listen to me?

The wind howled,
"Whooree!
I blow as I wish
I wish
30 I wish
I'm bold and
I'm brash and
I'm cold and
I'm rash!"

35 I said to my friends,
"Please, call out with me,
Stop, wind, stop!"
    "STOP, WIND, STOP!"

Ah, *now* the wind listens
40 It brushes my hair
Chases clouds slowly
Sings in my ear,
"Whooree, whooree!"
Stretches out gently
45 Under the tree
Soothes little sister
And quiets the sea.

Unexpected Gifts

Drama

A gift is something that a person gives freely. Sometimes the best gifts are the ones you don't expect. In this unit, you will discover some unexpected gifts in two very different dramas.

Dramas are plays. The best way to enjoy a play is to watch it acted on a stage. The actors tell the story through their words and actions. In this unit, you will read the written forms of plays, or **scripts.** Try to imagine that you are watching the actors. By reading their words and actions, you will discover their story.

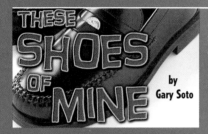

THESE SHOES OF MINE

BY GARY SOTO

MANUEL THINKS HE WANTS NEW SHOES. BUT COULD SOMETHING ELSE MAKE HIM HAPPIER?

Connect to Your Life

Have you ever wanted something very badly? Did you finally get what you wanted? How did you feel?

Key to the Drama

Most dramas have these special parts:
- **cast of characters:** a list of the characters in the play. The list often includes a short description of each character.
- **dialogue:** the words that characters say to each other. The words each character says are written next to his or her name.
- **stage directions:** instructions (in italics) for actors. They describe the setting and tell about the action.
- **scene:** a section of the play that happens in one time and place.

Vocabulary Preview

Words to Know
dejectedly   immigrant
impress

> Read the lists of characters, sets, props, and costumes. Read the first stage directions too. Both will help you understand this play.

Cast of Characters

Manuel
Mother
Angel, the school bully
Elena, Manuel's sister
Manuel's relatives
Tío José, Manuel's uncle
Ceci, the girl whom Manuel likes
Partygoers

Sets

Living room of Manuel's house
A street in the neighborhood
Bedroom of Manuel's house

Props

A sewing machine
A clunky pair of boy's shoes
A new pair of penny loafers
A letter
A wrapped birthday present
Two cots with pillows

props
(prŏps)
objects used in
a play

Costumes

Everyday clothes

THINK IT THROUGH

What information do you learn about this play from the lists?

(Manuel *paces back and forth in big clunky shoes while his mother sits at a table sewing patches onto a pair of pants.*)

Manuel (*indicating his shoes*). Look at them!

Mother. They're nice, *mi'jo* [my son].

Manuel. Nice! They're too big! They're old! They're ugly. (*stomps his feet*) And can you hear them?

Mother. They're like drums.

(Manuel *stomps louder.*)

10 **Mother.** No, like congas .

Manuel. Everyone will hear me. They'll laugh and say, "Here comes Manuel in his big ugly shoes."

congas
(kŏng' gəz)
very tall drums

Mother. *Mi'jo*, it will be like music from your feet.

Manuel (*kicking up a shoe*). And look. There's a start of a hole on the bottom. Rain will get in. (*desperately*) And they're from the thrift store .

thrift store
(thrĭft stôr)
store that sells
used items

Mother. Sure, they're a little bit used, but
20 these shoes are new for you.

Manuel. Mom!

Mother. Manuel, new things cost money.

(Manuel's *sister enters stage left, balancing three boxes of shoes and slowly walking across the stage.*)

Manuel. But look at Elena! She's got new shoes. Lots of them!

Mother. She saved her money for them. And what did you do with your money?

(Manuel *forces a moody face.*)

30 **Mother.** Come on. *Dime.* [Tell me.] Tell me.

Manuel (*low voice*). I bought a hundred ice creams.

Mother. Louder!

> **Manuel.** I bought a hundred ice creams for my friends. (*pause*) I should have bought a bicycle. Then I could ride by real fast and no one would see that I have ugly shoes.
>
> **REREAD**
> What does this tell you about Manuel?

(*Telephone rings, and the mother gets up to answer it. Her face brightens as she hears a relative's voice.*)

40 **Mother.** *¿Quién es? ¿Pablo? ¿Dónde está? En Chula Vista. Pues, Fresno no es muy lejos. Por Greyhound dos días, no más.* [Who is this? Pablo? Where are you? In Chula Vista. Well, Fresno is not very far. No more than two days by Greyhound (bus).]

(*Her voice fades, but she keeps talking into the telephone.*)

Manuel (*to audience*). Mom's always helping relatives from Mexico. (*mocking*) "Please, stay with us. Don't worry. We have room for you." And me? I
50 get stuck with old shoes or . . . (*looking at table piled with sewing, among it a patched-up pair of old pants*) or jeans like these.

THINK IT THROUGH
What are two reasons why Manuel can't afford new shoes right now? Which reason seems to bother him more?

Discover what happens when a bully sees Manuel with new shoes.

(*Lights fade, then come up on* Manuel *and his mother.* Manuel *holds up a pair of brand-new loafers.*)

Mother. Take care of them. They're for your birthday, except early.

Manuel. Thanks, Mom! They're really nice.

(*He hugs his mother, kicks off his old shoes, and starts to put on the new loafers.*)

60 **Mother.** They're called loafers. *Mira* [Look], you can put pennies in them.

Manuel. Where?

Mother. Here. In these slots. (*bends to put in pennies*) That's why they're called penny loafers.

(Manuel *clicks the heels of his penny loafers;* Mother *leaves stage.*)

Manuel. But why should I put pennies in? I'd rather have dimes!

(Manuel *bends to insert two shiny dimes in the slots.*
70 *He walks around the stage, admiring his*
shoes. Transfixed *by the shoes, he doesn't*
notice Angel, *the school bully, who has*
come onstage, "tagging" walls.)

> **transfixed**
> (trăns fĭkst′)
> made motionless
> by amazement

Angel. What's wrong with you, homes? You loco?

> **homes**
> (hōmz)
> slang for
> homeboy, friend

Manuel. Oh, hi, Angel!

Angel. There's something different about
    you. . . . (*circles* Manuel) How come you're
    wearing those kind of shoes? You look like a
80   nerd, homes.

Manuel. They're penny loafers. Stylish, huh?

Angel (*pointing*). What's that?

Manuel. What's what?

Angel. That shine! Looks like dimes. Give 'em up!

Manuel (*whining*). Angel.

Angel. Come on! Give 'em up. I could use a soda.
    Yeah, a root beer would make me feel real happy.

(Manuel *squeezes the dimes from his shoes. He hands*
the dimes over to Angel, *who leaves, flipping*
90 *the coins.* Manuel *walks* dejectedly *back*
to his house. He takes the shoes off and
throws them into a box.)

> **dejectedly**
> (dĭ jĕk′ tĭd lē)
> *adv.* sadly

THINK IT THROUGH

Why do you think Manuel puts away his new shoes?

How can a party make Manuel change his mind about his new shoes? Read to find out.

Manuel (*to audience*). Months pass. My mom keeps taking in relatives from Mexico, and I keep on wearing my old shoes.

(Relatives *march in a line across the stage; then his mother appears holding a letter. She sniffs the letter.*)

Manuel (*to audience*). And you know what else happens? I grow two inches. I get big. I can feel my
100   shoulders rise like mountains . . . well, more like hills. But still, they get bigger. . . . Then, I get an invitation.

Mother. Manuel, here's a letter . . . from a girl.

Manuel. A girl wrote to me?

Mother (*holding it under the light*). Yeah, it says—

REREAD

Read these lines aloud. Show the actors' emotions in your voice.

Manuel. Mom! It's personal!

(Manuel *takes the letter from his mother, who leaves stage.*)

110 **Manuel.** Wow! An invitation to Ceci's birthday party. "Games and dancing" and "Dress to impress ."

impress

(ĭm prĕs')
v. make people have a good opinion of you

(Manuel *runs offstage.* Mother *and* Tío [Uncle] José, *a Mexican* immigrant , *enter.*)

immigrant

(ĭm' ĭ grənt)
n. person who moves to another country to live

Mother. Let me show you your room. You'll share it with Manuel.

Tío José (*looking about*). Nice place, *¡Y qué grande!* [And how big!]

(*The two exit;* Manuel *enters wearing a tie and holding* a *wrapped gift. He looks down at his old shoes.*)

Manuel. I can't wear these shoes.

(*He turns to the box holding his loafers. He takes out the loafers, fits in two dimes, and then struggles to put them on.*)

Manuel. Hmmm, kind of tight. Guess my feet were growing with the rest of me.

(Manuel *walks around stage, taking hurtful steps.*)

Manuel. But I got to go to the party! It's going to be a good one.

(Manuel *walks painfully, crawls, swims, then gets back to his feet.*)

Manuel. Maybe if I walk backward, my toes won't feel so jammed.

(Manuel *begins to walk backward, sighing with relief.*)

Manuel. Wow, the world looks different. The birds look different, and the cars, and those kids over there on their bikes.

(*As* Manuel *absorbs the world in his backward walk,* Ceci *and* Partygoers *come onstage.* Manuel *bumps into* Ceci.)

Manuel. Sorry, Ceci.

Ceci. That's okay. How come you're walking backward?

Manuel. Oh, you know, to see how the world looks from the other direction. (*pause*) Also, I'm inventing a dance.

Ceci. You're what?

Manuel. A new dance. It's called . . . the Backward
150 Caterpillar.

(Manuel *demonstrates by cha-chaing backward*. Ceci
and Partygoers *fall in line and cha-cha backward, too.*)

Ceci. Look at Manuel slide in his new shoes!

THINK IT THROUGH
Why does Manuel invent a new dance?

(Partygoers *ad-lib* "*Cool shoes,*" "*Look at the dude slide,*" "*Manuel's the best!*" Partygoers *cha-cha off the stage. Lights dim, then come up on* Manuel *and* Tío José *in their beds, ready to go to sleep, their hands folded behind their heads.*)

Manuel. Doesn't that crack on the ceiling look like
160   lightning?

Tío José. *Sí* [Yes], it does. And that one over there looks like a pair of scissors, *¿qué no* [doesn't it]? (*pause*)
You have a good life, *muchacho* [boy]. A nice house and plenty to eat. Your mama's a good cook.

Manuel. I am lucky. And I had good luck at Ceci's party.

> **REREAD**
> Do you think Manuel has thought about his good luck before?

Tío José (*getting up*). Wish me luck tomorrow. I'm going to Modesto. I think I got a job in a restaurant there.

170 **Manuel.** How will you get there?

(Tío José *sits up.*)

Tío José (*hooking thumb into a "hitchhiking" manner*). *Un poquito de éste* [A little of this] and lots of walking. *Pero mira, mis huaraches son rasquachis.* [But look, my sandals are cheap, worn out.] (*laughing*) I hope they can make it to Modesto.

Mother (*offstage*). José! *¡Teléfono!* [Telephone]

(*When* Tío José *leaves,* Manuel
180 *examines his uncle's worn sandals.*
Manuel *scribbles a note as lights dim.*
Lights come up on Tío José *and* Manuel

> **REREAD**
> What do you think the note says? Why do you think so?

asleep; Tío José rises, sleepily rubbing his face. A rooster crows offstage.)

Tío José. It's morning already. (*eyes Manuel's shiny shoes at foot of bed*) What's this?

(Tío José *reads note and shakes his nephew awake.*)

Tío José. These shoes? For me? They're too nice for a worker like me.

190 **Manuel.** You have a long way to go, Tío, and you need good shoes.

(Tío José *is touched by this* gesture. *He puts on shoes and walks a few steps as he tries them out.*)

> **gesture**
> (jĕs′ chər)
> action that shows
> one's feelings

Tío José. They're perfect. *Adiós* [Goodbye], Manuel. These shoes will take me a long ways, and by the time they are worn out, you'll be as tall as your parents. They'll be looking up to you.

(Tío José *walks offstage and* Manuel *lowers his head*
200 *back onto the pillow.*)

THINK IT THROUGH

1. What does Manuel do for his uncle? Why?
2. Why does Manuel's uncle think that Manuel's family is rich?
3. Does Manuel have to give up anything to give his uncle a gift? Does that fact make the gift less important? Why or why not?

**Herbie knows
more than
other people.
Sometimes,
though, it's
better not to
know too much.**

Herbie

by Rod Serling

based on a story by Margaret St. Clair

Connect to Your Life

Have you ever known something you wished you didn't? What happened as a result?

Key to the Drama

This drama is called a teleplay. It appeared on a TV series called *Night Gallery*. The series showed science fiction stories. **Science fiction** is a form of literature. In science fiction, imaginary objects and events are based on real or possible science. In this way, the stories can make fantastic things seem real, like time travel and space aliens.

Vocabulary Preview

Words to Know

astronomy   predictions

Characters (*in order of appearance*)

Mr. Reed, TV director

Mr. Godwin, Herbie's grandfather

Mr. Wellman, head of TV studio

Herbie Bittman, young person

Secretary

Announcer

Dr. Alice Peterson, scientist

Make-up Man

SCENE: A television studio. The crew is getting ready to tape a program. One man is putting a table and chair in front of the cameras. Others are working on the lights. On one side of the stage is a viewing booth with a large window. Inside the booth, Mr. Reed, *the director, is watching the crew. An old man,* Mr. Godwin, *sits beside him. Suddenly,* Mr. Wellman *rushes into the booth. It is clear that he is the boss.*

REREAD
Read these stage directions carefully. Then draw a sketch of the TV studio.

10 **Wellman** (*to* Reed). When do you start taping?

Reed. In a couple of minutes, Mr. Wellman. (*He pauses.*) Mr. Wellman, I'd like you to meet Mr. Godwin.

(Godwin *stands up to shake hands with* Wellman. Wellman *ignores him.*)

Wellman (*to* Reed). What's the kid's name?

Reed. Herbie, sir, Herbert Bittman. Mr. Godwin here is his—

Wellman. What does the kid do?

20 **Reed.** Well, he talks about what's going on in the world.

Wellman (*angrily*). You mean he's a newsman? How old is this kid? Seven?

Reed. He's ten, Mr. Wellman.

Wellman (*more and more angrily*). A ten-year-old newsman! That's beautiful, Reed! You plan to show this at eight o'clock tonight, right? Wednesday night, right? The toughest hour of prime time! And how are we going to beat the other stations? With a ten-
30 year-old newsman?

> **REREAD**
> Why is Wellman so angry?

Reed (*nervously*). Mr. Wellman, this is Herbie's grandfather, Mr. Godwin. (*to* Godwin) This is Mr. Wellman, the head of the station.

Godwin (*quietly*). The boy has a special talent.

Wellman. Is that a fact? (*to* Reed) He'd better have a special talent! Prime time on Wednesday night!

THINK IT THROUGH
Why is Herbie at a TV studio?

FOCUS ————
What can Herbie do that nobody else can? Read to find out.

(*In the television studio, the taping of the show begins. Herbie is sitting at the table, facing a camera.*)

Herbie. Hello. My name is Herbert Bittman. I've been
40 reading a good book. It's called *The Count of Monte Cristo*. I think almost anybody might like it. I've

also started a book on astronomy . It has made me want a telescope.

astronomy
(ə strŏn′ ə mē)
n. the study of planets and stars

(Reed *looks very nervous as he watches from the viewing booth.* Wellman *sits with his mouth open. He can't believe what he's hearing.*)

Herbie. My grandfather says maybe I can have a small telescope. But I have to work hard and get good grades in school. If I get a telescope, I'll tell you
50   what I can see with it.

(*In the viewing booth,* Wellman *is shaking his head.*)

Wellman. I don't believe this! A telescope! (*to* Reed) That's what they'll need to find you after I kick you out of here! Do you know what you've done to me?

Herbie (*continuing his broadcast*). Later this evening, Gwendolyn Fox will be found. She's that little girl who's been lost in the Sierra Mountains since Thursday. Her leg is broken, but she is
60   still alive. (*He pauses.*) If I get a telescope, I want to—

REREAD
Why do you think Herbie is suddenly talking about a little girl?

Wellman (*to* Reed *in the viewing booth*). This is a joke, isn't it, Reed? You're not really planning to show this tape, are you?

Reed. Mr. Wellman, the boy makes predictions . And they always come true. Ask Mr. Godwin.

predictions
(prĭ dĭk′ shənz)
n. statements about what is going to happen

Wellman. He tells me to ask Mr. Godwin.

Godwin. Just listen to Herbie, Mr. Wellman.

70 **Herbie** (*in the studio*). I guess that's all for tonight. Oh, there's one more thing. There will be an earthquake tomorrow morning. It will happen in Los Angeles at one minute before six o'clock. I'm sorry to have to give you this kind of news.

Wellman (*very angrily*). And I'm sorry to have to give you this news, Mr. Reed. The kid has done his first and last show. And you no longer have a job with this station.

THINK IT THROUGH
What is Herbie's special talent?

FOCUS
Do you think Herbie's predictions will come true? Read to see if you're right.

Reed. Please, Mr. Wellman. I checked him out. His
80 predictions come true. Several colleges have wanted to study him.

Wellman. You're the one who should be studied! You want me to put this program on during prime time? A ten year old who makes up horror stories? (*making fun of* Herbie's *voice*) Gwendolyn Fox will be found alive with a broken leg. And there's going to be an earthquake in Los Angeles tomorrow morning.

REREAD
Read Wellman's words aloud. Show his scorn for Herbie in your voice.

90 **Godwin.** You should give the boy a chance, Mr. Wellman.

Wellman. Really? I should fall down an elevator shaft!

Godwin. My grandson has a special talent. You could call it a gift. It was his idea to share it.

Wellman. You share it, Grandpa! Put him in a carnival or something. I'm not interested in his gifts!

(*He walks out and down the hall to his office. He slumps at his desk. His* Secretary *enters.*)

Secretary. Mr. Wellman, Mr. Reed just called. He
100   wants you to turn on your television set.

Wellman. You tell Mr. Reed that I—

Secretary. He says it's a news bulletin.

(Wellman *turns on a television set. The screen shows a helicopter over a mountain peak. The voice of a television* Announcer *can be heard.*)

Announcer. The helicopter is near the little girl now. We don't know if she is hurt. But the pilot says she is alive. He saw her waving. I repeat, Gwendolyn Fox has
110   been found alive. The helicopter is about to make the rescue.

REREAD
How do you know that Herbie really can see the future?

Secretary (*smiling*). Isn't that wonderful? Who would have thought they'd find her alive?

Wellman. Herbie! Herbie Bittman! He would have thought. (*He pauses.*) It could be just luck.

Announcer. As you can see, the child is being carried to the helicopter. She has a broken leg, but she is alive.

120 **Wellman** (*turns off the television set*). We'll wait until tomorrow.

Secretary. Wait for what, Mr. Wellman?

Wellman. To see if they get the shakes in Los Angeles. If they do, I'm signing Herbie Bittman to a twenty-five year contract.

> **contract**
> (kŏn' trăkt')
> written agreement to hire someone

THINK IT THROUGH

Why is Mr. Wellman's feeling about Herbie changing?

FOCUS

Discover what happens to Herbie after his predictions come true.

(*The next morning, there is an earthquake in Los Angeles.* Herbie *starts appearing on "The Herbie Bittman Show." He predicts things like election results, plane crashes, and winners of sports events. Several* 130 *scientists want to study him. One of them is* Dr. Alice Peterson. *She has come to* Wellman's *office.*)

Peterson. I admit that I have some doubts about Herbie.

Wellman. Of course you do. I did, too, at first. But he's been right every time. He has some special kind of talent.

Peterson. What is the boy like?

Wellman. He's as normal as you or I. He comes here with his grandfather twice a week to do the show.

He never gives us any trouble. He's been on the
140 show for a year and a half. During that time, he's
made one hundred and six predictions. And every
one of them has come true!

Peterson. Can I see him now?

Wellman. Of course. He goes on the air in twenty
minutes. We'll go right into the studio.

(*They go to the studio. The crew is getting ready for
the show.* Herbie *sits with his grandfather.* Wellman
leads Dr. Peterson *over to them.*)

Wellman. Hello, Herbie. I'd like you to meet Dr.
150 Peterson. She's from the university that wants to
study you. And this is Mr. Godwin, Herbie's
grandfather. (Godwin *and* Dr. Peterson *shake
hands.*) Give us another great show, Herbie. I'll see
you later. (*He leaves.*)

THINK IT THROUGH
Why did Herbie get his own TV show?

FOCUS —————————————————————
Find out how Herbie makes his predictions.

Peterson. Do you feel like talking now, Herbie?

Herbie. They told us last week we were going to be
investigated.

Peterson (*smiling*). Not investigated. We want to
study you. I think you can teach us a lot about
160 extrasensory perception. ESP. (*She
takes out a notebook.*) Do you have
any idea how this works?

> **ESP**
> knowing things
> without using the
> senses of sight,
> hearing, smell,
> taste, and touch

Herbie. You mean my predictions? It just sort of happens.

Peterson. Do you see something in your head?

Herbie. No. It isn't pictures, and it isn't words. It just sort of comes into my mind. There is one thing I've noticed. I can't predict anything unless I already know something about it. I can predict an earthquake, because I know what an earthquake is. I knew Gwendolyn Fox was missing. If I hadn't known that, I wouldn't have known she'd be found.

170

REREAD
What does Herbie have to do before he can make a prediction?

Also, I can't tell what's going to happen more than two days before it happens.

Peterson. You can't predict something unless you know something about it?

Herbie. I guess so. It makes a kind of spot in my mind. But I can't tell what it is. It's like looking at a light with your eyes closed. You know a light is there. But that's all you know about it. That's why I read so many books. The more things I know about, the more things I can predict.

180

THINK IT THROUGH
Explain what Herbie needs in order to make predictions.

Reed (*comes over*). Herbie, it's time to get your make-
up on.

Herbie. Excuse me, Dr. Peterson. (*He goes to his chair
and table, where his* Make-up Man *is waiting.*)

Peterson (*to* Godwin). What is it like living with such
a famous grandson?

190 **Godwin.** Is that really important?

Peterson. Not really. I just want to learn all I can
about Herbie.

Godwin. That's the problem. He has become public
property. He gets thousands of letters every week.
They come from public leaders, bookies ,
sick people. They call him on the phone,
they write, they come to the house. (*He
points to a man in a corner of the studio.*)
See that man? He's with the FBI. He's here
200 during every show. If Herbie says something that
might be a government secret, he'll stop the taping.
(*He looks at* Herbie, *who is having make-up put on
his face.*) Herbie doesn't seem changed by all this.
And yet, I can't help wondering.

> **bookies**
> (bŏŏk' ēz)
> people who
> make bets for
> others

Peterson. Go on.

Godwin. What is it like being able to look into
tomorrow? Imagine the strain it must put on him.
Suddenly, he knows about a disaster that hasn't
happened yet. And he can't do anything about it.
210 That must be hard for an eleven year old.

THINK IT THROUGH
What problems does fame bring Herbie? Which problem does
Herbie's grandfather think is the hardest?

Read to find out about a new problem that Herbie may be having.

(Reed *has been talking with* Herbie. *Now he comes over to* Godwin.)

Reed. Mr. Godwin, would you come over here?

Godwin. A problem?

Reed (*upset*). I'm not sure.

(Godwin *and* Reed *walk over to* Herbie. Peterson *follows them.*)

Godwin. What's the matter, Herbie?

Herbie. Grandfather, take me home.

220 **Wellman** (*running into the studio*). What's the trouble? What's going on? (*To* Herbie.) Now, what's the problem, Herbie? They say you don't want to do the show.

Herbie. I want to go home.

Wellman. Are you tired? Don't you feel well?

Herbie. I feel all right. But I just—can't do it today. (*He stands up.*) I have to go home, Grandfather.

Godwin. Then that's what we'll do.

Wellman. Just like that? Take a walk? What about our
230 schedule? What about the time and money we've put into this? If he's not sick, there's no excuse—

Godwin. The excuse is that Herbie just doesn't want to do it today. Come on, Herbie.

Wellman. Wait a minute! Herbie, what about all your fans? They sit and wait for you. They need you. If you don't go on, they'll get scared. They'll imagine all sorts of awful things. You can see that, can't you?

REREAD

Read these lines aloud. What does Wellman make Herbie think about?

Herbie **91**

Herbie. Maybe you're right.

240 **Wellman.** Herbie, after this show, we'll talk about a
vacation. Anywhere you want to go. The station will
pay for it. But, right now, you've got to do this show.

Herbie. All right, Mr. Wellman. I'll try. (*to Godwin,
who looks worried*) It's all right, Grandfather. (*He
tries to smile.*) It's really all right.

(*The show goes on.* Herbie *talks about what he did in
school that day.* Wellman *looks worried. He's afraid*
Herbie *won't make any predictions.*)

Herbie. Now I want to tell you about tomorrow. It's
250 going to be different from anything that's ever
happened. Tomorrow will be the start of a new and
better world. There won't be any more wars. We'll
begin living side by side like brothers and sisters.
We'll begin to see the end of hunger and disease.
There's going to be a kind of garden growing all over
the world. People will live a long time and be happy.
When they die, it will be from old age. Pretty soon,
we'll send out spaceships. We'll go to Venus and the
other planets. Someday, we'll visit the stars.
260 Tomorrow is going to be the beginning of all that.
(*He pauses.*) That's all for now. Good-by. Good night.

(Herbie *and* Godwin *go to a hotel to get away from
the public. Crowds of people are celebrating in the
streets.* Herbie *watches them from the window of the
hotel room.*)

THINK IT THROUGH
Were you surprised that Herbie gave such a good prediction?
Why or why not?

Godwin (*entering*). Herbie? Dr. Peterson is here.

(Herbie *turns to face them.*)

Peterson. Herbie? You told me you couldn't see into the future for more than forty-eight hours.

270 **Herbie.** That's right.

Peterson. Then how could you know all the things you predicted today?

Herbie. Do you really want me to tell you?

Peterson (*after a pause*). Yes, I do.

Herbie. If I hadn't read an astronomy book, I wouldn't have known. I'd only have known that something big was going to happen. (*He pauses.*)

Tomorrow the sun will be different. I think it's better this way, Dr. Peterson. I

280 wanted the people to be happy. That's why I lied to them.

> **REREAD**
> What did Herbie do differently this time?

Peterson (*moving toward* Herbie). What are you trying to say? What's going to happen tomorrow?

Herbie. I've forgotten the word. It's when a star becomes a billion times hotter than it was before.

Peterson (*whispering*). A nova?

Herbie. That's right. A nova.

Godwin. What does that mean?

Peterson. The sun explodes!

290   **Herbie** (*putting his hand on* Godwin's *arm*). Don't be scared, Grandfather. It will happen so quickly, we won't even feel it. Nobody else will feel it either. They will just expect it to be a better day. Maybe afterward, that's what it will be.

THINK IT THROUGH

    1. What is really going to happen tomorrow?
    2. What gift does Herbie give to the people?
    3. Do you think Herbie does the right thing? Why or why not?

The End

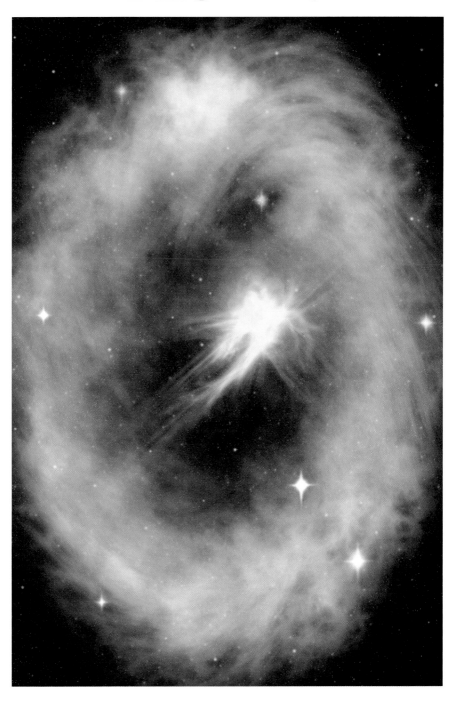

Family Snapshots

Unit 5

Mixed Genres

Do you have a photo album? Does it include snapshots of your family and friends? Snapshots help you remember certain times in your life and the lives of your family and friends.

In this unit, you'll read two short stories, a folk tale, a poem, and an anecdote. All will give you "snapshots" of different families.

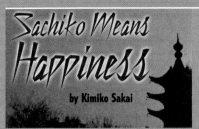

Sachiko Means Happiness

by Kimiko Sakai

幸子

People change. But how do you deal with change in a loved one?

Connect to Your Life

Has illness changed someone close to you? How did the changes affect you?

Key to the Short Story

"Sachiko Means Happiness" is an example of **realistic fiction.** The story is made up, but the characters act like real people. They have the same kinds of problems that people have in real life.

Sometimes older adults get a disease that causes them to lose their memory. They may even forget who they are and who their family members are. In this story, a granddaughter has to face changes in her grandmother. Read to find out how she handles it.

Vocabulary Preview

Words to Know

impatiently	wicked	reassure
crossly	recognize	

 Reading Coach CD-ROM selection

FOCUS

Sachiko doesn't like evenings. Read to find out why.

I don't like sunsets, even if they are so beautiful. Trouble always comes in the evening. In the evening it always begins.

"Sachiko, where are you? Come and help me," called Mother.

So it began as usual.

"Here I am." I opened the door and entered the kitchen.

Mother looked at me with relief. "Sachiko, please
10 talk with Grandmother for a while. I am busy preparing supper."

Grandmother and I have the same name, Sachiko. This name means happiness in Japanese. I was her first granddaughter. When I was born, she was very glad and gave her name to me. She loved me very much. She always looked at me lovingly and gave me special attention.

But she has changed, changed much. Now, even when I stand by her side, she does not seem to notice me.

THINK IT THROUGH

Why does Sachiko feel the way she does about evenings?

How has Grandmother changed?

20   "Hello, Grandma," I said to her.

She didn't look at me. She only said, "I should go home. It's already late. Mother will be worried."

Mother? Whose Mother was she talking about?

"Hello, Grandma," I said again impatiently.

She turned to me and cried angrily, "I am not Grandmother!"

> **impatiently**
> (ĭm pā′ shənt lē)
> *adv.* in an irritated manner

Not Grandmother? Who is she then? Why does she say she is not Grandmother? Why does she say she 30 should go home? Why does she make so much trouble for me?

"I am Sachiko—five years old!" she said firmly.

I felt like crying. I was tired, very tired.

> **REREAD**
> Why is Sachiko upset?

"Why should I take care of her?" I thought crossly. "She says she doesn't know me. Well, then I don't know her either."

As I looked at her, a wicked idea came to me. If she doesn't want to be my 40 grandmother, she doesn't have to stay here. She can go anywhere she wants. It is her problem.

> **crossly**
> (krôs′ lē)
> *adv.* in an angry way

> **wicked**
> (wĭk′ ĭd)
> *adj.* bad; evil

"You can go home," I said.

Her face lit up with joy.

"Do you know the way to your home?" I asked.

"Of course I know."

We went out. The air was fresh and cool and smelled of autumn.

"You are very kind," said Grandmother. "May I 50 know your name?"

"Sachiko," I said coldly, but she didn't seem to mind.

"We have the same name. I like you very much," she said, just as if she were singing.

I didn't know where she was going, so I just followed her. When I was little she sometimes took me for a ride on her back. Her back was strong and warm then. I was her "little Sachiko" then.

We walked and walked. Suddenly, she stopped and cried, "I can't find the way. I can't!" She turned to 60 me. She was in tears.

"What's the matter?" I asked.

"I don't know. I don't know. I can't find anything." She continued weeping.

I did not know what to do. I had never seen a grownup cry like this. I looked into her eyes trying to find the Grandmother I once knew. I saw instead a small, lost child, frightened and alone. She did not **recognize** anyone, not even me, and she was scared.

> **recognize**
> (rĕk′ əg nīz′)
> v. know

THINK IT THROUGH

Grandmother was happy for a while. What made her sad?

70   Slowly I began to understand. She is no longer Grandmother. She is a little girl, only five years old. But when she was five, I was not born yet. I am a stranger to her. And Mother, Father and the neighbors are strangers to her too.

"It must be very hard," I thought, "to suddenly discover that everyone is a stranger to you." I blinked back tears, but they were not tears of anger.

I looked at her for a long time. At last I hugged her and said, "Would you stay with me

80 tonight? Surely my mother knows your house. She will call your mother and tell her you are staying with us."

reassure
(rē′ ə shŏŏr′)
v. make someone feel sure

She looked at me seriously and asked, "May I really stay with you?"

"Of course, you can," I answered and grasped her hand tightly to reassure her, this little five-year-old girl.

REREAD
What does Sachiko do to make Grandmother feel better?

We began to walk slowly. When we got to our corner, I saw my father getting out of his

90 car. He turned to us.

"What are you doing?" he asked.

Grandmother seemed uneasy. I patted her arm.

"Dad, this is Sachiko, my friend. Is it okay if she stays with us tonight?"

Father looked at me, and looked at Grandmother without saying anything. He nodded, "Of course, it's okay. We will be happy to have you stay with us."

Grandmother smiled at me, relieved. "Thank you," she said timidly, "Thank you."

100   Again Father nodded, nodded knowingly. He took my hand and Grandmother's hand. The three of us walked together towards the house.

As we walked, I turned to Grandmother. The sunset was reflected on her face.

"Look at the sunset!" I said.

We stood looking at it for a while without saying anything. It was beautiful. For the first time, I thought, I liked it.

THINK IT THROUGH

1. What does Sachiko finally understand about Grandmother? Find the place in the story where she understands.
2. What details in the story show how Sachiko's feelings change toward Grandmother?
3. Why does Sachiko feel differently about sunsets at the end of the story?

A NOTE FROM THE AUTHOR: Kimiko Sakai

Everybody has two grandmothers. I also did. But my grandmothers are both dead, because I am far older than you. I have been an adult for many years.

Let me tell you about one of my grandmothers, my mother's mother. She was born in 1893—long ago. Like most women of her time, her life was not easy. She was a farmer's wife and worked very hard. She had ten children and eighteen grandchildren. Two of her daughters died of illness and one of her sons died in the war. She was a good mother and grandmother—a strong, quiet woman who never complained about anything. Everybody loved her.

Soon after she turned eighty years old, she got a disease that caused her to lose her memory. My grandmother was very kind and strong, but this disease changed her. I could not understand this disease or this change. I just kept looking at her, not knowing what to do. I was a child then. But now I am an adult and now I feel I could do something for her if she were here. That is why I wrote this story.

FROM CHILDHOOD

BY BILL COSBY

WHEN CAN A BED TURN INTO A BOXING RING? WHEN YOU HAVE TO SHARE IT WITH A SISTER OR BROTHER.

"This is my side of the bed," I told him one night, "and I don't want you on it."

"What do you mean your side of the bed?" said Russell. "Ain't nobody owns a side."

"Well, *I* do an' this is it, an' I'm tellin' you I don't want your body touching my body on my side of the bed."

"An' I'm tellin' *you* I'll move to any side of the bed I want: the right side, the left side, or any of the others."

10 "Any but my side. I don't want you touching anything, like me."

Doesn't this scene make your own children's fights seem like leaps of intellect?

"How come all of a sudden you don't want anybody touching you?" said Russell.

"For a very good reason," I told him. "Because you are not really my brother."

He seemed surprised by this news; he had presumed we were closely related.

20 "Well, I'm *somebody's* brother."

"That could be. You just don't happen to be mine."

REREAD

Does Russell really believe he isn't Bill's brother?

"How do you know? You look it up or somethin'?"

"Because you weren't born here."

"An' who brought me here? The *stork?*"

"No, the police. They said, 'Take care of this boy until he starts touching.'"

It was not possible for Russell and me to take to a 30 lower level what was already the most stupid conversation in the history of sibling rivalry. Both of

presumed
(prĭ zōōmd´)
v. thought something was true; past tense of *presume*

us, however, were eager to continue, so we now gave a new dimension to the exchange: violence.

"I can touch your raggedy old body anytime I want to," said Russell, emphasizing his point by belting me in my chest.

"You take that back!" I said.

"No, I won't; it's all yours."

"Okay then, you take *this*. And I got you last!"

"Not anymore," he said with another punch.

The bed had become a boxing ring with two feebleminded flyweights.

"Well, I'm hitting you *two* times last!" I said.

"And I'm hitting you *three* times last!" he replied.

feebleminded
(fē′ bəl mīn′dĭd)
stupid

flyweights
(flī′ wāts′)
boxers who weigh no more than 112 pounds

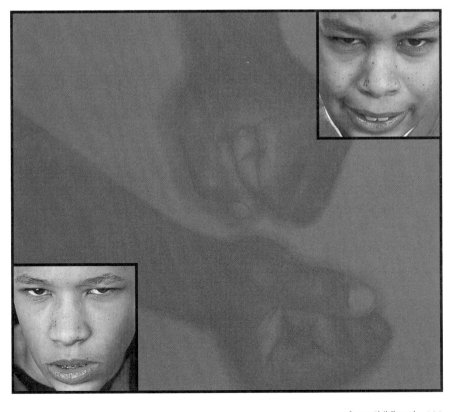

The two of us were nicely proving that Darwin had been wrong. With nitwit dedication, we kept trying to top each other in landing the most final blows until Russell had to stop to blow his nose because he was crying.

THINK IT THROUGH
Does Bill and Russell's fight remind you of anything you've done or heard? Explain.

FOCUS
Read to find out what happens next.

"Be quiet, you fool!" I said, a suggestion that made him cry even louder, until there came a voice from outside the room that I'd been expecting:

"What's going *on* in there?"

"Oh, that ain't us, Dad," I said.

"Well, you take a message to whoever it is. You tell 'em if they don't quiet down, I'm comin' in with my belt."

"I'll be happy to tell 'em, Dad, if I happen to see 'em."

And then I turned to Russell and fiercely whispered, "You don't shut up, Dad's comin' in with his belt an' it'll rip the meat off your bones. You'll wish *I* was hittin' you again."

"You hit me in the eye," he said through his whimpers, "an' my *eyeball* fell out."

REREAD
How do Bill and his brother exaggerate?

"Well, if it did, I'm sorry an' I'll find it for ya. It's gotta be right here in the bed."

"You always hit people in the face."

"That's a lie: I hit Fat Albert an' I can't even reach his face. Nobody can. Look, I said I'm sorry. Now if

you don't take my apology , I'm gonna
bust you one."

"Sure, hit a *little* guy."

"That's the only guy in the bed."

"You hit me in the face an' I'm
tellin' Dad."

"Good. Commit suicide."

"Hey, why'd you pull the covers offa me?"

80   "'Cause I don't have none on this side."

"Well, don't take mine."

"Look, Russell, I'm gettin' tired of you wettin' the
bed an' then I roll over in the cold spot."

"It ain't always cold."

"By the time *I* get there, it is."

"I hate you! I hate *all* brothers!"

"That includes you."

Suddenly, the bedroom door opened and my father
appeared. "Okay, you two, what's goin' on in here?"

90   "Nothing, Dad—really *nothing*," I said, buying
time for a miracle to save us, perhaps Philadelphia's
first tidal wave.

"Then why is Russell crying?"

"He fell out of bed, Dad, and right on his eye.
Didn't you, Russ?"

"Yeah, Dad, I think that's what happened," said
Russell. "See, I was up on the bed—"

"Havin' a bad dream," I said.

"Right, havin' a bad dream. An' I fell
100 down in the dream an' he tried to catch
me an' my eye hit his fist 'cause it was
my side of the bed."

"That's the most stupid story I ever
heard," my father said.

---

apology

(ə pŏl′ ə jē)
n. act of saying
one is sorry for
doing something
wrong

REREAD

With a partner,
reread this
passage aloud.
Try to make Bill
and Russell's
dad believe
your story.

Some philosopher once said, "Children and fools cannot lie." He, of course, was one of the latter. Do you want to be certain that your children are telling the truth? Then limit your questions to the names of their schools.

110   "It only *sounds* stupid," I said. "You gotta understand he kept sayin' they were his covers."

"But you said the police brought me and this ain't really my father."

"Now listen to me, you two. If I hear any more cryin' or arguin' or heavy breathin', I'm comin' in here with The Belt or maybe a machete. Go to *sleep!*"

> **RERED**
> Do you think Bill and Russell's father is serious? Why or why not?

THINK IT THROUGH

What excuses does Bill give for the noise he and Russell make?

FOCUS

Read to find out if Bill and Russell obey their father.

"And *another* thing" said Russell after Dad had left, for the thing that best defines a child is the total

120 inability to receive information from anything not plugged in, "get your cold feet off me, man."

"That's the temperature feet are supposed to be, you jerk," I said.

"Not *human* feet. Get 'em *off!*"

"Be quiet. Dad's at the door with a machete."

> **machete**
> (mə shĕt′ ē)
> large knife

"What's that?"

"An Italian machine gun."

"Hey, you know what *I* can do?"

130 "I don't care, unless it's leavin' the bed and goin' to sleep on the roof."

"I can jump up and down on the bed and almost hit my head on the ceiling."

"Russell, your head ain't workin' right *now*. You wanna break it even more?"

"Wanna see me do it?"

"Sure, I never saw the inside of a head."

For the next couple of minutes, Russell put everything he had into trying to fracture his skull by

140 using the bed as a trampoline. At least he soon would be asleep.

"I betcha we could do it *together*," he said after one of his landings. "'Cause that's a lotta bodies, an' if we get a lotta bodies bouncin', it'll really go up."

Although Russell's grasp of physics was hardly Newtonian, I let him grab my hand as we began jumping together. Moments later, one of our landings

150 produced a great crack that I hoped was in Russell and not in the bed; but unfortunately, he was fine.

> **physics**
> (fĭz′ ĭks)
> *n.* science of how matter and energy act together. Sir Isaac Newton developed many physics concepts.

> **REREAD**
> Do you think the fight is over? Why or why not?

"Oh, man," he said, "now you done it: you broke the bed!"

"*I* broke the bed?" I cried. "*You* started the jumpin'."

"But it's broke on your side."

"An' you better help me fix it or your face is gonna be broke on your side."

"I think I'd like to do a little face breaking too,"

160 said a familiar voice as the door flew open.

This time, Russell and I both ducked under the covers of the tilted bed.

THINK IT THROUGH
How do Bill and Russell break the bed?

"If my sons are anywhere near this broken bed,"
said the voice, "I'd like to know if they have any
last words."

"Dad, I gotta tell ya what happened," I said,
intending to do no such thing as I reappeared. "Some
man came in here and just started jumpin' on the bed.
He came right through the *window.*"

170   "You really want me to believe that, don't you?"

"Dad, I could never lie to you because you're
beautiful."

My father knew, however, that I could have lied to
Marilyn Monroe.

"It was his side of the bed that broke, Dad,"
said Russell.

"Okay, here's the story," my father said. "If I have
to come back in here once more, you'll both be
sleeping on hospital beds."

180   The moment Dad left, I thought about a
reconciliation with Russell, but decided
against it.

"You're the most stupid brother in the
history of human families," I said. "And
maybe the other kind too."

"I have to go to the bathroom," he replied.
"And don't take my side of the bed while I'm gone."

This was one of those times when Russell decided to
use the bathroom instead of the bed, a sign that he
190 might have been growing up. When he returned,
however, he gave a different sign by spitting a
mouthful of water on me.

"That's it!" I cried. "I'm gonna *kill* you now!"

"I'll do it for you," said my father, "and I'm not

> **reconciliation**
> (rĕk′ ən sĭl′ ē ā′
> shən)
> *n.* act of getting
> back together
> after a fight or
> argument

even gonna ask you where all that water on the bed came from."

"And I'm gonna tell ya, Dad," I said, "'cause I think you should know. A man came in here and dumped a whole bucket of water on us."

200 "The same man who jumped on the bed?"

"That's the one! Dad, he's no good."

"Okay, since you boys wanna spend the night breakin' beds an' spittin' water an' greetin' people who come in the window, I'm gonna let ya get out of bed."

"Oh, good," said Russell. "We don't gotta sleep any more, Dad?"

"Right: you'll both stand here for the rest of the night. An' if I catch either of you movin', I'm gonna kill ya or do

210 somethin' even worse. You understand?"

REREAD

How does Bill's father exaggerate?

My father had not been gone for more than thirty seconds when Russell turned to me and said, "An' I don't want you touchin' my side of the *floor,* neither."

THINK IT THROUGH

1. Suppose the story continued. Tell what would happen next.
2. Do you think Bill really thinks his father will believe his excuses? Why or why not?
3. Pick a passage from the story that you thought was funny. Find a sentence in the passage that contains exaggeration.

The Boondocks

Boondocks copyright © 2000 Aaron Mcgruder. Distributed by Universal Press Syndicate. Reprinted with permission. All rights reserved.

Three Hundred Pesos

by Manuela Williams Crosno

No goal is impossible to reach. But what will it cost in the end?

Connect to Your Life

Have you ever wanted to save money or wanted a better grade in a class? In either case, you set a goal. What did you do to reach your goal? How long did it take?

Key to the Folk Tale

"Three Hundred Pesos" is a folk tale. A **folk tale** is a story that has been told for many years. It can have people or animals as characters. A folk tale often teaches a lesson about what is really important.

In this story you will read about a man who is a miser. A miser is a person who is very greedy about money.

Vocabulary Preview

Words to Know

peso	distress	shortage
misfortune	doom	profit

"Just to keep one peso Anastacio would let
his own brother starve!" Emil Perea was
talking to his sister, Berta.

peso
(pā' sō)
n. Mexican
money that is
similar to a dollar
in the United
States

"And how do you know this, brother?"

"I know it from yesterday, Berta. When
we were children it was not so."

"Well do I remember those happy days," sighed
Berta. "But what is this you say of our brother?" she
asked. "How do you know he will not give food to
10 his brother or his sister who have need?"

"I went to Anastacio only yesterday because my
little Pedro is sick. For three days now he will not
even taste of the milk from the goats.

I asked our brother Anastacio for a
peso to buy medicine to make my Pedro
well again—"

niños
(nē' nyōs)
Spanish word
meaning
"children"

"He will not give it to you?"

"No, he will not give it. He said,
'Emil, go away and do not bother me. *I*
20 did not marry. *I* have no *niños* to worry
me. I also have no pesos to give you. I
am busy now.' That is how he talked
with me."

REREAD
Why does
Anastacio feel he
shouldn't have
to give Emil a
peso?

"Our brother is no good," said Berta. "But do not
worry. I will give you a peso to get medicine for Pedro."

At this very moment, their brother, Anastacio, was
walking across his field of corn. The year had been a
good one with much rain. He saw that his crop was
good, and green, and he was certain it would pay him
30 well when it ripened in the fall.

Soon he would have those three hundred pesos! All
his life, it seemed, he had been working hard for this

exact amount. He would have it now because the corn was good. He would sell it for a high price!

High in the warm, blue sky a crow flew over the field. It sped away toward the dark mountains to the west.

Anastacio shook his fist at the bird. "My corn is not for *you!*" he shouted. 40 "You are like my brother and my sister— nothing have I to give any of you!"

REREAD

What do you think of the way Anastacio treats his brother and sister?

THINK IT THROUGH

How do Emil and Berta feel about Anastacio? How does he feel about them?

FOCUS

What is Anastacio's plan?

Again, as many times before, his thoughts went back to the day when his plan had been born.

He was a small boy and had asked the storekeeper, "How is it you do no work?"

"I am the storekeeper," the man had replied, smiling.

For several days, the small Anastacio thought about this amazing piece of information. *His* father worked hard in the fields, as did all of their neighbors.

50 Again he went to the storekeeper. "How much does it take to make the store?"

"Oh, a man can begin with about three hundred pesos." The storekeeper looked at the serious boy. "But that is a lot of money," he warned.

From that day, Anastacio's goal had been set. He *must* earn three hundred pesos! But this had not been easy to do. Although he held onto his money like a

miser, he had made some investments which were not good. And misfortune was his
60 shadow in other matters of business. One time, someone had stolen money from his home. Now he kept his pesos in a leather bag under his shirt, tightly tied to his trouser belt.

Anastacio removed the leather bag from his belt. He counted his money. Two hundred pesos! From the sale of his corn he might make fifty more! He looked out across the field and was satisfied.

investments
(ĭn věst′ mənts)
money put into something, such as property or stocks, in order to make more money

misfortune
(mĭs fôr′ chən)
n. bad luck

THINK IT THROUGH
| Why has Anastacio's goal been difficult to reach?

FOCUS ——————————————————
| Read to find out two things that happen to Anastacio's corn.

That night hail came. The people in the valley
70 declared they had never before seen hailstones so big. Window panes were broken, the trees were stripped. The corn in the field of Anastacio was in shreds!

Anastacio stood beside his field and wondered what to do. Along came his brother, Emil.

"Brother," said Emil, "my corn is ruined, too. It is a sad loss. But corn is not everything in life. We can plant more corn. Come home with me and join us for a hot supper of tortillas and chili."

Anastacio was angry. He wanted to place the blame
80 for the hail on his brother. He felt that in some strange way Emil was responsible for this loss. Perhaps if he had given him money for the sick *niño*—?

"Go!" he shouted at his brother. "I have no time to eat with you!"

REREAD
How does Anastacio react to Emil's kindness?

Shortly afterward, Anastacio replanted his field. In July of that year, his sister, Berta, came to see him. She was slight and frail and seemed very nervous. Berta sat down, pulling a thin, black shawl over her head and around her shoulders. Her small face,

90 peering out from the shawl, made her look like a starving bird.

Anastacio looked at her and wished that he had no relatives to bother him. It was clear that his sister was in distress.

> **distress**
> (dĭ strĕs′)
> *n.* trouble

"Why do you come here?" he asked harshly. He had decided to bring the interview to a quick end.

"A tree has fallen on the roof of my *casa.*"

"So?"

100 "We have no money now for materials to make the repairs. If you can lend us but a few pesos, we will pay you back shortly."

Anastacio thought of the money he had—of his pesos. He thought of the store he would some day own.

"I have no money—to give you," he said. "Nor do I have room for you and your husband in my small *casa.* But go to our brother, Emil. Perhaps *he* can give you money. Perhaps *he* can take you in."

Berta went silently from the house. As she walked

110 away, the wind blew her shawl and lifted it above her shoulders. Her shadow, on the ground, looked like that of a great, black bird. Anastacio shook off a feeling of coming doom.

> **doom**
> (do͞om)
> *n.* very bad ending

The next day, he discovered that his field had been invaded by wandering sheep. The corn was completely ruined. Most of the tender stalks had been eaten or trampled, and it was too late to plant again.

Later, Anastacio saw Berta on her way to the village. Emil and his family were with her. Anastacio wanted, somehow, to place the blame for the ruined corn on Berta. If he had given her money? If he had allowed her to stay?

He looked bitterly in Berta's direction, but her face was calm and peaceful. If she saw her brother, she gave no sign of recognizing him.

THINK IT THROUGH
Why can't Anastacio sell his corn? Whom does he blame?

FOCUS
Read to find out what Anastacio does next.

During the winter of that year, Anastacio made fifty pesos by cleverly trading some horses. By spring, he lacked just fifty pesos of the amount he desired. He did not see his brother or his sister. "May I never be bothered with them again!" he said to himself.

When spring came, and snow in high places began to melt and run in streams down into the valleys, Anastacio planted his field. This time he put in pinto beans. He had heard they would bring a good price, for there had been a shortage the season before.

shortage
(shôr′ tĭj)
n. not enough of something

No one saw Anastacio all summer, so busy was he guarding his field from possible damage. All day he
140 worked in the field, and at night he lay down beside it to be there should anything happen.

In the fall the pods were dry. Then Anastacio harvested his pinto beans. He placed them in open wooden boxes and loaded them into his wagon. He had a large crop of fine beans ready to sell.

He started for the village. If he were lucky, he might make fifty pesos. This would complete the amount he needed—three hundred pesos! At last! Yes, it would be his best winter! With the money he could buy a
150 store. On cold winter days he would sit near the fire. He would have little to do and plenty to eat.

Although he had these pleasant thoughts, Anastacio was not a happy man. He would need to guard his store carefully. If he did not, Berta and Emil would beg all of his profit from him. They would think the food in his grocery store was free. They would think it was to be shared by all of them!

profit
(prŏf′ ĭt)
n. money left after spending for supplies and equipment

THINK IT THROUGH
Anastacio has almost reached his goal. Why is he still not happy?

> Read to find out if Anastacio's new plan will work.

160 Anastacio drove along a winding road. It rose higher and higher before descending into the valley where he intended to sell his beans. Finally, Anastacio reached the top. He then started down at once, urging on his exhausted horses with a snap of the reins.

Anastacio turned round a curve on the downward side of the road. Suddenly, he was struck from behind by a fast moving horseless wagon. The driver had not seen Anastacio in time. He banged into the back of the wagon, tearing off the board that 170 held the boxes of beans in place. This frightened the horses. They reared, tipping the wagon, and hurling Anastacio into the air. He fell against the trunk of a tree, heavily striking his head and shoulders. The horses ran wildly along the side of the road, scattering beans everywhere.

horseless wagon
car

reared
(rîrd)
rose up on the hind legs

By spring, he lacked just fifty pesos of the amount he desired. He did not see his brother or his sister. "May I never be bothered with them again!" he said to himself.

Anastacio was dazed. But looking ahead, he saw that the horses had finally stopped in a grove of trees near the home of his brother, Emil.

180 Anastacio turned around. He saw that, except for the broken board, the wagon was not damaged. It appeared that the horses had not been hurt either. This was good, but his crop was lost again! All of the boxes had been thrown from the wagon. Beans were scattered in the dirt and in the ditch beside the road.

At this moment, the man in the horseless carriage returned. He apologized for causing the accident. Then, seeing the beans along the road, he asked how much they had been worth.

190 "Fifty pesos!" gasped the unhappy Anastacio.

"Done!" said the traveler, handing over the money. He was glad to pay this amount and escape without further trouble.

Anastacio was satisfied. When he was again alone, he took from his belt the leather bag. He held the bag in one hand and the fifty pesos in the other. There were two hundred and fifty pesos in the bag, and now he had fifty pesos more. He could buy the store at

200 last! He was a rich man!

REREAD

The story is not over yet. How do you think it will end?

He sighed and sat down on a stump. How his head ached! His chest burned from the blow he had received. It seemed so hard to breathe—

Suddenly, he fell forward and lay quite still in the warm sunshine. Overhead, three large, black birds circled slowly about.

The horses belonging to Anastacio stopped a short distance from a field. There, Emil and his wife and Berta were working. It was a warm morning, the crop was

210 plentiful, and the three people were very happy indeed.

"Look!" shouted Emil. "The horses of our brother!"

"But where is he?" asked Emil's wife.

"Let us see!" exclaimed Berta.

Together they hurried up the road. Soon they came to the body of their brother. It was lying so still, they knew he was dead.

"Poor Anastacio!" cried Emil. "What is this terrible thing that has happened to you?"

220 "Poor brother!" Berta grieved. "I remember the little boy you were and how we loved you then."

REREAD

Does their reaction surprise you? Why or why not?

Emil drew from his brother's clenched hand the money bag and pesos.

"Much money!" he said, when he had counted it. "Fifty pesos!"

Berta opened the bag and removed the money.

"Two hundred and fifty pesos more!" she gasped in astonishment.

"Three hundred pesos!" they exclaimed, all together.
230 "What a beautiful funeral this will give for him!"

THINK IT THROUGH

1. How does Anastacio reach his goal?
2. **Irony** is the difference between what you expect to happen and what actually does happen. What is the irony in the last line of the story?
3. Contrast the way Emil and Berta treat Anastacio with the way he treats them. Use examples from the story.
4. What message about life do you get from this story?

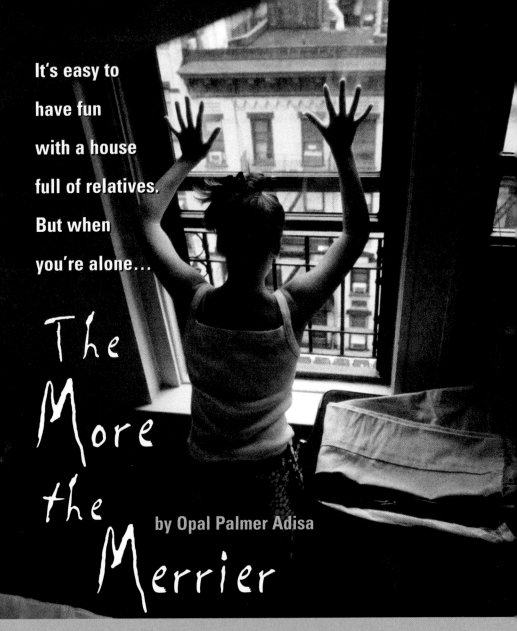

It's easy to
have fun
with a house
full of relatives.
But when
you're alone...

The More the Merrier

by Opal Palmer Adisa

▮ Connect to Your Life

Have you ever been home alone? What rules did you have to follow? Were you lonely? scared? bored?

▮ Key to the Poem

 **Reading Coach
CD-ROM selection**

In a poem, the voice that talks to the reader is called the **speaker.** The speaker in this poem tells about feelings you may have had yourself.

   This poem is an example of free verse. In **free verse**, the poet does not use rhyming words. The lines may have different lengths to emphasize certain words or phrases.

sitting on the
windowsill
looking down
on the street
5 watching folks
go by
wanting
to be there
in the midst
10 of it all
but stuck up
here all by myself
no friend
no sister
15 no brother
not even a dog
to talk to

mama off
somewhere
20 doing chores
papa still
at work

just me
all by myself
25 warned not to
go anywhere
told not
to let anyone in
not even a friend
30 especially if
he's a boy

rules
nothing but rules
not allowed
35 to choose
not allowed
to decide for myself

i guess
the more the merrier
40 only applies
to relatives
who come to visit
on holidays

THINK IT THROUGH

1. Who is speaking in this poem? Where does the speaker live?
2. What seems unfair to the speaker? Why?
3. What rules does the speaker have to follow? How are these rules the same or different from rules you have to follow?
4. What do you think the speaker would do if she didn't have rules?

PHOENIX FARM

by Jane Yolen

Connect to Your Life

Has someone ever disappointed you? Did you ask the person why? Or did you pretend he or she no longer existed?

Key to the Short Story

A **symbol** is a thing that stands for something else. Anything can become a symbol by taking on a special meaning. In this story, a phoenix has special meaning.

The phoenix is a bird from Greek myths. Some people believed the bird lived for 500 years. In the myths, the phoenix would burn itself up at the end of its long life. Then another bird would rise from the ashes. Now the phoenix is a symbol for new life.

Vocabulary Preview

Words to Know

vanity	pulse
recession	seared
refugees	

**Reading Coach
CD-ROM selection**

BAD THINGS HAPPEN TO GOOD PEOPLE. HOW YOU HANDLE YOUR PROBLEMS IS WHAT MATTERS.

Read to find out what happened in the narrator's life.

We moved into Grandma's farm right after our apartment house burned down along with most of the neighborhood. Even without the fire, it had not been a good California summer, dry as popcorn and twice as salty, what with all the sweat running down our faces.

I didn't mind so much—the fire, I mean. I had hated that apartment, with its pockmarked walls and the gang names scribbled on the stoop. Under my bedroom window someone had painted

10   the words "Someday, sugar, you gonna find no one in this world gonna give you sweet." The grammar bothered me more than what it said.

REREAD
What do you think this sentence means?

Mama cried, though. About the photos, mostly. And about all her shoes having burned up. She has real tiny feet and her one vanity is shoes. She can buy the model stuff for really cheap. But it's not just the photos and the shoes. She cries about everything these days.

vanity
(văn′ ĭ tē)
n. something that one takes great pride in

20   It's been that way since Daddy died.

Ran off. That's what Nicky says. A week before the fire. *Couldn't take it. The recession and all. No job. No hope.*

recession
(rĭ sĕsh′ ən)
n. period of time when businesses lose money

Mama says it won't be forever, but I say he died. I can deal with it that way.

And besides, we don't want him back.

THINK IT THROUGH
What two serious events have happened? How does the narrator feel about them?

So we got ready to head for Grandma's farm up in the valley, with only the clothes we'd been wearing; our cat, Tambourine; and Mama's track medals, all fused

30   together. She found them when the firefighters let us go back upstairs to sort through things. Nicky grabbed a souvenir, too. His old basketball. It was flat and blackened, like a pancake someone left on the stove too long.

> souvenir
> (sōō′ və nîr′)
> reminder of a person, place, or event

I looked around and there was nothing I wanted to take. Nothing. All that I cared about had made it through the fire: Mama, Nicky, and Tam. It was as if we could start afresh and all the rest of it had been burned away. But as we were going

40   down the stairs—the iron stairs, not the wooden ones inside, which were all gone—I saw the most surprising thing. On the thirteenth step up from the bottom, tucked against the riser, was a nest. It was unburnt, unmarked, the straw that held it the rubbed-off gold of a wheat field. A piece of red string ran

Mama says it won't be forever, but I say he [Dad] died. I can deal with it that way. And besides, we don't want him back.

through it, almost as if it had been woven on a loom. In the nest was a single egg.

It didn't look like any egg I'd ever seen before, not dull white or tan like the eggs from the store. Not even a light blue like the robin's egg I'd found the one summer we'd spent with Grandma at the farm. This was a shiny, shimmery gray-green egg with a red vein—the red thread—cutting it in half.

"Look!" I called out. But Mama and Nicky were already in the car, waiting. So without thinking it all the way through—like, what was I going to do with an egg, and what about the egg's mother, and what if it broke in the car or, worse, hatched—I picked it up and stuck it in the pocket of my jacket. Then, on second thought, I took off the jacket and made a kind of nest of it, and carefully carried the egg and my jacket down the rest of the stairs.

When I got into the car, it was the very first time I had ever ridden in the back all alone without complaining. And all the way to the farm, I kept the jacket-nest and its egg in my lap. All the way.

THINK IT THROUGH

What was so unusual about what the narrator found?

How does each family member adjust to living in a new home?

Grandma welcomed us, saying, "I'm not surprised. Didn't I tell you?" Meaning that Daddy wasn't with us. She

70 and Mama didn't fight over it, which was a surprise on its own. Neighbors of Grandma's had collected clothes for us. It made us feel like refugees, which is an awkward feeling that makes you prickly and cranky most of the time. At least that's how I felt until I found a green sweater that exactly matched my eyes and Nicky found a Grateful Dead T-shirt. There were no shoes Mama's size. And no jobs nearby, either.

80 I stashed the egg in its jacket-nest on the dresser Mama and I shared. Nicky, being the only boy, got his own room. Mama never said a word about the egg. It was like she didn't even see it. I worried what she'd say if it began to smell.

But the days went by and the egg never did begin to stink. We got settled into our new school. I only thought about Daddy every *other* day. And I found a best friend right away. Nicky had girls calling him after dinner for the first time. So we were OK.

90 Mama wasn't happy, though. She and Grandma didn't exactly quarrel, but they didn't exactly get along, either. Being thankful to someone doesn't make you like them. And since Mama couldn't find a job, they were together all day long.

REREAD
What does this tell you about the relationship between Grandma and Mama?

refugees
(rĕf′ yŏŏ jēz′) *n.* people who must leave home to find protection or shelter somewhere else

THINK IT THROUGH
Why doesn't Mama adjust as well as Nicky and the narrator?

Then one evening my new best friend, Ann Marie, was over. We were doing homework together up in my room. It was one of those coolish evenings and the windows were closed, but it was still pretty bright outside, considering.

100   Ann Marie suddenly said, "Look! Your egg is cracking open."

I looked up and she was right. We hadn't noticed anything before, because the crack had run along the red line. When I put my finger on the crack, it seemed to pulse.

pulse
(pŭls)
v. beat regularly

"Feel that!" I said.

Ann Marie touched it, then jerked back as if she had been burned. "I'm going home now," she said.

110   "But, Ann Marie, aren't you the one who dragged me to see all those horror movies and—"

"Movies aren't real," she said. She grabbed up her books and ran from the room.

I didn't even say good-bye. The egg had all my attention, for the gray-green shell seemed to be taking little breaths, pulsing in and out, in and out, like a tiny brittle

120 ocean. Then the crack widened, and as if there were a lamp inside, light poured out.

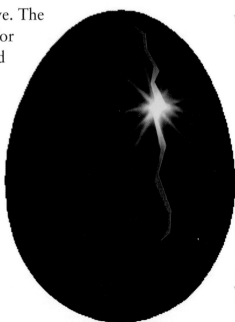

Nicky came in then, looking for some change on the dresser.

"Neat!" he said when he saw the light. "Do you know what kind of bird it's going to be? Did you look it up in Dad—" And then he stopped, because all of

130 Daddy's books had been burned up. Besides, we didn't mention him anymore. And since we hadn't heard from him at all, it was like he really *was* dead.

"No," I said. "And I don't think it's any *ordinary* bird that you would find in an *ordinary* book."

"A lizard, you think?"

Never taking my eyes off the egg, I shook my head. How stupid could he be? With that light coming out? A dragon, maybe. Then the phone rang downstairs and he ran out of the room, expecting, I guess, that it

140 would be Courtney or Brittany or another of his girlfriends named after spaniels. Talking to them was more important to him than my egg.

REREAD
What kind of egg do you think it is?

spaniels
(spăn' yəlz)
kinds of dogs

THINK IT THROUGH
How do Ann Marie and Nicky feel about the hatching egg?

FOCUS
What happens next?

But I continued to watch. I was the only one watching when it hatched. How such a large bird got into such a small egg, I'll never know. But that's magic for you. It rose slowly out of the egg, pushing the top part of the shell with its golden head. Its beak was golden, too, and curved like one of those Arabian

150 swords. Its eyes were hooded and dark, without a center. When it stared at me, I felt drawn in.

The bird gave a sudden kind of shudder and humped itself farther out of the egg, and its wings were blue and scarlet and gold, all shimmery, like some seashells when they're wet. It shook out its wings, and they were wide enough to touch from one side of the dresser to the other, the individual feathers throwing off sparkles of light.

REREAD
Try to picture this bird in your mind. Why is it so unusual?

160 Another shudder, and the bird stood free of the egg entirely, though a piece of shell still clung to the tip of one wing. I reached over and freed it, and it seared my fingers—the touch of the feather, not the shell. The bird's scarlet body and scaly golden feet pulsed with some kind of heat.

seared
(sîrd)
v. burned; past tense of *sear*

"What *are* you?" I whispered, then stuck my burnt fingers in my mouth to soothe them.

170 If the bird could answer me, it didn't; it just pumped its wings, which seemed to grow wider with each beat. The wind from them was a Santa Ana, hot and heavy and thick.

Santa Ana
strong, dry, hot wind blowing from southern California toward the Pacific Ocean

I ran to the window and flung it wide, holding the curtain aside.

The bird didn't seem to notice my effort, but still it flew unerringly outside. I saw it land once on a fencepost; a second time, on the roof of Grandma's barn. Then it headed straight toward
180 the city, the setting sun making a fire in its feathers.

When I couldn't see it anymore, I turned around. The room smelled odd—like the ashes of a fire, but like something else, too. Cinnamon, maybe. Or cloves.

> **unerringly**
> (ŭn ûr′ ĭng lē)
> without stopping or making any wrong moves

THINK IT THROUGH

How is this bird like a phoenix? Use details from the story to support your answer.

FOCUS

What does the narrator find out?

I heard the doorbell. It rang once, then a second time. Grandma and Mama were off visiting a neighbor. Nicky was still on the phone. I ran down the stairs and flung the door wide open.

Daddy was standing there, a new beard on his face and a great big Madame Alexander doll in his arms.
190 "I got a job, baby. In Phoenix. And a house rented. With a real backyard. I didn't know about the fire, I didn't know where you all had gone. My letters came back and the phone didn't connect and . . ."

"Daddy!" I shouted, and he dropped the box to scoop me up against his chest. As I snuggled my face against his neck, I smelled that same smell: ashes and cinnamon, maybe cloves. Where my burnt fingers tangled in his hair they hurt horribly.

> **REREAD**
> What else smelled like this?

200 Grandma would be furious. Nicky and Mama might be, too. But I didn't care. There's dead. And there's not.

Sometimes it's better to rise up out of the ashes, singing.

THINK IT THROUGH

1. Why did the narrator's father come back?
2. How is the phoenix a symbol of new life in this story?
3. What do you think the narrator means by "Sometimes it's better to rise up out of the ashes, singing"?

Travelin' Man

by Nikki Grimes

We're on the road
just Dad and me
in his dusty black MG.
We're going
5   it doesn't matter where
as long as we go there
together.
Sometimes
when he leaves alone
10   I worry that
he might be gone
forever.

Getting the Upper Hand

Unit 6
Fiction

A person who "gets the upper hand" is in control. In this unit, you will meet characters who try to get control. As you read, decide what you like or don't like about these characters.

You will read two stories and two folk tales. A **folk tale** is a story that has been told for many years. It can have people or animals as characters. It often teaches a lesson about life.

Whitewashing a fence
is an awful job.
But someone has to do it.

Whitewashing the Fence

by

Mark Twain

retold by

Sue Baugh

Connect to Your Life

Have you ever had to do a job you hated? What was it? Did you try to get out of doing it?

Key to the Story

"Whitewashing the Fence" is an example of a **novel excerpt**. It is from a book called *The Adventures of Tom Sawyer*. The book tells about a young boy who lived in Missouri in the 1800s. In this excerpt, the author tells about a humorous event. The word *humorous* means "funny." As you read the story, decide which parts are funny to you.

Vocabulary Preview

Words to Know
suits   fussy

 Reading Coach CD-ROM selection

Saturday morning dawned fresh and clear. All the trees were in bloom. The smell of their blossoms filled the air. The bright summer day put a song in every heart. Or almost every heart.

Tom walked out of his house with a slow, heavy step. He had a bucket of whitewash in one hand and a long-handled brush in the other. He looked at his Aunt Polly's fence. All hope left him. The wood fence was thirty feet long and nine feet high.

10

whitewash
mixture of lime, water, and white chalk. It is cheaper than paint.

With a sigh, he set the bucket down. He dipped the brush in the whitewash. He made a white stripe along the top of the fence. He dipped the brush again and painted another stripe. Then he stepped back. The white stripes looked so small, and the fence looked so big. Feeling gloomy, Tom sat down on a wooden box.

THINK IT THROUGH
| What problem does Tom have?

He had a bucket of whitewash in one hand and a long-handled brush in the other. He looked at his Aunt Polly's fence. All hope left him.

Read to find out one way Tom tries to solve his problem.

At that moment Jim came out of the house and passed by. Jim was a young man who worked for Aunt Polly. He was singing and carrying a tin pail in 20 his hand. His job was to bring water home from the town pump. Tom usually hated going for water, but not today.

"Say, Jim! I'll get the water if you'll whitewash some of this fence."

Jim shook his head.

"Can't. Miss Polly told me to go get water. I can't be fooling around with anybody. She said if you ask me to help, I just mind my own business."

REREAD
How does Aunt Polly know what Tom will do?

30 "Oh, come on. Give me the pail. I won't be gone a minute. *She* won't know."

"I don't dare. Miss Polly will be after me for sure."

"She wouldn't hurt anybody. I tell you what. I'll give you a white marble."

Jim began to weaken.

"Say! That's a mighty fine marble. But Miss Polly—"

"If you help me, I'll show you my sore toe."

That was too much for Jim. He put down his pail. He took Tom's white marble and bent down to look at 40 the boy's toe. Tom carefully took off the bandage.

At that minute Aunt Polly came out of nowhere. Jim took one look at her stern face and went flying down the street. Tom quickly picked up the brush. He started whitewashing like a windmill. Aunt Polly went back into the house, smiling to herself.

Tom's energy didn't last long. He thought about all the fun he'd planned for the day. The more he

thought about it, the sadder he got. The
other boys would come by soon. They
50 would make fun of him for having to
work. The idea burned him like fire.

REREAD

How does Tom
feel about the
other boys see-
ing him work?

He took everything out of his pockets
and looked at what he had. Bits of toys, marbles, and
trash. Not enough to pay anyone to work for him.

Then, in his darkest hour, a great idea burst upon
him. An amazing, truly wonderful idea!

THINK IT THROUGH

What have you learned about Tom's personality?

FOCUS

What do you think Tom's new idea might be? Read to
find out.

Happy now, he picked up the brush and calmly
went to work. Soon Ben Rogers came up the street. He
was eating an apple and pretending to be a steamboat.
60 When he saw Tom, Ben pulled up to watch.

Tom went on whitewashing.

Ben said: "*You're* in a real fix, ain't you?"

No answer. Tom looked at his last stripe with the
eye of an artist. He added a touch of whitewash. Ben
came up beside him. Tom's mouth watered for that
apple, but he kept on painting.

Ben tried again. "Too bad you got to work."

Tom turned around in surprise.

"Why it's you, Ben! I didn't see you."

70 "Say, *I'm* going swimming. Don't you wish *you*
could? But of course you'd rather *work*, wouldn't
you? Course you would."

Tom looked at Ben a bit, then asked, "What do you call work?"

Ben pointed to the fence. "Why, ain't *that* work?"

Tom started whitewashing again and said in a calm voice, "Well, maybe it is and maybe it ain't. All I know is, it suits Tom Sawyer."

"Oh, come on. You don't mean you
80 *like* it?"

Tom's brush kept moving. "Like it? Well, I don't see why I shouldn't like it. Does a boy get a chance to whitewash a fence every day?"

That put the job in a new light. Ben stopped eating his apple. Tom moved the brush lightly back and forth. He stepped back to check his work. He added a touch here and there. Ben watched every move. He was getting more and more interested.

suits
(so͞ots)
v. pleases

THINK IT THROUGH
How does Tom get Ben interested in whitewashing the fence?

Finally he said: "Say, Tom, let *me* whitewash a little."

90   Tom thought about it. He was about to say *yes,* then changed his mind.

"No—no—it wouldn't do, Ben. You see, Aunt Polly's awful fussy about this fence. It's right on the street, you know. If it were the back fence, she wouldn't mind. Yes, she's awful fussy about this fence. It has to be done just right. There's only one boy in a thousand, maybe two thousand, who can do it the way it ought to be done."

fussy
(fŭs' ē) *adj.* hard to please

100   Ben's eyes lit up.

"No—is that so? Oh, come on—let me just try. Only just a little. I'd let *you* if you were me, Tom."

"Ben, I would like to, honest. But Aunt Polly—well, Jim wanted to do it. She wouldn't let him. Sid wanted to do it. She wouldn't let Sid. Can you see my problem? If you were to paint this fence and anything happened to it—"

"Oh, shucks, I'll be just as careful. Let me try. Say—I'll give you the core of my apple."

110   Tom seemed to weaken. "Well . . . No, Ben, now don't. I'm afraid—"

"I'll give you *all* of it!"

Tom slowly gave up the brush. His face looked unsure, but his heart was happy. While Ben worked in the hot sun,

REREAD

Is Tom really unsure, or is he just pretending?

Tom sat on a barrel in the shade. He bit into the apple and made plans. He wanted other friends to help paint the fence.

He didn't have long to wait. Boys came by every so

120   often. They came to tease, but they stayed to whitewash.

By mid afternoon, Tom was a rich boy. He owned a kite, twelve marbles, a piece of blue glass, a key, six firecrackers, a kitten with only one eye, and many other treasures. He'd had a lot of fun, and the fence had three coats of whitewash on it!

REREAD

How do you feel about the trick Tom has played on his friends?

Most of all, Tom had learned a great law of human nature. The best way to make someone really *want* something is to make the thing hard to

130 get. He stood up. The day had turned out just fine after all. Tom went into the house to tell Aunt Polly the job was done.

THINK IT THROUGH

1. What words would you use to describe Tom? Use examples from the story to support the words you choose.
2. What does Tom learn about people? Do you agree with him? Why or why not?
3. What did you enjoy most about this story? Why?

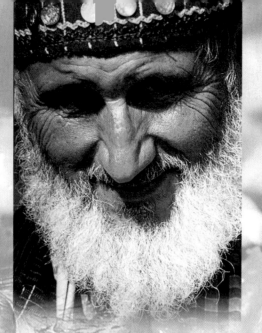

A Dinner of Smells

retold by Penny Cameron

Can you steal a meal without eating it?

Connect to Your Life

Have you ever been accused of something you didn't do? How did you prove that you didn't do anything wrong?

Key to the Folk Tale

A **folk tale** is a short story that is told for fun. Most folk tales have characters that are people or animals that act like people. Like myths and fables, folk tales may also teach lessons about life.

The **plot** tells what happens in a story. Often the plot tells about a problem a character has. In this tale, you will read about a man with a problem.

One day a poor man came into a little town. He was very hungry. Every time he saw food, his mouth watered. But he had no money.

The poor man stopped outside a fine restaurant. The food at the restaurant smelled delicious. He sniffed and sniffed the wonderful smell.

The owner of the restaurant came into the street.

"Hey! You!" the owner called. "I saw what you did! You smelled my excellent food! I

10 don't pay cooks to make food for you to smell! You stole the smell of my food. Are you going to pay for it?"

REREAD
How do you feel about the owner's statements?

The poor man replied, "I cannot pay. I have no money. I took nothing!"

The owner of the restaurant did not listen to him. "I'm taking you to the judge," he said. And he took the poor man to court.

The judge listened to the story. "This is very

20 unusual," he said. "I want to think about it. Come back tomorrow."

The poor man was very worried. He had no money. "What can I do?" he asked himself. He could not sleep at all.

THINK IT THROUGH
What problems does the poor man have?

The next morning the man got up and said his prayers. Then he went slowly back to the
30 court. On the way he met the wise mullah, Nasrudin.

| mullah |
| religious leader or teacher |

"Nasrudin," the poor man cried. "Please help me. People say that you are very clever. I am very unhappy and very worried." He told Nasrudin his story.

"Well, well," wise Nasrudin said. "Let's see what happens." The two men went to court.

The judge was already there. He was with the owner of the restaurant. They looked very friendly
40 with each other. When the poor man arrived, the judge began to speak. He said the poor man owed the restaurant owner a lot of money.

Nasrudin stepped forward. "This man is my friend," he said. "Can I pay for him?" He held out a bag of money.

The judge looked at the restaurant owner. "Can Nasrudin pay?" he asked.
50 "'Yes," the restaurant owner said. "Nasrudin has money. The poor man does not. Nasrudin can pay!"

Nasrudin smiled. He stood next to the restaurant owner.

Nasrudin held the bag of money near the restaurant owner's ear. He shook it so the coins made a noise.

"Can you hear the money?" he asked.

60   "Of course I can hear it," the restaurant owner said.

"That is your payment," the mullah said. "My friend smelled your food, and you heard his money."

And that is the end of the story.

THINK IT THROUGH

1. How does Nasrudin solve the poor man's problem?
2. Do you think the way Nasrudin solves the problem is fair? Why or why not?
3. What lesson do you think the author wanted to teach?

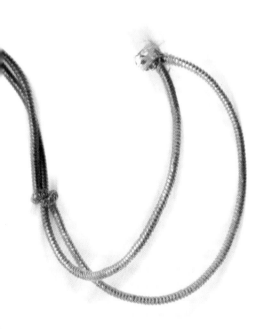

The Debate in Sign Language

retold by Syd Lieberman

Connect to Your Life

Have you ever had a misunderstanding with someone? Did the misunderstanding cause something funny to happen?

Key to the Folk Tale

In this story, two people have a debate. A debate is a discussion about a subject. Each person tries to prove that his or her opinion is right. However, the debate in this story is very different from most debates.

Sign language is a language in which people do not talk aloud. Instead, they move their hands to spell words and show symbols of what they mean.

 Reading Coach CD-ROM selection

FOCUS ───────────────────────────────
| Read to find out what an evil king plans to do.

Once there was an evil king who decided he wanted to throw the Jews out of his land. And the way he would do it was this: He would have a debate with one of them—in sign language.

He said to the Jewish community, "I will give you three signs. If someone can read my three signs and answer me correctly, all of you can stay here for the rest of your days. But if not, all of your people will have to go."

10 Well, the Jewish community was up in arms. No one knew what to do. There were arguments and discussions but no volunteers. After all, who could debate a king, let alone debate a king in sign language?

| up in arms
| angry

So, finally, after days of arguments going up and back, Yankel, a little chicken man, said, "Look, if no one will do it, I'll do it." And so the Jews agreed. Off went Yankel to the debate.

| chicken man
| man who raises and sells chickens

THINK IT THROUGH
| Why is it so hard to find someone to debate the king?

FOCUS ───────────────────────────────
| Read to find out what happens at the debate.

20 A huge platform had been set up in the center of town. Everybody surrounded it. The king stood on one side, little Yankel on the other. The king said, "Okay, I will give you three signs. If you get them all

correct, you can stay with your people in this land. If you don't, all of you will have to leave.

"Here is the first sign."

The king threw an arm in the air and stretched out the fingers of his hand. Yankel looked at the king and put a fist in front of his face.

30 The king said, "Correct. I'm amazed. Here is the second sign."

He threw his arm toward Yankel with two fingers straight out, and Yankel put one finger up in front of his nose.

REREAD
With a partner, make the signs that the king and Yankel make.

The king said, "Correct again. If you get the third sign right, you and all of your people will be able to remain." And he reached into the folds of his robe and pulled out a piece of cheese. Yankel looked at the king, shrugged, and pulled out an egg
40 from his pouch.

The king gasped. "Correct again. The Jews can stay!"

THINK IT THROUGH
What is the result of the debate?

FOCUS
What has the debate been about?

That night in the castle the whole court gathered around the king and asked, "What was the debate about?"

The king replied, "It was astonishing that the Jews had a little chicken man who could read my signs. I put out my hand with my fingers spread to show him that Jews were scattered all over the world. But he

put up a fist to show me that they were one in the
50 hand of God.

"Then I held up two fingers to show him that there
were two kings, one in heaven and one on the earth.
But he held up one finger to show me there was only
one king, the king in heaven.

"So I brought out a piece of cheese to show him
that the Jewish religion had grown old and moldy, but
he brought out an egg to show me that it was fresh
and whole.

"It was amazing."

60 Meanwhile, at Yankel's, everybody crowded into the
chicken store and asked, "What was the debate about?"

Yankel replied, "I don't know! It wasn't much of a
debate. I mean, the king reached out to grab me so I
put up a fist to show him I'd punch him if he touched
me. Then the king held up two fingers to poke out my
eyes, so I held up one to block him. I guess he knew I
was going to stand up to him, so he brought out his
lunch and I brought out mine!"

THINK IT THROUGH

1. Compare the men's thoughts about the meaning of
   each sign.
2. Did the ending of the story surprise you? Why or why not?
3. Do you think there is a message in this story? If so,
   what do you think it is?

by Eve Merriam

Argument

Good morning.
    Hmm.
Nice day.
    Dim.
5 Sorry.
    Glad.

Hadn't.
    Had.
Go.
10   Stay.
    Work.
Play.

Pro.
    Con.
15 Off.
    On.
Front.
    Back.
    Taut.
20 Slack.
Open.
    Shut.
And.
    But.

25 Over.
    Under.
Cloudless.
    Thunder.
Detour.
30   Highway.
New way.
    Thruway.
Byway . . . ?
    MY WAY!

FIFTEEN MINUTES

by LARRY CALLEN

IS FIFTEEN MINUTES ENOUGH TIME TO MAKE ONE OF THE MOST IMPORTANT DECISIONS OF YOUR LIFE?

Connect to Your Life

Have you ever had a hard time choosing between two things? What did you finally decide? What helped you make your choice?

Key to the Short Story

A short story often has a problem that a character has to solve. This problem is called a **conflict.** In "Fifteen Minutes," the main character has a conflict with his friend. As you read the story, you will learn about the conflict through dialogue. **Dialogue** refers to the words that the characters say to each other.

Vocabulary Preview

Words to Know

personal	preference
expression	jabbering
distracted	whirled

 Reading Coach CD-ROM selection

A boy named Pat has to make a choice. Read to find out what it is.

"You've got fifteen minutes to make up your mind," Mom said. She put the red toothbrush and the green toothbrush on the table, side by side. "If you haven't decided by the time Violet gets here, I'll do the deciding."

My old toothbrush had been yellow, and its bristles were soft and bent. These two looked pretty good. Maybe the red would be best. I sat down at the table and studied them.

10   Two minutes later Violet Deever walked in, big smile on her face like she owned the world.

"What're you doing?" she asked.

"Nothing."

She saw the toothbrushes on the table. She reached for one, but I pushed her hand away.

"Pat, stop that," she said. "I asked your mother to buy me a toothbrush. One of those is mine."

Mom heard her and shouted from the kitchen that I had asked first so I had first choice.

20   "Twelve minutes left to decide, Pat."

"Oh," said Deever. She sat down on the other side of the table and studied the toothbrushes.

"They're both nice, aren't they?" she asked. "You know which one you're going to take yet?"

"Whichever one I want," I said. I wasn't going to have her trying to make me take the one *she* didn't want.

"Maybe you ought to take the red one," she said, touching the end of the red handle. "It's very nice. The bristles look very straight."

30 Then a sly look crossed her face and I knew she was playing one of her games again. She was going to try and trick me. Well, this time I wasn't going to be tricked. This time I would do the tricking.

REREAD
What do you learn about the relationship between Pat and Violet?

"Deever, don't touch them. Mom said I had first choice, and that means first touching, too."

I looked closely at the green one. If she wanted me to take the red one, she must've seen something special about the green one. Or maybe she just liked 40 the color best.

The green one looked a little bit longer than the red one. But maybe it was just where I was sitting. I moved them closer together to compare size.

"It doesn't seem right that you can touch them and I can't," she said. "One of them is going to be mine, isn't it? Well, I don't want you touching my toothbrush. A toothbrush is a very personal thing, Pat. People don't go around touching other people's 50 toothbrushes."

personal
(pûr' sə nəl)
adj. used by one person only

All her talk was getting in the way of my deciding which one I wanted.

"Mom, make Violet stop talking. I can't think when she is talking."

Deever looked at her wristwatch. "You've got only ten more minutes to decide, Pat."

Now she was really trying to get me confused.

THINK IT THROUGH
Do you think Violet is as serious as Pat is about the toothbrushes? Find examples in the story to support your answer.

| Read to find out how Violet makes Pat's choice harder.

"Mom, do I really have only ten more minutes?"

But Mom didn't answer, and Deever smiled and
60 pointed to her watch. Then she drew a little circle
around the red toothbrush with her finger. She didn't
say a word, but she might as well have.

I looked at the toothbrushes and then I looked at
her. She kept telling me the red one was best. She
wanted me to think she wanted the green one. But
suppose it was one of her tricks? Maybe it was the red
one she wanted. Well, two could play at that game.

"I haven't really decided yet, but I think
that I might just take the green one," I said.

70 The expression on her face didn't change
a whit. Not an eyelid flickered. She
stared me in the eye, daring me to guess
what she was thinking.

expression
(ĭk sprĕsh' ən)
n. look

REREAD
What is Pat trying to do?

"You have nine minutes left, Pat,"
she said.

But I wasn't going to be
rushed into anything. I stood up
and went to the kitchen for a
glass of water. Mom was slicing
80 tomatoes and cucumbers and
celery for a salad.

"Mom, do I *have* to decide in
fifteen minutes?"

"Decide about what, dear?"

"Aw, Mom. You know. The
toothbrush. Violet is sitting
right there, trying to get me to
take the one she doesn't want."

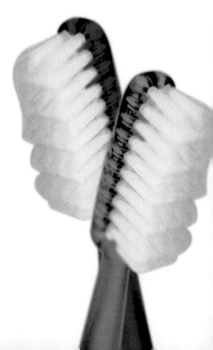

Now Mom was washing lettuce at the sink.

90 "I can't see what difference the color of a toothbrush makes, Pat. Just pick one and be done with it."

But she didn't understand. I went back into the dining room. And I saw right away that Deever had moved both brushes. The green one had been closest to where I was sitting. Now the red one was closest.

"A fly lit on it," she said.

"What?"

"I wouldn't take the green one if I were you, Pat.
100 While you were gone a fly lit on it. Maybe it laid some eggs. How would you like brushing your teeth with a bunch of fly eggs?"

REREAD
What is Violet trying to do?

"I'm not listening to that kind of stuff, Deever. I'm picking the one I want. Not the one you *don't* want."

"Know what color fly eggs are, Pat?"

I was looking at the toothbrushes. The bristles of both were snowy white. It looked like there might be a fleck of something on the bristles of the green one,
110 but it surely wasn't fly eggs. Maybe dust is all.

"They are green. That's what color fly eggs are."

I flicked the bristles of the green toothbrush with my finger and whatever was on them disappeared. But if I took the green one, I would wash it with scalding water anyway.

THINK IT THROUGH

Does Pat believe Violet's story about the fly? How do you know?

FOCUS

Who is E. J.? What does he think of Pat and Violet's problem?
Read to find out.

The screen door slammed in the kitchen and I could hear my brother, E. J., asking Mom if he had time to take a shower before dinner. Then he rushed into the dining room. When he saw us, he slowed.

120   "What are you two doing?" he asked.

"Pat is selecting a toothbrush," said Deever. "He has been at it for exactly seven minutes so far."

E. J. wasn't interested in what we were doing. He kept on walking. A minute later he came back into the room, holding his own toothbrush.

"Mom," he called, "I think I need a toothbrush worse than anybody. Could I have one of those on the table?"

"I get one," I told him. "Mom says Violet gets
130 the other."

"But if you *could* have one, E. J., which one would you take?" asked Deever.

He stopped at the table and stared down at the two brushes.

"That all the colors there are? Mine is orange. I'd like another orange one."

"Don't you think Pat ought to take the red one?" asked Deever.

E. J. didn't answer. When he had gotten a promise
140 out of Mom to buy him an orange toothbrush, he headed back to the shower.

"I think he secretly wants the red brush, Patrick," said Deever. "But you have first choice."

I'd already wasted more than half of my time and I still didn't know which one I wanted. I like red. It's a bright, kind of loud color. I wouldn't want red

clothes, except maybe a tie. Dad's got a red sport coat that he wore one time only, and then swore he would never wear again because everybody kept making
150 jokes about it. But a toothbrush is different. I never heard a toothbrush joke in my whole life.

"Pat, have you ever broken a tooth?" asked Deever.

I was just getting started on my thinking and she got me distracted again.

distracted
(dĭ străk' tĭd)
adj. having one's attention turned to something else

THINK IT THROUGH
Do you think Pat is being silly? Find examples in the story to support your answer.

FOCUS
The words in italics show Pat's thoughts. Read to find out what he is thinking.

Mom's not going to fool around. At the end of the fifteen minutes, she's going to decide who gets what color.

"The reason I asked, Pat, is that when you break a tooth, it means a friend will die. I had that happen to
160 me when I was only six years old. It wasn't exactly a person-friend. It was a hamster. But it broke my heart. You know what my hamster's name was, Pat?"

"Deever, will you please let me think?"

She says I ought to take the red one. She knows I'm not going to take the one she wants me to. That means she knows I'll take the green one. And *that means she wants the red one. If she just keeps quiet a little bit longer, I'll have this thing puzzled out.*

REREAD
Do you agree with Pat's thinking? Why or why not?

170 "Red is a very lucky color, Pat. Did you know it can even help you if you have a poor

memory? All you have to do is tie a red string around a finger on your left hand—"

"And remember why you tied it there," I snarled. She just wouldn't shut up.

"Mom, what time is it?"

"You have five minutes left, Pat," said Deever. "You are surely taking a long time to make up your mind."

She got up and went into the kitchen. I could hear
180 low voices and laughter. Then she came back, crunching on a celery stick.

She says I should take the red one. But she also knows I won't do it, because she is telling me to do it. But if I'm smart enough to figure that out, then I'll take the red one, and she'll be left with the green one.

Suppose she's figured out that I'll figure it out. Which one does she really want, then?

I was getting confused.

I looked at her. She was still chewing on the celery.
190 Was she trying to say something to me with that green stick? She smiled at me, still chewing.

Maybe I ought to get back to thinking about which one I want, instead of which one she wants. The green one is pretty. Kind of a grass green. I've got to get that business about fly eggs out of my mind. That's just trickery.

Lots of nice-looking things are green. Lawns are green. Leaves are green. Olives. Emeralds. Watermelons.

200 *Watermelons.*

But the sweet part on the inside is red.

"Do you know anything about rotten garbage, Pat? It's ugly and slimy and probably full of fly eggs. Did I ever tell you that once I had a possum for a pet? Possums eat garbage. Did you know that? And they have funny green stuff growing all over their teeth."

THINK IT THROUGH
List three things Violet does to confuse Pat.

I used to like brushing my teeth. Made them feel clean. And I like the taste of toothpaste. They put something in it that tickles your tongue. Sometimes 210 when we run out of toothpaste, I brush with salt, and I even like the taste of that. But I wasn't looking forward to brushing my teeth ever again.

"What time do you think it is, Pat?" she asked.

"All right, Deever. Which one do you *really* want?"

"Oh, I don't have a real preference. I just thought the red one would be nice for you."

220   I balled my fist. I knew she wasn't going to tell me the truth.

> **preference**
>
> (prĕf′ ər əns)
> *n.* choice of one thing over another

> **REREAD**
>
> Do you think Violet is telling the truth? Why or why not?

"You're just saying that, right? I'll take the red one, and then you will get the green one, which is the one you really want. I know what you're trying to do, Deever."

She tilted her head, lifted her eyebrows, and kind of sniffed, like she was saying I had a right to my opinion even if I was wrong.

"Ma!" called E. J. from the bathroom. 230 "There's a big green fly in here."

"See there!" said Deever. "I told you so."

Mom came to the rescue with a flyswatter clutched in her hand. I heard a single *whack!,* and she came walking out with a grin of victory on her face.

"Two minutes to go, Pat," she said as she passed.

"Mom, it's not fair to put all this pressure on me. I
240 haven't had a single minute to think. Deever's been
here jabbering away the whole time."

"I'll be back in two minutes," Mom said.

I whirled on Deever. I wanted to yell at
her to go away, but she wasn't smiling like
she was winning the war or anything.
There was a kind of hurt look on her face.

"I thought I had been helping you, Pat,"
she said.

jabbering
(jăb′ ər ĭng)
adj. talking very fast

whirled
(hwûrld)
v. spun around
very fast; past
tense of *whirl*

"Deever, a guy doesn't need help to pick the right color for a toothbrush."

"All right, then. I won't say another word." She sat back in her chair and looked at me. The hurt look stayed on her face. Now she was trying to make me feel guilty.

"One minute!" called Mom.

Which one? Red one? Green one? Ruby one? Emerald one? Somehow I knew she wanted the red one. I just knew it.

I could hear Mom stirring around in the kitchen. She was going to come marching out here any second.

"All right. I've decided," I said.

I stretched my hand out over the toothbrushes. I paused over the red one and looked at Deever's face, but I couldn't tell a thing. Then I moved my hand over the green one. Still nothing.

I scooped my hand down and grabbed the green one, watching her from the corner of my eye. Her face lit up like a Christmas tree.

"Good!" she said.

Now I knew. I dropped the green toothbrush and grabbed the red one. I pulled it close to me. This time I had won.

"Time's up!" yelled Mom.

I grinned at Deever and waited for her smile to fade. But it didn't happen.

She reached out in her dainty way. With two fingers she plucked the green toothbrush from the table.

"Wonderful!" she said. "Green is my favorite color."

1. Which do you think is more important to Pat—picking the toothbrush he likes or tricking Violet? Use examples from the story to support your answer.

2. Violet says "wonderful" when she gets the green toothbrush. What do you think her reaction would be if she got the red one?

3. How would you describe Violet? Would you want her as a friend?

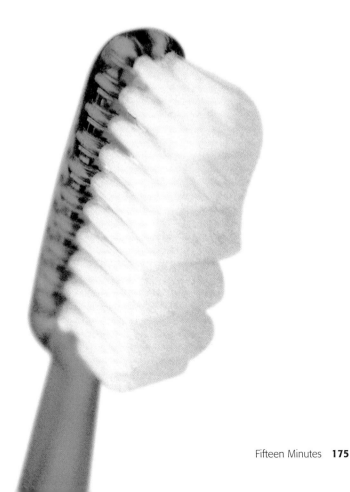

You Can If You Try

Unit 7

Nonfiction

Who is your favorite athlete? What do you admire about that person? Athletes who do well work hard and don't give up. In this unit, you will read about three successful athletes. You will read these kinds of nonfiction.

- **Feature Article:** an article in a magazine or newspaper about an interesting person or event

- **True Account:** writing that tells about real people, places, and events. The writer tells it like a story to make it interesting.

- **Biography:** a story about a person's life written by someone else

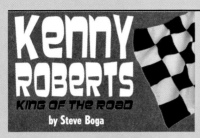

Kenny ROBERTS

KING OF THE ROAD

BY STEVE BOGA

DO YOU THINK YOU'RE TOO SMALL FOR BASKETBALL? TOO TALL FOR ICE-SKATING? THINK AGAIN.

Connect to Your Life

Has your size ever kept you from playing a sport or taking part in some other activity? Did you give up the activity, or did you try harder to take part?

Key to the Feature Article

The following article is a **feature article.** A feature article can appear in a magazine or a newspaper. It usually tells about an interesting person or event. Unlike a news story, a feature article tells more than just facts. The article may also include some of the author's own thoughts and feelings.

Vocabulary Preview

Words to Know

dazed	spleen
cocky	pushy
courses	

 Reading Coach CD-ROM selection

Kenny Roberts sits on his motorcycle at the starting line. He is wearing a red and white leather suit and a white helmet. He is not the biggest racer. He may even be the smallest. But he is the best. Yet it wasn't always so. Kenny will always remember one of his first races just as if it were happening today. There were thirty other bikers in that race. Everyone was opening and closing their throttles, revving their

10 engines. The roar was so loud, Kenny couldn't talk to the guy next to him.

> **throttles**
> (thrŏt' lz)
> pipes that control the flow of fuel in engines

At last they were off! Thirty riders on thirty motorbikes were trying for the lead. The air was filled with the spray of sand. And the noise was loud, like a swarm of giant bees.

> **revving**
> (rĕv' ĭng)
> increasing the speed of

Kenny was first off the starting line. He was leading the race at the halfway mark. Then his front tire hit a hole. He spun out of control. Then another bike hit him

20 on the side. He flew from his bike like a shot. He hit the track, then rolled and bounced. Ramming into a wall head first, he went limp.

As he lay there, dazed, dozens of bikes skid and slid within inches of his head. Dirt filled the air. Suddenly, another rider rammed into Kenny's bike. The twisted metal flew over Kenny's body.

> **dazed**
> (dāzd)
> *adj.* confused or shocked because of a heavy blow

After that, Kenny learned how to stay on his bike.

THINK IT THROUGH
What happened to Kenny in his motorcycle race?

Some say Kenny started racing when he was born.
30 Even then he had a quick start. He was born two
weeks early. His parents blamed it on a hit-and-run
driver who smashed into the family car before Kenny
was born. Some say Kenny has been getting back at
bad drivers ever since.

As a boy, Kenny was small and loved horses. Most
people thought he would become a jockey. He says, "I
was a cowboy. I liked horses, not motorbikes."

When he was 12, a friend got a mini-bike for a
present. At first Kenny did not want to try it. But his
40 friend kept pushing him. So Kenny rode the bike, but
only for a minute. He says, "The first thing I did was
drive it into a house trailer. It scared me to death. It
also thrilled me."

It thrilled him so much that he tried again. After
that he decided he wanted to be a good rider. So he
practiced all the time. "Two months later, I built my
own mini-bike out of a bicycle frame and a lawn
mower engine," he says.

At age 14, Kenny began racing the dirt tracks of
50 central California. Even as a young rookie,
he was very cocky and very good. By the
time he was 16, he was known in all the
small valley towns. He was beating
everyone his own age. They even made
Kenny start behind the other racers just to make it
fair. Still he won. People either loved or hated him.
But they came to watch him race.

> **cocky**
> (kŏk′ ē)
> *adj.* too sure of
> oneself

THINK IT THROUGH
What made Kenny change from horses to motorcycles?

The rules did not allow him to turn pro until he
was 18. But he did not care. He says, "Motorbikes
60 were just fun to me. It wasn't a job. I was working in
a repair shop and riding the canals with my friends. I
was having fun. The faster I went, the more fun it
was. And since I was good, people put faster bikes in
front of me. They would say, 'Ride this!' It was fun to
show them I could."

At first no pro team wanted him. They
thought he was too small to race
motorbikes. The big bikes weighed about
300 pounds. Kenny then weighed 110 pounds. But he
70 had a great feel for motorbikes. When Yamaha did
sign him to a pro contract, he turned out to be the
best rookie in the country.

REREAD
Why don't pro
teams want
Kenny?

Kenny says, "Being big doesn't help." (He should
know. He is now 5 feet, 5 inches tall and weighs 135
pounds.) "Good riders are not big guys. To race, you
need good reflexes and quick muscles, like a
boxer. But you also need to dare to go 45
minutes full out. You can't ever relax. Racing
is hardest on legs, wrists, and forearms."

reflexes
(rē' flĕk sĭz)
unplanned body
responses, such
as a sneeze

80 As a biker, Kenny sits a lot. But he still
has to be in great shape. Weeks before a race, Kenny
starts working out. He runs, plays racquetball, hits a
punching bag. Sometimes he lifts weights.
But most of the time he rides motorbikes.
He rides a mini-bike for reflexes and a
motorcross bike to build muscles.

**motorcross
bike**
special bike for
riding on steep
hills and around
sharp curves

By the time he was 26, Kenny was the
best cycle racer in America. He was married

and making more than $300,000 a year. He was
90 happy. But Yamaha, his sponsor, wanted him to race
in Europe. That was the big time. That was where he
could make real money. So he took his wife and kids
and went to Europe. He was off to be a
Grand Prix motorbike racer.

   At first, the European racers did not pay
any attention to little Kenny Roberts. Why
should they? He did not look like much.
And this was the Big Time. Speeds were more than
180 miles per hour. And it took years to learn the
100 courses. Nobody went to Europe and
started winning right away.

   Nobody, that is, except Kenny. He won
three of his first five races. Then he went on
to win the whole thing. He was the Grand Prix World
Champion.

   He was the first American and the first rookie ever
to become champion. After that, the other racers
noticed him. In fact, they tried not to let him out of
their sight. And they gave him a nickname. They
110 called him "King Kenny."

THINK IT THROUGH
Why is Kenny's success so surprising? Find at least three reasons.

Many racers like
this one now drag
their knees on
turns because of
Kenny Roberts.

For the next six seasons, Kenny really was the king. He was the best road racer in the world. And he was exciting to watch. On turns, he would lean his bike so far over that his knee would drag on the road. Before Kenny, no one else dragged his knee. Soon everyone was doing it.

Kenny says, "It is a game of inches. Lean an inch too far and the bike scrapes the ground. They then scrape me off the pavement. An inch the other way and I lose the race."

120

REREAD
Why are inches so important in racing?

Sometimes an inch can cost more than a race. It happened when Kenny was testing a new Yamaha bike in Japan. He was all alone on the track. Maybe that was the problem. Maybe without other riders he relaxed.

He came into a right turn. He hit the front brake and his bike slowed to 120 miles per hour. He had done it a million times before. But this time was different. He suddenly lost control of the bike. It slid out from under him. He was thrown hard against a guard rail and knocked out.

130

He hurt his spleen, broke his foot and his back. He nearly died. But Japanese doctors saved him. They put him in a cast and sent him home three weeks later. They told him, "You will never race again."

spleen
(splēn)
n. organ in the human body. The spleen helps to clean the blood and also produces white blood cells.

Three weeks later, when he went to the hospital for X-rays, the doctors were surprised. His back was healed.

140

"Good," Kenny said. "I'm racing in Austria in a few days."

"Impossible," the doctors said.

"Watch me!" said King Kenny.

So six weeks after he almost died, Kenny showed up in Salzburg, Austria. People thought he was there to watch. When he pulled his leather suit on over his back brace, they knew he was there to race.

He raced and he won! The other riders could only shake their heads in awe.

150   The next week, he finished second. Then he won three straight races in Italy, Spain, and Yugoslavia. He went on to win his second straight World Championship. He did it wearing a back brace.

THINK IT THROUGH
Why didn't the accident end Kenny's career?

FOCUS ———
Why does Kenny feel he has been so successful?

How did he do it? How did he come back? Lots of people would have just quit. But Kenny had no quit in him. "Breaking my back was just a hurdle that I had to get over. It was something to make me better," he says.

He could not have been too much better. In all, he
160 won the World Championship three times. He became a star. In Japan and Europe, he was treated like a king. They sold thousands of posters of King Kenny leaning his bike into a turn.

He says, "People do not know me in America. I am not famous in the United States like I am in other countries. I can walk down the streets of my home town. Most folks do not even know me."

Kenny has always been serious about motorbikes. He has made millions of dollars being serious about them. But he is also a man who loves his fun. He loves to joke and laugh. A child at heart, he once broke his leg goofing around on a motorbike with his kids. "The most fun you can have on a bike is just riding around with your buddies or your kids," he says.

Kenny has won races by going faster than other riders. He says though that the real thrill of riding is not high speeds. It is learning how to do it right. "I enjoy taking a 20-mile per hour curve at 30 with perfect brake, gear, and line. It's better than going 170 miles per hour on a straight road," he says.

REREAD

What is most important to Kenny?

Most people sitting on a 150-horsepower bike would die of fear before it ever reached 170 miles per hour. Yet Kenny, who has hit 190 and had a blowout at 170, says he has never been afraid on a bike.

horsepower
(hôrs′ pou′ ər) unit for measuring the power of an engine

He says, "I have felt excitement, but not fear. During a race there's no time to be afraid. I have been nervous before a big race and worried about doing well. But that's not fear. And after a near miss, I have thought, 'Hey, I could be dead.' But then it's not fear anymore, is it?"

For a little man, Roberts is very strong in the arms and legs. But he thinks he has won most of his races because he has a strong mind. Kenny says, "The mind has to focus. Sometimes I get near my limit, and I know I could die. But I still think hard about doing it right. You see, this is what I do. I race bikes. It is an exciting sport because I have to get it just right. A good guess does not make it."

Yes, Kenny is tough both in body and mind. He says, "I can be nasty. I have always been very pushy. As a kid, I was mean and stubborn."

For proof, Kenny points to his very first race. He says, "I was riding a nasty old bike, a 50-cc clunker. It died on me not far into the race. I got off and kicked it."

That was the last time Kenny got off his bike before the finish line.

THINK IT THROUGH

1. What reasons does Kenny give for his success?
2. Why do you think the author wrote this article?
3. How does the author feel about Kenny? Do you agree with his opinion? Why or why not?

Water Woman

by S. A. Kramer

Muscle cramps, breathing problems, unkind teammates—all of these things could keep Amy Van Dyken from winning at the Olympic Games. Will she let them?

400-Meter Free Relay

4x100-Meter Medley Relay

100-Meter Butterfly

50-Meter Freestyle

Connect to Your Life

Did anything ever keep you from doing something you really love? Or were you able to follow your dreams anyway?

Key to the True Account

"Water Woman" is a **true account.** The article gives facts about a real person, places, and events. But the writer presents the information as a story.

Asthma is an illness that makes it hard to breathe. A person having an asthma attack may cough or take very short breaths. Dust, certain drugs, and even exercise can bring on an attack. Yet many people with asthma play sports with the help of medicine.

Vocabulary Preview

Words to Know

meters	awkward
strokes	depressed

 Reading Coach CD-ROM selection

Read to find out what happens to Amy Van Dyken when she swims in her first Olympic event.

Atlanta, Georgia. The 1996 Olympic Games. The 100-meter freestyle is almost over. Amy Van Dyken is behind—but she's not giving up. This is her first Olympic event, and she wants to do well. Twenty-three-year-old Amy has a dream—to take home a gold medal.

Just a few meters to go. Amy strokes furiously. Her head's so low in the water,
10 fans see only her cap. She's tired, but somehow she turns up the speed. Amy always gives everything she's got.

This time it's not enough. Amy finishes fourth. No gold, no silver—not even a bronze. But as she leaves the pool, she isn't thinking about losing. Her burst of speed has made her muscles cramp. The pain is so bad, she can't even stand.

Amy falls to the pool deck. Cramps
20 shoot into her back and neck. She gasps for air. Trainers have to carry her off on a stretcher.

100-meter freestyle

a swimming event. The swimmer decides which stroke to swim. One hundred meters (about 328 feet) is the length of the pool and back.

meters

(mē' tərz) *n.* units of measure; each one is equal to 39.37 inches

strokes

(strōks) *v.* moves the arms and legs to swim

THINK IT THROUGH
What happened to Amy after she lost the event?

Find out how Amy's high school experiences affect her.

What a way to start the Olympics! Amy can't believe her bad luck. But it's not the first time her health has gotten in her way.

Ever since she was little, Amy's had asthma (you say it like this: AZ-mah). Asthma is an illness that makes it hard to breathe. Amy's lungs have never worked right.

As a child, she was always out of breath. Climbing
30 just one flight of stairs left her huffing and puffing. But when she was seven, her doctor said swimming might help her. So Amy headed straight for the pool.

Her talent didn't show right away—far from it. Even at twelve, she could hardly finish a race. She'd often have to stop in the middle to catch her breath.

Things weren't much better in high school. Amy coughed all the time. She was also awkward, skinny—and six feet tall! Her classmates made fun of her. Amy felt like
40 a nerd.

> **awkward**
> (ôk′ wərd)
> *adj.* clumsy

Somehow she made the school swim team. But then the coach put her on a relay with three other girls.

The girls weren't happy. They complained to the coach. To get Amy to quit, they threw her clothes into the pool. Once they even spat at her.

Amy felt awful. But she didn't leave the team. Later she said, "I'm really stubborn. If someone tells me I stink, I'm going to try to prove them wrong." She
50 vowed that one day she'd make those girls respect her.

THINK IT THROUGH

How did Amy react to the actions of her high school teammates?

In college at Colorado State, Amy joined the swim team. Fighting her asthma, she got all the way to the 1990 junior nationals. But she wasn't fast enough to make the 1992 Olympic team.

Amy kept trying. She got faster and faster. But in 1993, she flopped in the NCAA championships. And after that, she caught a terrible virus.

NCAA
stands for National Collegiate Athletic Association

Amy was depressed. All her training 60 hadn't made her a champion. She told herself, "This is too hard. I want to be normal." For a few months she quit swimming. But she didn't stay away for long. She missed it too much.

depressed
(dĭ prĕst′)
adj. unhappy, sad

Amy charged back into the pool. She learned to make her starts faster and to stroke with more power. To boost her speed, she kept shaving the hair off her body. She said, "If I miss the hair on my knee, it could cost me a hundredth of a second."

70 Her all-out attitude paid off. In the 1994 world championships, she won a bronze medal in the 50-meter freestyle. The same year, she was named female NCAA swimmer of the year. Then in 1995, she broke the U.S. records for both the 50-meter and 50-yard freestyle.

Amy was on a roll. In 1996 she won a place on the Olympic team. This time none of her teammates complained. In fact, she became their leader. Her horrible high school years seemed long ago.

THINK IT THROUGH

How did Amy change? Give at least three examples.

Now she's at the Olympic Games, lying on a
80 stretcher. Her teammates are worried. But Amy has
come back from worse. She calls herself "the tough
girl." Sure enough, two hours later her cramps ease
up and she's feeling fine.

Her next race is a relay—the 4x100-meter freestyle.
There's no way Amy's going to let her teammates
down. She hopes those high school girls are watching
their TVs today.

The U.S. wins the gold! The team couldn't
have done it without Amy. The very next day
90 she wins the 100-meter butterfly by 1 100th
of a second.

And she's still not finished. She takes
golds in the 50-meter freestyle and the
4x100-meter medley relay, too. That's four
in all! Amy is the first and only American
woman ever to win four gold medals in one
Olympics.

No one makes fun of Amy anymore. In
fact, she's almost too popular. Fans won't
100 leave her alone. At hotels, she uses a fake
name so strangers can't keep calling her.

Her asthma still makes her sick. Some days, she has
to stay out of the water. When she pushes herself too
hard, she ends up in the hospital. Even now, Amy
takes medicine three times a day.

She often thinks about her future. She may teach
biology, or work with deaf children. But one thing
she knows for sure. Swimming will always be part of
her life.

butterfly
swimming stroke
in which the
swimmer's arms
move through
the water in
large, wide circles

**4x100-meter
medley relay**
swim event in
which four team
members take
turns, with each
member
swimming a
different stroke
for 100 meters

1. What record does Amy hold in the Olympics?
2. What made Amy return to swimming after she gave it up?
3. What do you think the author's message is?

Editor's Note: Amy Van Dyken also swam at the 2000 Olympic Games in Sydney, Australia. She won gold medals in two events—the 400-meter freestyle relay and the 400-meter medley relay. Jenny Thompson, Amy's teammate, beat Amy's record of four gold medals at the 1996 Olympics. Jenny won six medals in swimming at the 2000 Olympic Games.

The Swimmer

by Constance Levy

The sun
underwater
makes chains of gold
that rearrange
5   as I reach through.
I feel at home
within this world
of sunlit water, cool and blue.
I sip the air;
10   I stroke;
I kick;
big bubbles bloom as I breathe out.
Although I have no tail or fin
I'm closer than I've ever been
15   to what fish feel
and think about.

SATCHEL PAIGE

by Patricia
and Fredrick
McKissack

THE BEST ARM IN BASEBALL

In professional sports, most players can only play for about 15 years before their skills start to fade. One baseball pitcher played for 30 years.

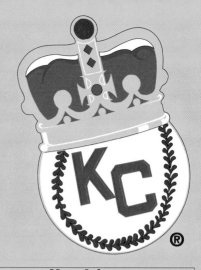

Connect to Your Life

Sports announcers often argue about who's the best player in a sport. Who do you think is the best soccer player, best basketball player, or best golfer? Compare your opinions with your classmates' thoughts. Does everyone agree?

Key to the Biography

When someone writes the story of another person's life, the story is called a **biography.** The events in a biography are usually told in the order that they happened.

Satchel Paige lived during a time when segregation made it hard to reach his goals. *Segregate* means "to keep apart." Segregation laws kept blacks and whites from living in the same neighborhoods, going to the same schools, or playing together.

Vocabulary Preview

Words to Know

contract	rookie
gaining	retire

 Reading Coach CD-ROM selection

FOCUS _____
| Read to find out what Satchel's childhood was like.

When Satchel Paige was born he was named Leroy
Paige. Leroy grew up in a large family. He had ten
brothers and sisters. His parents worked very, very
hard. His father earned money as a gardener. His
mother washed and ironed clothes for money. But the
family was still poor.

The Paiges lived in a small house on Franklin Street in
Mobile, Alabama. It was called a shotgun house. There
were four rooms, one behind the other. "A straight shot
10 from the front door to the back," Satchel said.

When Leroy was seven years old, he earned money
at the train station. He carried traveler's bags,
sometimes called satchels, for money. He carried so
many at one time, his friends said he was a "satchel
tree." Pretty soon he was just called Satchel.

When he wasn't working, Satchel liked to throw
things. It was fun hitting trees and cans with rocks. He
became good at it. First, he took aim. Then he threw
the rock. Zap! He hit the mark almost every time.

THINK IT THROUGH
| How would you describe Satchel's childhood? Find details to
| support your answer.

FOCUS _____
| Find out how stealing affects Satchel's life.

20 Satchel didn't like school. So, he didn't go very
often. Then he was caught stealing toys. In 1918,
when he was twelve years old, a judge sent him to the

> # When he wasn't working, Satchel liked to throw things. It was fun hitting trees and cans with rocks. He became good at it.

Industrial School for ⟨Negro⟩ Children at Mount Meigs, Alabama. He stayed there until he was seventeen.

"It was the best thing that happened to me," Satchel said later. "I was running around with the wrong crowd."

30 At Mount Meigs, he stopped throwing rocks and learned how to throw a baseball on the school baseball team. That was the beginning. Satchel Paige would still be throwing baseballs thirty years later.

When Satchel left Mount Meigs he was about 6 feet and 3½ inches tall. He weighed 140 pounds. "I was so tall and thin everybody called me 'The Crane,'" he said.

Satchel wanted to play baseball, so he joined the Mobile Tigers. All the players were black. Wilson Paige, one of Satchel's brothers, played for the Tigers, too. Satchel was the team's star pitcher.

THINK IT THROUGH
How did the Industrial School change Satchel's life?

40   In the 1920s the United States was segregated. There were laws that kept blacks and whites from going to school together. They could not live in the same neighborhoods. And they could not play professional sports in the same leagues. African Americans played baseball in the "Negro Leagues."

Being a Negro League ball player wasn't easy. The team traveled in old cars and run-down buses. They weren't welcome in most hotels and restaurants. Many times the team had to sleep on the ball
50 park benches.

White fans came to see the black teams play. Sometimes those fans shouted unkind things to the black players. But when they saw Satchel Paige pitch, they cheered. His best pitch was the fast ball. He called it his
60 "bee ball," because it hummed like a bee. He also threw a hard breaking curve ball and a fast slider.

REREAD
For what did Satchel become famous?

In 1926, he joined the Chattanooga Black Lookouts. He earned
70 $50 a month. "Big money for me then,"

Satchel said. But he was restless. He moved from team to team. From 1926 to 1934, Satchel Paige pitched for teams in Birmingham, Alabama and Cleveland, Ohio. Satchel proved how good he was with the Pittsburgh Crawfords between 1931 and 1934. Satchel helped the Crawfords win the Negro National League title in 1933.

80   During off-seasons, Satchel played for teams in the Caribbean, Mexico, and South America. He was known as a "traveling man."

    On October 26, 1934, Satchel married Janet Howard. They did not live together very much. Satchel liked to travel. He could not settle down. Soon the marriage ended.

    Now Satchel was getting older. Some people thought his pitching arm had burned out. The Kansas City Monarchs signed him to a contract anyway. The Monarchs were

90 smart. Satchel had many more seasons left to pitch.

> **contract**
> (kŏn′ trăkt′)
> *n.* legal agreement

THINK IT THROUGH
Why was Satchel such a popular player in the Negro Leagues?

FOCUS
Read to find out how successful Satchel's career was.

    Between 1939 and 1942, the Monarchs won the Negro American League championship every year. Satchel was a big part of it. The Monarchs beat the Homestead Grays and won the Negro World Series in 1942. Satchel pitched the winning game. He was older now, but he was as good as ever.

Satchel did not make a whole lot of money. But he made more than most black ball players did in the 1940s. If Satchel had been white, he would have pitched for one of the major league teams. But he could only play in the Negro Leagues.

Satchel was one of the best pitchers who ever played the game. And he was the first to say it! Satchel loved to brag as much as he liked to make people laugh. Satchel said and did funny things on and off the baseball field. One of his most famous sayings was, "Don't look back. Something might be gaining on you."

REREAD
What qualities did Satchel have?

gaining
(gā′ nĭng)
v. getting closer

Satchel spent a lot of money, too. He went back to visit his mother in Mobile. She was still living in the same small shotgun house. One day he took her out for a ride. He showed her a large house and asked her if she liked it. She said it was too big. Satchel said it was hers. He had already bought it for her. At last, he moved his mother out of the shotgun shack.

Satchel's girlfriend, Lahoma Brown, wanted him to spend his money wisely. She talked him into buying a large home in Kansas City. On October 12, 1947, they were married in Hays, Kansas.

THINK IT THROUGH
What details show that Satchel was a great ball player even though he didn't play in the major leagues?

In 1947 Jackie Robinson was chosen as the first black player to start in the all-white National League. He played for the Brooklyn Dodgers.

Satchel was hurt that he had not been the first black player in the National League. He had worked long and hard for the chance to be that player. But a lot of people thought he was too old.

130 Satchel finally got his chance in the majors on July 9, 1948. He signed up with the Cleveland Indians. That made him the first black pitcher in the American League. At 42 years old, he was also the oldest rookie.

Satchel won six games and lost one during his first season. His team won the American League Championship. They also won the 1948 World Series against the Boston Braves.

rookie
(rŏŏk' ē)
n. first-year player

If Satchel had been white, he would have pitched for one of the major league teams. But he could only play in the Negro Leagues.

Satchel only got to pitch one inning in the World
140 Series. It was enough for him. He said, ". . . it felt
great!" Satchel was very proud. Even at his age, he
could still throw a baseball hard, fast, and straight.

Satchel retired after the 1949 season. But not for
long. He played whenever he could for many more
years. Finally, he became a coach for the Atlanta
Braves. And in 1968, he really did retire.

All his life, Satchel had heard: "We sure
could use a pitcher like you. If you were
white." But he was never bitter. "I don't
150 look back," he said often.

> **retire**
> (rĭ tīr')
> v. stop working

Satchel won many honors for his work in baseball
on and off the field. His greatest honor came in
August 1971. Leroy "Satchel" Paige was accepted
into the Baseball Hall of Fame.

Most great Negro League baseball players were
part of their own Hall of Fame. They were still
segregated. Satchel Paige was a great pitcher. He was
placed alongside other great major league players like
Babe Ruth and Jackie Robinson. For the first time,
160 nobody said, "If he was only white." His skin color
didn't matter.

Satchel Paige lived in Kansas City with Lahoma the
rest of his life. He died on June 8, 1982.

THINK IT THROUGH

1. Why was Satchel's career with a major league team
   so remarkable?
2. Make a chart that shows the order of events in
   Satchel's life. Include only the events you think are
   most important.
3. Why was Satchel voted into the Baseball Hall of
   Fame? Do you think he deserved it? Use details
   from his biography to support your opinion.

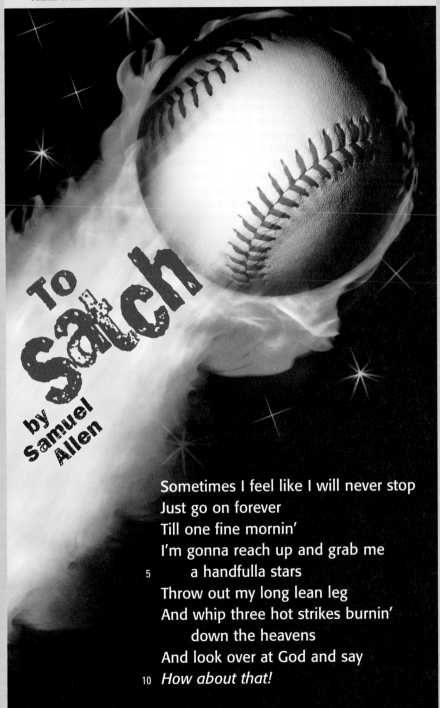

To Satch

by Samuel Allen

Sometimes I feel like I will never stop
Just go on forever
Till one fine mornin'
I'm gonna reach up and grab me
5   a handfulla stars
Throw out my long lean leg
And whip three hot strikes burnin'
     down the heavens
And look over at God and say
10 *How about that!*

Making a Difference

Mixed Genres

A single act can help change a law or make a difference in who wins a war. In this unit you will read a **short story,** an **autobiography,** and a **true account.** Each story tells about people whose actions caused changes in a neighborhood, a country, or the world.

City Green

by DyAnne DiSalvo-Ryan

Connect to Your Life

What do you do when you see a
problem in your community? Do you
ignore it? Do you take action yourself or
ask others for help?

Key to the Short Story

The time and place in which a story takes
place is called the **setting.** The setting
can be in the present, past, or future. The
writer may use words that give details
about the time of day or words that
describe sights, sounds, and smells. As
you read, notice words that describe the
setting in this story.

    The person who tells the story is the
narrator. A narrator always tells a story
from a certain point of view. "City Green"
is told from the **first-person point of
view.** That means the narrator is a
character in the story. As you read, you'll
find out about the narrator's feelings.
You'll also learn about the feelings of the
people around her.

Vocabulary Preview

Words to Know
stoop   petition
hardware

What would you do with an empty lot?
Your choice may be different from
someone else's. But together, one
neighborhood has to decide.

There used to be a building right here on this lot. It
was three floors up and down, an empty building
nailed up shut for as long as I could remember. My
friend Miss Rosa told me Old Man Hammer used to
live there—some other neighbors too. But when I
asked him about that, he only hollered, "Scram."

Old Man Hammer, hard as nails.

Last year two people from the city came by, dressed
in suits and holding papers. They said, "This building
10 is unsafe. It will have to be torn down."

By winter a crane with a wrecking ball was parked
outside. Mama gathered everyone to watch from our
front window. In three slow blows that building was
knocked into a heap of pieces. Then workers took the
rubble away in a truck and filled the hole with dirt.

Now this block looks like a big smile with one
tooth missing. Old Man Hammer sits on
his stoop and shakes his head. "Look at
that piece of junk land on a city block,"
20 Old Man Hammer says. "Once that
building could've been saved. But nobody
even tried."

And every day when I pass this lot it makes me sad
to see it. Every single day.

stoop
(stō͞op)
n. small porch

How do you think the neighbors feel about losing the
building? Find examples in the story to support your answer.

Then spring comes, and right on schedule Miss
Rosa starts cleaning her coffee cans. Miss Rosa and I
keep coffee cans outside our windowsills. Every year
we buy two packets of seeds at the hardware store—
sometimes marigolds, sometimes zinnias,

30 and one time we tried tomatoes. We go to
the park, scoop some dirt, and fill up the
cans halfway.

> **hardware**
> (härd' wâr')
> *n.* tools

This time Old Man Hammer stops us on
the way to the park. "This good for nothin' lot has
plenty of dirt right here," he says.

Then all at once I look at Miss Rosa. And she is
smiling back at me. "A *lot* of dirt," Miss
Rosa says.

"Like one big coffee can," I say.

> **REREAD**
> What do you
> think Miss Rosa
> and the narrator
> will do?

40 That's when we decide to do
something about this lot.

Quick as a wink I'm digging away,
already thinking of gardens and flowers. But Old
Man Hammer shakes his finger. "You can't dig more
dirt than that. This lot is
city property."

"Look at that piece of junk land on a city block," Old Man Hammer says. "Once that building could've been saved. But nobody even tried."

Miss Rosa and I go to see Mr. Bennett. He used to work for the city. "I seem to remember a program," he says, "that lets people rent empty lots."

50   That's how Miss Rosa and I form a group of people from our block. We pass around a petition that says: WE WANT TO LEASE THIS LOT. In less than a week we have plenty of names.

petition
(pə tĭsh' ən)
n. written request to the government from a person or group

"Sign with us?" I ask Old Man Hammer.

"I'm not signin' nothin'," he says. "And nothin' is what's gonna happen."

But something did.

The next week, a bunch of us take a bus to city
60   hall. We walk up the steps to the proper office and hand the woman our list. She checks her files and types some notes and makes some copies. "That will be one dollar, please."

We rent the lot from the city that day. It was just as simple as that.

THINK IT THROUGH

Describe the process of renting an empty lot.

Saturday morning I'm up with the sun and looking at this lot. My mama looks out too. "Marcy," she says, and hugs me close. "Today I'm helping you and Rosa."

After shopping, Mama empties her grocery bags
70 and folds them flat to carry under her arm. "Come on, Mrs. B.," Mama tells her friend. "We're going to clear this lot."

Then what do you know but my brother comes along. My brother is tall and strong. At first, he scratches his neck and shakes his head just like Old Man Hammer. But Mama smiles and says, "None of that here!" So all day long he piles junk in those bags and carries them to the curb.

Now, this time of day is early. Neighbors pass by
80 and see what we're doing. Most say, "We want to help too." They have a little time to spare. Then this one calls that one and that one calls another.

"Come on and help," I call to Old Man Hammer.

"I'm not helpin' nobody," he hollers. "You're all wastin' your time."

Sour grapes my mama'd say, and sour grapes is right.

Just before supper, when we are good and hungry, my mama looks around this lot.
90 "Marcy," she says, "you're making something happen here."

sour grapes
pretending not to want something that one really does want

Next day the city drops off tools like rakes and brooms, and a Dumpster for trash. Now there's even more neighbors to help. Miss Rosa, my brother, and I say "Good morning" to Old Man Hammer, but Old Man Hammer just waves like he's swatting a fly.

REREAD
Why do you think more people join the project?

"Why is Old Man Hammer so mean and cranky these days?" my brother asks.

100 "Maybe he's really sad," I tell him. "Maybe he misses his building."

"That rotten old building?" My brother shrugs. "He should be happy the city tore down that mess."

"Give him time," Miss Rosa says. "Good things take time."

Mr. Bennett brings wood—old slats he's saved—and nails in a cup. "I knew all along I saved them for something," he says. "This wood's good wood."

Then Mr. Rocco from two houses down comes,
110 carrying two cans of paint. "I'll never use these," he says. "The color's too bright. But here, this lot could use some brightening up."

Well, anyone can tell with all the excitement that something is going on. And everyone has an idea about what to plant—strawberries, carrots, lettuce, and more. Tulips and daisies, petunias, and more! Sonny turns the dirt over with a snow shovel. Even Leslie's baby tries to dig with a spoon.

For lunch, Miss Rosa brings milk and jelly and
120 bread and spreads a beach towel where the junk is cleared. By the end of the day a fence is built and painted as bright as the sun.

THINK IT THROUGH

Compare your prediction with what happens to the lot. What is the same? What is different?

Later, Mama kisses my cheek and closes my bedroom door. By the streetlights I see Old Man Hammer come down his steps to open the gate and walk to the back of this lot. He bends down quick, sprinkling something from his pocket and covering it over with dirt.

In the morning I tell my brother. "Oh, Marcy," he 130 says. "You're dreaming. You're wishing too hard."

But I know what I saw, and I tell my mama, "Old Man Hammer's planted some seeds."

Right after breakfast, I walk to the back of this lot. And there it is—a tiny raised bed of soil. It is neat and tidy, just like the rows we've planted. Now I know for sure that Old Man Hammer planted something. So I pat the soil for good luck and make a little fence to keep the seeds safe.

Every day I go for a look inside our garden lot. Other 140 neighbors stop in too. One day Mrs. Wells comes by. "This is right where my grandmother's bedroom used to be," she says. "That's why I planted my flowers there."

I feel sad when I hear that. With all the digging and planting and weeding and watering, I'd forgotten about the 150 building that had been on this lot. Old Man Hammer had lived there too.

I go to the back, where he planted his seeds. I wonder if this was the place where his room used to be.

I look down. Beside my feet, some tiny stems are sprouting. Old Man Hammer's seeds have grown! I run to his stoop. "Come with me!" I beg, tugging at his hand. "You'll want to see."

160   I walk him past the hollyhocks, the daisies, the peppers, the rows of lettuce. I show him the strawberries that I planted. When Old Man Hammer sees his little garden bed, his sour grapes turn sweet. "Marcy, child." He shakes his head. "This lot was good for nothin'. Now it's nothin' but good," he says.

REREAD
What do you think Old Man Hammer means?

Soon summertime comes, and this lot really grows. It fills with vegetables, herbs, and flowers. And way in the back, taller than anything

170 else, is a beautiful patch of yellow sunflowers. Old Man Hammer comes every day. He sits in the sun, eats his lunch, and sometimes comes back with supper.

Nobody knows how the sunflowers came—not Leslie, my brother, or Miss Rosa. Not Mr. Bennett, or Sonny, or anyone else. But Old Man Hammer just sits there smiling at me. We know

180 whose flowers they are.

THINK IT THROUGH

1. How does Old Man Hammer change from the beginning of the story to the end? What causes the change?
2. How is the setting important to the action of this story?
3. What message do you think the author wants to share?

IN THE HARDWARE STORE

by Pam Koo

In the hardware store
I asked,
"Gramma, want to plant a garden this year?"
She said,
5   "Tend vines, fight white flies?
Watch everything dry in the sun?"

Eyeing each other, smiling,
I rattled a seed packet,
and she marched
10   to the clerk,
two envelopes—melons and tomatoes—
in each hand.

I Am Rosa Parks

by Rosa Parks with Jim Haskins

For most people, getting arrested is scary. Would you be willing to get arrested for breaking a law you thought was unfair?

Connect to Your Life

Are there laws in your community that you don't think are right? How do you think they should be changed?

Key to the Autobiography

A person's story of his or her own life is called an **autobiography.**

Besides telling her own story, Rosa Parks tells some history about the United States. She became famous for her role in the civil rights movement. As you read, you will learn about this particular time in history.

MONTGOMERY CITY CODE

6, § 10

c. 10. Separation of races—Required.

Every person operating a bus line in the
qual but separate accommodations for v
egroes on his buses, by requiring the em
ereof to assign passengers seats on the v
harge in such manner as to separate the
he negroes, where there are both white a
ded however, that negro

Rosa Parks is telling about an experience from her life. Find out why she gets arrested.

I Get Arrested

Many years ago black people in the South could not go to the same schools as white people. We could not eat in white restaurants. We could not even drink from the same water fountains. We had to stay apart from white people everywhere we went. This was called segregation.

Segregation was the law in the South. If we broke the law, we could be arrested, or hurt, or even killed.

When we rode a bus, we could only sit in the back
10 seats. The front seats were just for white people. If all the front seats were filled with white people, we black people had to give up our seats to the next white people who got on the bus. That's the way we rode the buses in the South when I was younger.

I rode the buses and obeyed the laws that kept me apart from white people. But I did not think they were right.

REREAD
What is Rosa Parks's opinion of the laws?

One day I was riding on a bus. I was sitting in one of the seats in the back section for black
20 people. The bus started to get crowded. The front seats filled up with white people. One white man was standing up. The bus driver looked back at us black people sitting down. The driver said, "Let me have those seats." He wanted us to get up and give our seats to white people. But I was tired of doing that. I stayed in my seat. The bus driver said to me,

"I'm going to have you arrested."

"You may do that," I said. And I stayed in my seat.

Two policemen came. One asked me, "Why didn't
30 you stand up?"

I asked him, "Why do you push us black people around?"

The policemen took me to jail. They took my picture. They put my fingers on a pad of ink and rolled my fingers onto white cards. That way, they had my fingerprints. Then they put me in a jail cell. I did not have to spend the night in jail. My husband came to get me. A friend paid my bail money. That meant I could go free for now. The police told me to 40 come to court in three days.

I went to court. The judge said I was guilty of breaking the law. I was fined ten dollars, plus four dollars in court costs. I never paid it. I did not feel I had broken the law. I thought black people should not have to give up their seats on the bus to white people. I thought the law should treat black people and white people just the same way. I always wanted rules to be fair, even when I was small.

THINK IT THROUGH
Why does Rosa Parks feel she did not break the law?

Rosa Parks being fingerprinted after her arrest on February 22, 1956

How I Grew Up

50 I was born on February 4, 1913. I grew up in a place called Pine Level, Alabama. I was named Rosa Louise McCauley, after my grandma Rose. My little brother was named Sylvester, after my grandpa. My mother's name was Leona. She was a schoolteacher. My father was a builder of houses. His name was James.

We lived on a farm with my grandma and grandpa. They owned their own land, and grew vegetables and raised chickens on it. I liked to go fishing with Grandma and Grandpa. They could not see very well, so I would put the worm on the hook for them.

60 Pine Level was too small to have buses or public water fountains, or even a library. But there was segregation just the same.

Sylvester and I went to school for black children. It had only one room. White children went to a bigger school. There was a school bus for the white children. There was no school bus for us. Sometimes when we walked to school, the bus would go by carrying the white children. They would laugh at us and throw trash out the window. There was no way to stop them.

70 One day a white boy named Franklin tried to hit me. I picked up a brick, and I dared him to hit me. He went away. My grandma was angry. She told me not to talk back to white folks. I thought I was right to talk back.

REREAD
Why did Rosa's grandmother tell her not to talk back?

When I grew up, I married a man named Raymond Parks. The year was 1932. He was a barber. He lived in the city of Montgomery, Alabama.

Sylvester and I went to school for black children...White children went to a bigger school. There was a school bus for the white children. There was no school bus for us.

I was proud of my husband because he worked to
80　help black people. He helped get lawyers for people who had been arrested. I began to work to help black people too. I wrote down their stories when they were hurt by whites. I asked young black people to try to use the white library. It was very hard work. It was also very sad work, because nothing we did really helped make our lives better.

Then came that day on the bus when I would not give up my seat to a white person. I was tired of black people being pushed around. Some people think I kept
90　my seat because I'd had a hard day, but that is not true. I was just tired of giving in.

THINK IT THROUGH
What events in her childhood was Rosa thinking about when she decided not to give up her seat?

We Stay Off the Buses

Many black people heard that I had been arrested. They were very angry. They thought it was time to fight for new laws.

A woman named Jo Ann Robinson said we should not ride the buses if we had to give up our seats to white people. She passed out leaflets asking all black people in the city of Montgomery to stay off of the buses
100 for one day. This was called a boycott.

> **REREAD**
> What point were black people trying to make by boycotting?

The day of the boycott came. The buses were almost empty. Very few black people were on them.

A man named E. D. Nixon called a big meeting of black people. The meeting was held in a church. A young minister named Dr. Martin Luther King, Jr., told all the black people to keep off the buses. Everyone at the meeting cheered, and the boycott went on. We walked to work or took taxis. We got
110 rides from our friends. But we did not ride the buses.

Christmas passed. It was very cold, but we did not ride the buses.

White people were very angry. They wanted us to ride the buses again. Some black people even lost their jobs because they would not ride the buses. Some black people were arrested. Some were beaten up. I got telephone calls from people who would not give their names. They said they wanted to hurt me.

> **REREAD**
> Why were the white people angry?

120 Spring came. Now it was nice weather for walking. All the black churches had station wagons to drive the people who could not walk. Summer came. The buses

had stopped running. There were not enough riders without the black people.

Mr. Nixon and Dr. King got lawyers to take our case to court. They took our case all the way to the Supreme Court in Washington, D.C. The Supreme Court said that the segregation laws were wrong. Black people should not have to give up their bus
130 seats to white people.

Our boycott worked, and we had won. We went back to the buses at last. We did not have to give up our seats anymore. We had stayed off the buses for a whole year.

THINK IT THROUGH
How did the boycott help change the law?

FOCUS
What happens after the boycott?

Since the Boycott

Many white people were angry that we had won. My brother was worried about our safety. My husband and I left Montgomery to find work and be near my brother. We moved up North, to Detroit, Michigan. My mother moved with us.

Back in the South, Dr. Martin Luther King, Jr., decided
140 to fight against segregation in other ways. He led black people in the fight to vote and to eat in restaurants, just as white people did. He was fighting for their rights. This fight was called the civil rights movement.

REREAD
What was the civil rights movement?

Some white people joined the fight. Most went down South from the North. But some white people in the South joined the civil rights movement too.

I helped out by making speeches. I told about being arrested. I went down South for some of the big
150 marches for black people's rights. The civil rights movement won many rights for black people. New laws for equal rights were passed. The old segregation laws were over. Today I still make many speeches, and I receive many awards. Some people say I started the whole civil rights movement because I would not give up my seat on the bus. I know that many people started the civil rights movement. And many people worked very hard to win the rights that black people have today. But I am glad that I did my part.

160 There is still much work to be done. The laws that kept black and white people apart have been changed. But there are still many people who have not changed their hearts.

I hope that children today will grow up without hate. I hope they will learn to respect one another, no matter what color they are.

THINK IT THROUGH

1. How did Rosa Parks help the civil rights movement?
2. Does Rosa Parks think that changing the laws is enough? Why?
3. What do you think was Rosa Parks's purpose in writing about this event?

Mr. Nixon and Dr. King got lawyers to take our case to court. They took our case all the way to the Supreme Court in Washington, D.C. The Supreme Court said that the **segregation laws were wrong.**

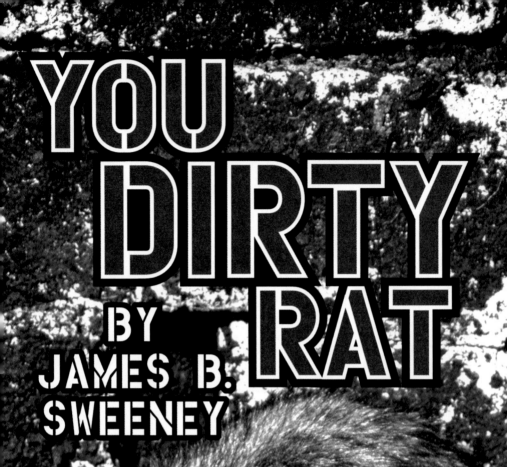

YOU DIRTY RAT

BY JAMES B. SWEENEY

Connect to Your Life

Did your friends ever choose you to solve a dangerous problem? Did you refuse? Or did you think of a solution?

Key to the True Account

"You Dirty Rat" is an example of a **true account**. The article is about real people, places, and events. But the author presents the information as a story to make it interesting. The conflict in this story comes out in the conversations between the characters.

These events take place during World War II. The terms below will help you understand some of the groups in World War II.

French Underground: secret group who opposed the Germans

Nazis: the political party that ruled Germany

Luftwaffe: the German air force

Allies: armed forces of the United States, England, Russia, and other nations

Gestapo: the German police

Vocabulary Preview

Words to Know

smuggle	intrigued
conceal	comical
torture	

 Reading Coach CD-ROM selection

WHAT GOES THROUGH YOUR MIND WHEN YOU READ THE TITLE OF THIS STORY? YOU MIGHT THINK DIFFERENTLY AFTER YOU READ THIS STORY.

Three men were hunched over a candle. They spoke in whispers. Their lives depended on not being discovered by German storm troopers. For these three were members of the French Underground.

"It's past midnight," Pierre Pinault complained. He was a squirrel-faced little man. He was also very nervous. "The curfew has been in force since nine this evening."

"Stop it!" Maurice Pomme hissed.

10 Obviously suited to his role as a spy, Pomme was a big man and tough. "Here in St. Jeane, we know every alley, every sewer leading to safety. There's no need to worry."

René Le Du chuckled. He was an escaped convict, a murderer, thief, and con man. "These Nazis, poof! For six months we have met in this abandoned wine cellar. They have not discovered us yet. Why tonight? So stop your whining, Pierre. Let's talk business instead."

20 "Agreed!" Maurice Pomme said. "Now, Le Du, you have stolen a German military map, yes?"

curfew
(kûr' fyōō)
law that requires people to be inside their homes by a certain time

REREAD
What do you think their business is?

"Well, yes. But only in a sense. You see, I have the map. But it is hidden in the castle occupied by the German Luftwaffe. I stole it off the general's desk. He was drunk. After that I slipped it under some loose floorboards."

THINK IT THROUGH
Why is the meeting a secret?

Maurice Pomme scratched his chin. He liked to think out loud. "So the problem remains.

30 We must somehow smuggle the map out of the building past the Nazi guards."

| **smuggle**
| (smŭg′ əl)
| v. take secretly

"And deliver it to the city of Caen. Underground members there will then get it to Britain," Le Du said.

"But is this map so important?" asked Pinault. "It could cost all of our lives."

"Important?" Le Du screamed. "This map shows the location of every German military unit in France. It also shows their defenses along the English

40 Channel."

"Yes, yes," Pomme added excitedly. "The Allies must have this map! They need it for their upcoming invasion of Europe. But how can we get it out of the

REREAD
Why is the map important?

castle? They search everyone leaving the building."

"But can't someone just wrap it around their bodies? Is it all that big?" Pinault asked.

"Big?" Le Du said. "But of course. It is a wall map. Even folded it's eighteen inches square.

50 Who could conceal that on their bodies?"

| **conceal**
| (kən sēl′)
| v. hide

"How thick is this folded map?" Pomme asked.

"Almost two inches. Not heavy, mind you—remember it is only paper. But it is thick."

THINK IT THROUGH
| What is the men's goal? What problems stand in their way?

FOCUS

Which man do you think will be sent to get the map? Read to
see if you are right.

Maurice Pomme looked at Pierre Pinault. "Your job
has always been to get information to our friends at
Caen. So I think the responsibility is yours."

Pinault was shocked. His voice quivered.
"But if the Gestapo catch me, they will

60 torture me. Then I would be forced to give
them your names. You remember what
those devils did to poor Lambot."

> **torture**
> (tôr' chər)
> v. make someone
> suffer a lot of
> pain

The other two nodded their heads sadly.
Everyone knew about Yves Lambot. He
was a French freedom fighter. The Gestapo had pulled
his fingernails out. Then they'd blinded him in both
eyes and broken his legs. Finally they had dragged
him to the public square and set him on fire.

René Le Du stood up. "I must leave. I'm the

70 maintenance man. My job is to put coal in the
fireplaces throughout the castle. Luftwaffe
members like their offices warm when they arrive
for work."

Maurice Pomme agreed. "Yes. Enough is enough.
Now each of us must think. How can we get the map
out of the castle? We will meet here again tomorrow
evening, yes?"

As they stood up, Maurice Pomme laid a huge hand
on Pinault's bony shoulder. "Remember, my skinny

80 little friend. You must get the map into my hands.
That is *your* job. So you had better come up with a
good plan."

A few hours later, René Le Du approached the
castle. He had gone home and picked up his lunch
bucket. Now he was walking slowly down the dark

road. He neared the castle entrance. German soldiers stopped him. They looked at his identification tag, then waved him on. Le Du entered the building. As he did, he noted some civilian

90 workers leaving the castle. They were being stopped and searched by other Nazi soldiers. It was impossible. There was not a chance the map could be smuggled out.

civilian workers (sĭ vĭl′ yən) people who are not in the military

---

THINK IT THROUGH
Why does getting the map out of the castle seem impossible?

FOCUS
Which man will have a plan? Read to find out.

That night the three spies met again. As usual, they gathered in the abandoned wine cellar. René Le Du told them what he had seen. "Those Gestapo guards are thorough . They search through everything and everyone leaving the castle. We have no chance."

thorough (thûr′ ō) very careful

100 This angered Maurice Pomme. He turned toward the frightened little Pierre Pinault. "And you," he snarled. "What have you got to say?"

Pierre Pinault was clearly uncomfortable. His hands shook. He squirmed in his seat. Then he said, his voice quivering, "I can get the map out of the castle without too much trouble."

Both Le Du and Pomme were amazed. "You can *what?*" Pomme shouted.

Pinault shrunk back. "Why, yes, I—ah—can get the

110 map out of the castle," he stuttered.

"How?" Pomme demanded.

Pierre shook his head. "You must do exactly as I tell you. Ask no questions. My plan is simple. But if one word leaks out, we'll all be killed."

Both Le Du and Pomme agreed. "We seem to have no other option," Pomme said. "What must we do?"

Pierre Pinault leaned forward. "Le Du, my friend. You said they do not search workers going into the castle. Only those going out, yes?"

120 "That is true."

"And you carry a lunch bucket?"

"Yes. But what has that got to do with the map?"

Pinault's voice still shook. "Starting tomorrow, in place of food, you will carry three large rats in your lunch pail."

"What?" Le Du gasped. "Dead rats in my lunch bucket?"

THINK IT THROUGH
How does Pinault surprise the other men?

FOCUS
Read to find out how the rats will be used.

"Not dead," Pinault said. "They will be asleep. Drugged. Get them to the general's office. Then hide
130 them in the woodwork. After a time, they will wake up. And they will start moving about."

Pomme was intrigued. "And how long must René continue doing this?"

"Last night," said Pinault, "I went to the city dump. I caught thirty-six huge rats. They are vicious and hungry."

"So you have enough for twelve days?"

> **intrigued**
> (ĭn trēgd′)
> v. interested; past tense of *intrigue*

"Yes," the little man said. "When the rats wake up, they will be active again."

140 "And then what?" Le Du asked.

"The Nazi general is certain to scream about all the rats," Pinault said. "You must see that his staff learns of me, the village rat catcher."

Both Le Du and Pomme stared at Pinault. "You, the village rat catcher? Why, for twenty years you have been a school teacher."

Pinault smiled nervously. "Yes, a teacher then, a rat catcher now. Just make sure I am called to the castle to catch rats."

REREAD

Why does Pinault say he is a rat catcher when he is really a teacher?

150 Pomme and Le Du were still uncertain. But they did as they were told. Le Du began to carry rats instead of food in his lunch bucket. For three days, little was said by the Nazi general. Just a comment or two about noisy rats inside the walls of the old building. On the fourth day, the general let out a howl. During the night, several of the rats had fouled on his desk. On the tenth day, rodents were running freely about the room. By the twelfth, it appeared they might take over.

160 *"Gott und himmel!"* the Nazi general roared. "Call in the exterminators . Have them fumigate the place."

exterminators
(ĭk stûr′ mə nā′ tərz)
people who get rid of pests such as insects and rats

THINK IT THROUGH
What is Pinault's plan for getting inside the castle?

FOCUS ——————————————————————

A new problem arises. Find out what it is.

René Le Du had kept his ear attuned for just this. He put in a quick appearance. "General," he said. "I will send for the village rat catcher. He will clean them out."

"*Nein!*" the general roared. "My own squad will clear them out."

170 Le Du had not expected this. He had to think fast. "No, no, General. These are French rats."

"French rats?"

"Yes. A special breed. They will respond only to the village rat catcher. Give him two days. Presto! They will be gone."

REREAD

Why does Le Du ask for two days?

After much talking on Le Du's part, the general finally agreed. "Two days, then. After that, I call in my own exterminators."

René Le Du had no idea if two days were enough.
180 He had no choice, however. That night, in the wine cellar, he hissed at the little rat catcher. "You must bring out the map within that time. Otherwise you will have failed the Underground."

Pinault turned pale. To fail the Underground was dangerous, even deadly. "Do not fear, Le Du. I will be at the castle by ten tomorrow morning. The job will be done."

Both Le Du and Pomme were startled. "In broad daylight? You plan to sneak the map out in broad
190 daylight?" they shouted.

The little man was quivering all over. He hated people to yell at him. "But yes, of course. My scheme is simple. You shall have your map by tomorrow evening."

Le Du and Pomme had no confidence in Pinault. He would blow the job for sure. But they had no choice.

THINK IT THROUGH
How does Le Du save the plan?

FOCUS
Read to find out what Pinault does next.

On the following day, a comical figure appeared at the gate of the castle. It was a runty little Frenchman in baggy coveralls. He had a net in one hand. In the other he
200 carried a large wooden box.

comical
(kŏm' ĭ kəl)
adj. funny

"Who are you?" the Gestapo sergeant of the guard asked.

"The rat catcher, Pierre Pinault."

The sergeant telephoned the castle. Then he let the Frenchman pass. Inside the castle Pinault was met by René Le Du, who asked, "Now what?"

"First," Pinault whispered, "help me catch rats. Stuff them into this wooden box. Then stand by with your map."

210 After the box had six active rats stuffed into it, the top was closed. "N—Now," Pinault said nervously, "I will leave with my rats."

Le Du was stunned. "But what about the map? I still have the map hidden."

"Sssh," Pinault cautioned. "I will be back shortly."

Le Du was puzzled. He trailed Pinault down to the front gate. "Halt!" a Gestapo guard shouted. "What have you got in that box?"

"NO, NO, NO," PINAULT CRIED OUT. "DO NOT OPEN THE LID."

Pinault fumbled about. He looked around uneasily. If ever a person looked guilty, he did. The Gestapo agent grabbed the box. He prepared to open the lid. "No, no, no," Pinault cried out. "Do not open the lid."

The little Frenchman made so much noise that the entire guard gathered around. "Open the lid," the sergeant ordered. "This man is trying to smuggle something out of the castle."

The lid flopped back. Out leaped the rats. They were big, mean, and very fast. The guards hollered and leaped aside. They cursed as the rodents raced among them. Within seconds, there wasn't a rat in sight.

"Gone," wailed Pinault. "Two hours of hard work for nothing. Now I must return and catch them again. And your general, he will say I have failed."

THINK IT THROUGH

Why does Pinault only bring out rats on the first trip?

FOCUS

Will Pinault be able to sneak the map out?

"Shut up," the Gestapo sergeant said. He was angry at himself and scared of the general. "Go catch your rats, and quit wailing."

Inside the castle, Pinault found Le Du. "Hurry," he said. "Where is that folded map?"

Quickly, it was produced. Pinault dropped it into
240   the box. It fit neatly on the bottom. "Now, quick, get more rats."

Le Du still didn't know what the school teacher was up to. But he did as Pinault asked. Soon, the box held another six rats. "Goodbye, my friend," Pinault whispered. "I will see you tonight."

Picking up the box, he walked toward the Gestapo guard. Again came the command, "Halt!"

"Would you like to see? I will open the lid," Pinault said.

250   The Gestapo sergeant was standing nearby. He realized what was happening. He raced over to the guard and yelled, "No. No more rats. Do not open the lid. Just get those filthy creatures out of here."

Pinault cringed . Then he hurried through the gate. Within minutes he was down the street and out of sight. With him went six angry rats and a map. Soon the rats would be free. And the map would be on its way to Britain.

> **cringed**
> (krĭnjd)
> stepped back in fear

THINK IT THROUGH

1. How did Pinault fool the guards?
2. The other two men had no confidence in Pinault. How did his behavior help him succeed?
3. Why didn't Pinault explain his plan to the other two men?
4. This event really happened. Why does it seem like fiction?

Games We Play

Unit 9

Poetry

Poetry expresses ideas, images, and feelings with only a few words. For this reason, poets choose their words carefully, so that they have just the right sound and meaning. In this unit, you will see how five poets have carefully chosen words about the games we play.

As in all poems, you will listen to a **speaker,** the voice that talks to the reader. In some poems you will find **imagery** that appeals to your senses and creates pictures in your mind. As you read, look for **themes,** which are important messages about life. Enjoy the sounds and word pictures that the poets created for you.

BEFORE THE GAME

BY PAUL B. JANECZKO

THERE'S MORE THAN BASEBALL GOING ON AT A BASEBALL GAME.

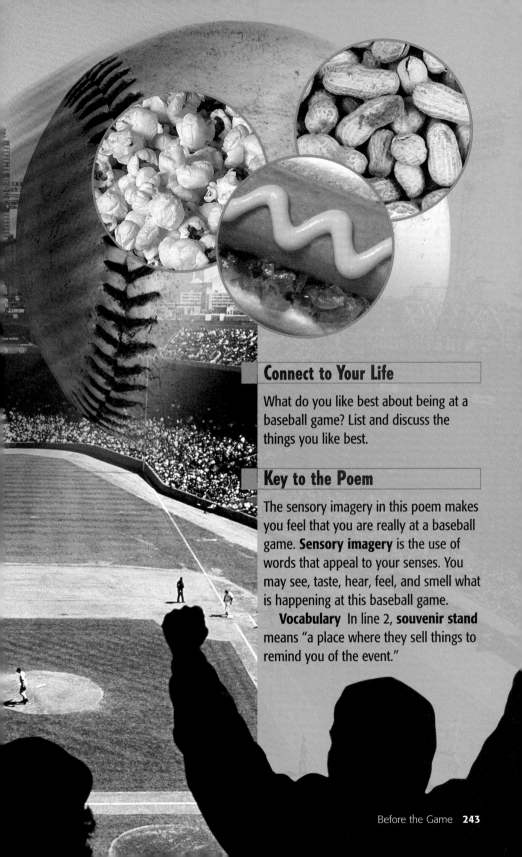

Connect to Your Life

What do you like best about being at a baseball game? List and discuss the things you like best.

Key to the Poem

The sensory imagery in this poem makes you feel that you are really at a baseball game. **Sensory imagery** is the use of words that appeal to your senses. You may see, taste, hear, feel, and smell what is happening at this baseball game.

    Vocabulary In line 2, **souvenir stand** means "a place where they sell things to remind you of the event."

BEFORE THE GAME BY PAUL B. JANECZKO

Pennants wave
on the souvenir stand

Sausages snap,
sizzle with onions on the grill

5 Girls with mitts
practice catches to be made

Scorecard
Ohhh-ficial scorecard

Boys, wearing caps of faraway teams,
10 laugh, shove

Peanut shells crunch
underfoot

Cheese oozes
over nachos

15 Joy
thick as the perfume
of popcorn and
boiled hot dogs
fills the air

20 as
ticket takers call,
This way
This way to the game

1. Which sense do you use on lines 7–8, when someone calls out *"Scorecard, Ohhh-ficial scorecard"*?

2. What images in the poem make you use your sense of smell? hearing? taste? touch?

3. Which image do you think makes you use only your sense of sight?

KARATE KID

by Jane Yolen

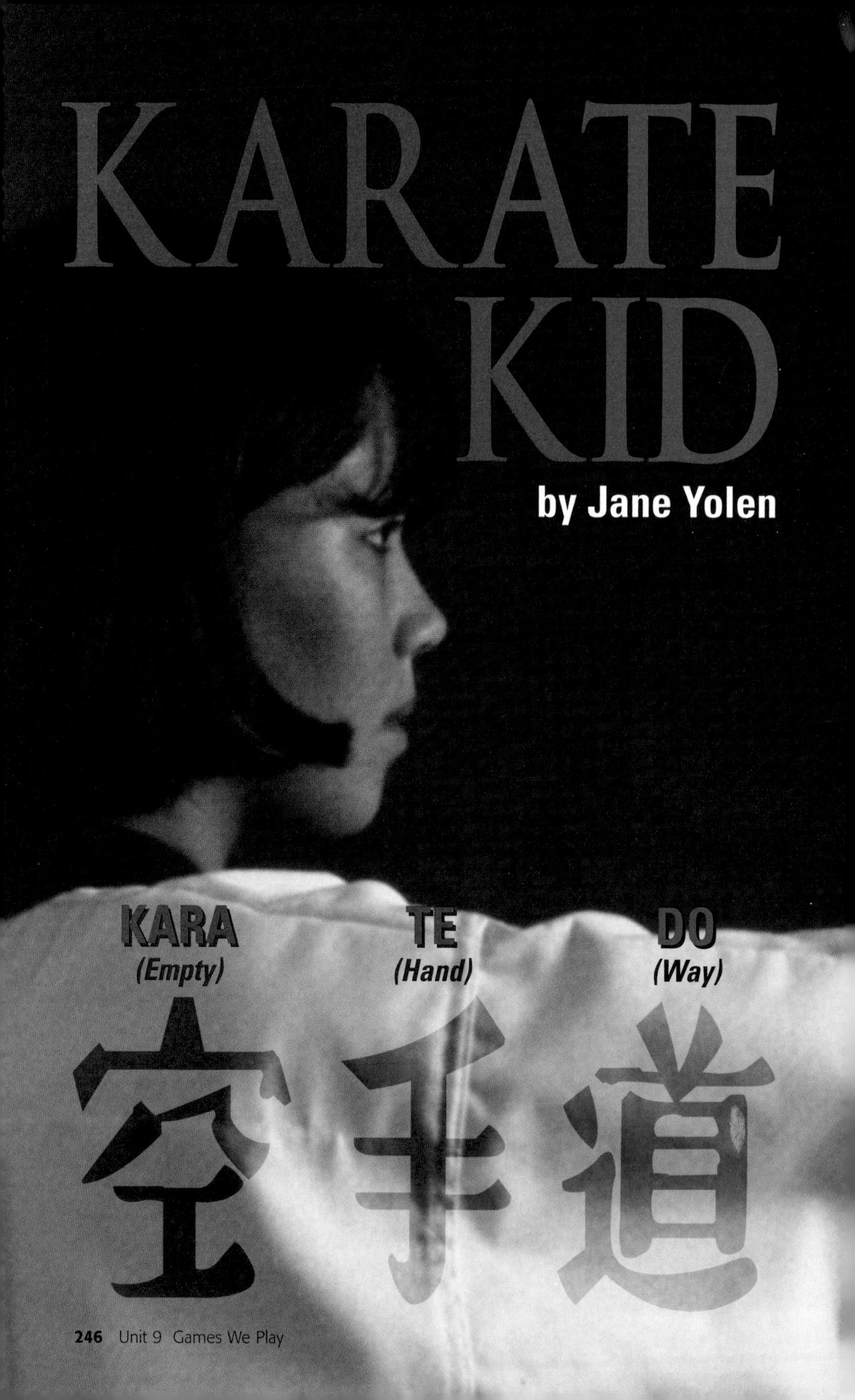

KARA
(Empty)

TE
(Hand)

DO
(Way)

空手道

You probably know some karate kicks. But do you know their real purposes?

Connect to Your Life

Have you ever taken karate lessons? Have you watched someone practice karate or seen it on TV? What do you think is the purpose of karate?

Key to the Poem

In a poem, the **speaker** is the voice that talks to you. In this poem, who does the speaker *claim* to be?

Reading Coach CD-ROM selection

KARATE KID

by
Jane Yolen

I am wind,
I am wall,
I am wave,
I rise, I fall.
5 I am crane
In lofty flight,
Training that
I need not fight.

I am tiger,
10 I am tree,
I am flower,
I am knee,
I am elbow,
I am hands
15 Taught to do
The heart's commands.

Not to bully,
Not to fight,
Dragon left
20 And leopard right.
Wind and wave,
Tree and flower,
Chop.
  Kick.
25   Peace.
    Power.

THINK IT THROUGH 空手道 空手道 空手道

1. When practicing karate, who or what does the speaker become?
2. Reread lines 7–8 and 15–18. According to these lines, what is the purpose of karate?
3. What feelings or ideas do you have about karate after reading this poem?

This Team the Silver Spokes

by
Arnold
Adoff

What kind of basketball team can spin and fly and pop wheelies?

This Team the Silver Spokes:

can   spin   and   fly   and   clutch
and   double
clutch

and

5 pop the s h a r p e s t wheelchair
wheeeelies   as
they

d r i b b l e pass c a t c h and
d r i v e on r o l l i n g   d o w n
10   the floor
to   block   and   pass   and   sh oo t   and   score.

I need to make that happen
on   my   m o v i n g   feet.

THINK IT THROUGH

1. Think about the title and lines 5–6. What is different about this basketball team? What other words give clues?
2. Why are the letters of some words in this poem spread out?
3. What are the "moving feet" in the last line?
4. What do you think are the challenges of playing basketball in wheelchairs?

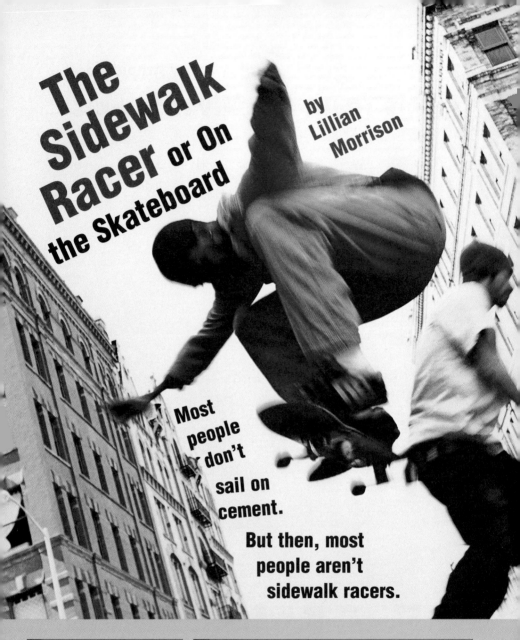

The Sidewalk Racer or On the Skateboard

by Lillian Morrison

Most
people
don't
sail on
cement.

But then, most
people aren't
sidewalk racers.

Skimming
an asphalt sea
I swerve, I curve, I
sway; I speed to whirring
5   sound an inch above the
ground; I'm the sailor
and the sail, I'm the
driver and the wheel
I'm the one and only
10   single engine
human auto
mobile.

THINK IT THROUGH

1. What is the speaker in this poem doing?
2. What is the shape of this poem?
3. Reread lines 6–12. When riding the skateboard, what does the speaker feel that he or she is?

FINAL SCORE

by Lee
Bennett
Hopkins

What can you do when
a game is over? Can
you change the score?

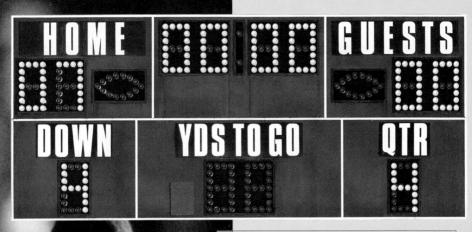

Connect to Your Life

Does it ever help to think about a game when it's over? Or is it better to forget the past and think only about the future? Discuss both sides of this issue with one or more classmates.

Key to the Poem

Some poems contain a **theme,** or important message about life. How can the end of a game be like other things in life?

 Reading Coach CD-ROM selection

FINAL SCORE

by Lee
Bennett
Hopkins

Eventually
there's
a final score
when
5 games
have ended

when
they're
over—

10 no more.

No more
  batting,
  kicking,
  tossing a ball—

15 No more
  stumbling,
  fumbling,
  rising up from a fall.

Games
20 have been played.

They're over.

    That's all.

THINK IT THROUGH

1. According to this poem, what can you do after the final score in a game? Can you change how you did something in the game? Why or why not?

2. What is the theme, or message, of this poem? How does the theme apply to something besides sports?

3. Think of someone who would benefit from hearing the message in this poem. Why would it help that person?

For the Sake of Others

Mixed Genres

Some people are willing to give up things they value to help others. Some even risk their lives. In this unit, you will read three stories, a poem, and a nonfiction article. All these selections tell what happens when people care about others more than they care about themselves.

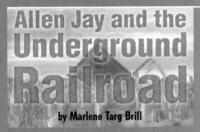

Femme à sa toilette (1889), Edgar Degas. Copyright © Edgar Degas/Wood River Gallery/PictureQuest.

THE GIFT OF THE MAGI

by C. G. Draper   *adapted from the story by O. Henry*

what makes a great gift? two people are about to find out.

Connect to Your Life

What is the one thing you own that you would never want to give up? Is there anything or anyone you might give it up for?

Key to the Short Story

The title refers to the Magi. According to Christian tradition, the Magi were wise men or kings. They went to Bethlehem to present gifts to the baby Jesus.

In reading some stories, you expect one thing to happen and then something entirely different happens. This is called **irony.** As you read "The Gift of the Magi," be on the lookout for events that you don't expect.

Della counted her money three times. She had only
one dollar and eighty-seven cents. That was all.
And tomorrow would be Christmas. What Christmas
gift could she buy with only one dollar and eighty-
seven cents? Della lay down on the old bed and cried
and cried.

Let's leave Della alone for a while and look at her
home. The chairs and tables were old and poor.
Outside there was a mailbox without mail, and a door
10 without a doorbell. The name on the door said MR.
JAMES DILLINGHAM YOUNG—Della's dear husband Jim.

Della knew that Jim would be home soon. She dried
her eyes and stood up. She looked in the mirror. She
began to comb her hair for Jim. She felt very sad. She
wanted to buy Jim a Christmas gift—something good.
But what could she do with one dollar and eighty-seven
cents? She combed her hair in the mirror and thought.
Suddenly she had an idea.

THINK IT THROUGH
Why is Della unhappy?

FOCUS

How will Della get money to buy a gift for Jim?

Now, Jim and Della had only two treasures. One was
20 Jim's gold watch. He was very proud of the watch. He
would take it out to check the time even when he knew
what time it was. The other treasure was Della's hair. It
was long and brown, and fell down her back. Della

looked in the mirror a little longer. Her eyes were sad, but then she smiled. She put on her old brown coat and her hat. She ran out of the house and down the street. She stopped in front of a door which said, MME. SOPHRONIE. HAIR OF ALL KINDS. The store was dark.

"Will you buy my hair?" Della asked.

30   "I buy hair," said Madame. "Take off your hat. Let's see your hair."

Della's hair fell down like water. Mme. Sophronie lifted Della's hair with a heavy hand. "Twenty dollars," she said.

"Give me the money now!" said Della.

Ah! the next two hours flew past like summer wind. Della shopped in many stores for the right gift for Jim. Then she found it—a chain for his gold watch. It was a good chain, strong and expensive. Della knew
40 the chain would make Jim happy. Jim had a cheap chain for his watch, but this chain was so much better. It would look wonderful with the gold watch. The chain cost twenty-one dollars. Della paid for the chain, and ran home with eighty-seven cents.

THINK IT THROUGH
Does Della feel bad about selling her hair? How can you tell?

At seven o'clock Della made coffee and started to cook dinner. It was almost dinner time. Jim would be home soon. He was never late. Della heard Jim outside. She looked in the mirror again. "Oh! I hope Jim doesn't kill me!" Della smiled, but her eyes were

50 wet. "But what could I do with only one dollar and eighty-seven cents?"

The door opened, and Jim came in and shut it. His face was thin and quiet. His coat was old, and he had no hat. He was only twenty-two, but he already had so many worries! Jim stood still and looked at Della. He didn't speak. His eyes were strange. Della suddenly felt afraid. She did not understand him. She began to talk very fast. "Oh, Jim, dear, why do you look so strange? Don't look at me like that. I cut my hair and

60 sold it. I wanted to buy you a Christmas gift. It will grow again—don't be angry. My hair grows very fast. Say 'Merry Christmas,' dear, and let's be happy. You don't know what I've got for you—it's beautiful."

"You cut your hair?" Jim spoke slowly.

"I cut it and sold it," Della answered. "Don't you like me now? I'm still me, aren't I?"

"You say that your hair is gone?" Jim asked again.

"Don't look for it, it's gone," Della said. "Be good to me, because it's Christmas. Shall we have dinner
70 now, Jim?"

Jim seemed to wake up. He smiled. He took Della in his arms.

THINK IT THROUGH
How does Jim seem to feel about Della's haircut?

FOCUS

Jim has a surprise for Della. Find out what it is.

Jim took a small box out of his pocket. "I love your short hair, Della," he said. "I'm sorry I seemed strange. But if you open the box you will understand." Della opened the box. First she smiled, then suddenly she began to cry. In the box were two beautiful combs. Combs like those were made to hold up long hair. Della could see that the combs came 80 from an expensive store. She never thought she would have anything as beautiful! "Oh, Jim, they are beautiful! And my hair grows fast, you know. But wait! You must see your gift." Della gave Jim the chain. The chain was bright, like her eyes. "Isn't it a good one, Jim? I looked for it everywhere. You'll have to look at the time one hundred times daily, now. Give me your watch. I want to see them together."

Jim lay back on the bed. He put his hands under his head, and smiled. "Della," he said, "let's put the gifts 90 away. They are too nice for us to use right now. I sold the watch to buy your combs. And now, let's have dinner."

REREAD

How has Jim bought his gift?

The magi were wise men—very wise men. They brought gifts to the baby Jesus. The magi were wise, so their gifts were wise gifts. Perhaps Jim and Della do not seem wise. They lost the two great treasures of their house. But I want to tell you that they *were* wise. People like Jim and Della are always wiser than others. Everywhere they are wiser. They are the magi.

1. **Irony** is a difference between what is expected and what actually happens. What is the irony in the gifts that Della and Jim buy for each other?
2. Why are Della and Jim willing to give up their treasures to buy each other gifts?
3. The author feels that Jim and Della are very wise. Do you agree? Why?

A rustling sound in a cornfield.
A gun pointed at your head. Even the
bravest person would be afraid.
How would an 11-year-old boy react?

Allen Jay and the Underground Railroad

by Marlene Targ Brill

Connect to Your Life

How would you feel if someone's life depended on your keeping a secret?

Key to the Story

Historical fiction is fiction that is set in the past. Such a story may refer to real people and events. *Allen Jay and the Underground Railroad* is about real people. But it is fiction, because the author didn't see what happened and doesn't know exactly what people said.

During the 1800s, people helped slaves in the South escape to freedom. Some of these people belonged to a religious group called the Society of Friends, or Quakers. The Quakers said "thee" and "thy" for "you" and "your."

Vocabulary Preview

Words to Know

courage	snorted
falsehoods	determined

 Reading Coach CD-ROM selection

One day Allen's life changes. Read to find out how.

July 1, 1842

Allen hung the last shirt on the line. His mother was too sick to do such heavy work. So the job fell to her eldest child. Every Monday Allen washed, boiled, starched, and hung out the clothes. Afterward he was free to play. This afternoon Allen headed for the barn to get his fishing pole. As he crossed the front yard, he saw a horse racing down the road toward the Jay farm. Within seconds the family doctor stopped at the front gate.

10   "Friend Jay! Friend Jay!" the doctor shouted.

Friend
member of the Society of Friends

Allen's father came out of the barn and walked quickly to the gate. "Thy horse has wings today," said Isaac Jay. "Thee seems in a hurry."

The doctor leaned toward Isaac. "A runaway slave is hiding in the woods," the doctor said in a low voice. "The slave's owner and his men are following close behind, and they have guns," he

REREAD
Is the doctor warning Isaac about the slave or the slave owners?

20   warned. The doctor grabbed Isaac's shoulder and added, "Be careful, my friend." Allen's father nodded. The doctor turned his horse and rode away.

Allen moved closer to his father and looked up into his troubled face. Allen wondered, Would the slave's owner come and shoot his father? He remembered stories about other Friends who helped runaways. Some Friends had been beaten. Others had had their homes burned.

30 Isaac Jay looked down at his son. "Allen," his father said, "thee may soon see a dark-skinned man. Take him into the cornfield behind the big walnut tree. The corn is high enough there to hide him. But if thee does this, thee must not tell me or anyone." Then Isaac Jay turned and walked back to the barn.

THINK IT THROUGH
What does Isaac tell Allen to do? Why do you think Isaac doesn't want to know what Allen does?

FOCUS
Discover whom Allen meets.

Allen could not move. What should he do now? A crackling sound from the woods broke into Allen's thoughts. He saw someone moving through the trees and brush. Allen walked quietly toward the sounds.
40 The rustling stopped.

Suddenly a man with a gun leaped out of the brush. Allen jumped back. The two of them stared at each other without speaking. The man had ragged clothes and bloody feet. His dark skin was cut and scarred with whip burns. "Is you Marster Jay's boy?" the man demanded. His eyes darted back and forth, watching the road and the house.

REREAD
Whom has Allen found?

"Yes," Allen stammered, "I'm Allen, his son." The man lowered his gun.

50 Allen gathered his courage to speak. He had always had trouble saying words clearly. Now it was more important than ever to be understood. "Follow me," Allen said slowly. "Father told me to take you to a hiding place."

courage
(kûr' ĭj)
n. ability to face danger

"I understand," the man said.

Allen led him along the edge of the woods to the back of the farm. They bent over as they ran deep into the cornfield. Allen brought the man to a clearing under the walnut tree. "Thee must stay quiet and out of sight," Allen whispered. "Someone will come for thee in time."

"Have mercy," the man begged. "My name is Henry James. I ran away day before last, and I ain't had nothing to eat or drink since." His eyes looked sad and tired. His lips were cracked from the heat.

"I will come back soon with some food," Allen told him. The boy looked around to make sure no one could see Henry James. He broke off a cornstalk and stirred the dirt behind him as he walked to cover any footprints. He checked that all the cornstalks were in place. Then Allen ran through the woods to the house. He hoped the slave owner was hours away. His father would need time to plan a safe escape for this runaway. Allen slowed his footsteps as he neared the barn. Someone might be watching, he thought.

THINK IT THROUGH
How does Allen help Henry James?

FOCUS
Allen has become involved. Read to see what happens next.

Allen opened the kitchen door. Milton, Walter, Abijah, and Mary were shelling peas at the table. His mother got up from her rocking chair. "Sit down, Allen," she ordered in a quiet voice. "I have something for thee."

"But, Mother," Allen protested.

"Hush, son," she said. Allen slid onto the bench next to Walter.

"Mary, please put some corn bread and bacon into a basket," Rhoda Jay said. Allen wondered how his mother knew to fix food at this odd hour of the day. And why were his brothers and sister all inside?

"Who gets the corn bread?" asked little Milton.

"Any friend who may pass our way," answered his
90 mother, smiling.

Rhoda Jay handed the filled basket to Allen. "Take this basket to anybody thee thinks is hungry," she said. Allen took the basket and grabbed a jug of milk. Then he hurried back to the cornfield.

REREAD

Why doesn't Allen's mother just tell him to give the corn bread to Henry?

As he got near the walnut tree, Allen heard stalks snapping. A dark gun barrel poked through the corn. Allen froze. Click! He knew the gun was ready to fire.

100 "Please, don't shoot," begged the boy. Henry lowered the gun and pushed the corn aside.

"You give me a scare," Henry said, his voice shaking.

Allen let out a deep sigh and moved closer. "Help thyself," Allen said, showing the man what he brought. Henry grabbed the jug. He took a long, hearty drink.

"This be mighty fine, Marster Allen," Henry James said thankfully.

110 "Thee may rest here until my father comes for thee. I must go now," Allen said.

THINK IT THROUGH

Why does Allen return to the cornfield? What danger does he face?

Allen Jay and the Underground Railroad **273**

Allen pushed through the corn to the edge of the field. He heard voices as he came through the woods. He ducked behind a pile of firewood before anyone saw him. Allen peeked through the logs and saw his father facing six men on horseback. The strangers had guns.

A man questioned his father roughly, "Are you sure you didn't see my runaway?"

Isaac Jay shook his head. "I told

120 thee once. I never speak falsehoods."

REREAD

Is Isaac Jay telling the truth?

The slave owner snorted in disbelief. "Then how about a look through your house?" he yelled.

"Thee are welcome," said Isaac Jay quietly. "But thee needs the correct papers."

"That could take some time," the owner shouted. "Expect us back by morning." Then he grumbled to his men, and they rode off in a hurry.

falsehoods

(fôls' hōōdz')
n. lies

snorted

(snôr' tĭd)
v. breathed through the nose in a noisy way, like a pig or horse; past tense of snort

130 Allen heard nothing more about the runaway slave or the angry men that afternoon. And he dared not ask. When Isaac Jay came inside for supper, he said little.

That night Allen's mother sent the younger children to bed early. Allen's father went out to the barn. A little while later, he came to the door and called Allen outside. Old Jack, their horse, stood in the yard harnessed to the buggy. "How would thee like to go to thy grandfather's house?" Isaac Jay said to his son.

140 "Go along with thee?" Allen asked, puzzled.

"No, by thyself this time," his father answered. Allen had never traveled through the woods in the dark before. There were bears, wildcats, and snakes out there. Now there might be slave hunters too. But Allen knew what his father wanted him to do.

Allen's mother came outside and clutched her husband's arm. "Thee must not send *him*," she said, "it's too dangerous."

"But I have to go, Mother," Allen said. "If the
150 owner and his men come back tonight, Father must be here."

"I'm proud of thee, son," Isaac Jay said. "If thee knows of anybody who ought to go along, thee had better take him too."

Rhoda Jay gave her son a long hug. Allen climbed into the buggy and grabbed the reins. "Go quickly, and stay on the main road," his father cautioned. "Thee can spend the night at thy grandfather's house."

THINK IT THROUGH
What does Isaac ask Allen to do? Why can't Isaac do it himself?

FOCUS
Look for details that tell what Allen's trip is like.

Allen guided Old Jack to the cornfield. He stopped
160 the buggy on the side of the field near the walnut tree. "It's Allen," he called softly. "We must hurry."

Henry James pulled himself into the buggy and squeezed into the space by Allen's feet. They rode past the warm light shining from the farmhouse windows. A cloud passed in front of the moon. Darkness closed around them on the bumpy road. Neither Allen nor Henry said a word. Would the slave hunters try to catch them? Allen tried not to think about how scared

he was. What if Henry shot him so he could steal Old
170 Jack? Allen tugged at the reins to make Old Jack go
faster. His hands felt wet. He bit his lower lip.

"Is you afraid to be with me?" Henry asked. Allen
could not answer. "Here, Marster Allen, you carry the
gun," Henry said. "If you see anybody coming, give it
back quick. I'll jump out as you drive. I don't want
you hurt." He handed the gun up to Allen. The boy
shook his head. He could not touch the gun. "I ain't
never goin' to go back," Henry vowed. "They all can
kill me, but I had my last whippin'."

180 Then Henry told Allen stories about being
a slave. Henry had worked all day and most
nights in the fields of Kentucky. He had seen
his brother beaten to death. His sister had been sold to
another owner far away. Now Henry was
determined to reach freedom in Canada.
Allen felt bad that he had not trusted
Henry.

determined
(dǐ tûr' mǐnd)
adj. firm in
pursuing a goal

REREAD
Why has Allen
changed his mind
about Henry?

All at once, Allen heard something
thrashing through the leaves. His body started to shake.
190 A shadow darted in front of the buggy. Old Jack reared
up on his back legs. Allen pulled back on the reins until
his fingers ached. Slowly the horse calmed down.

"What happened?" whispered Henry. "Do you need
the gun?"

"No," said Allen with a nervous giggle. "It was just
an old rabbit crossing the road." Henry didn't laugh.

Allen and Henry rode for more than an hour and a
half. Allen worried that every shadow was a slave
hunter. He was growing sleepy. His back ached. He
200 was cold from the damp night. And he was tired of
being afraid.

Finally Allen saw a light. It was coming from a cabin—Grandfather Jay's cabin. Allen jumped from the buggy and helped Henry out. Allen pounded on the door. His grandfather greeted them in his nightclothes. Grandfather Jay seemed surprised, but he knew what to do. "Hurry inside, you two," said the elder Jay. "Allen, wake thy uncle Levi."

Allen did as he was told. Uncle Levi dressed and left to saddle the horses. Grandfather bundled some food into a cloth sack for Henry. Henry thanked Grandfather Jay and followed him into the barnyard.

Before Henry and Levi rode away, Allen held out his hand to Henry. "May thee have a safe trip to Canada," Allen said, as carefully as he could. His words sounded strong and clear.

Henry James took the boy's hand. "I be remembering you, Marster Jay," he said, shaking Allen's hand. "You is a brave boy."

THINK IT THROUGH

1. Find examples in the story that show Henry and Allen's trust of each other.
2. Why is Allen's father able to tell the slave owner the truth?
3. Why is the trip to Grandfather Jay's house so dangerous? What might have happened to Allen and Henry if they were caught?

For some people, the longest trip
of their lives was the road to freedom.

HARRIET TUBMAN

by Eloise Greenfield

HARRIET TUBMAN by Eloise Greenfield

Harriet Tubman didn't take no stuff
Wasn't scared of nothing neither
Didn't come in this world to be no slave
And wasn't going to stay one either

5   "Farewell!" she sang to her friends one night
She was mighty sad to leave 'em
But she ran away that dark, hot night
Ran looking for her freedom

She ran to the woods and she ran through the woods
10 With the slave catchers right behind her
And she kept on going till she got to the North
Where those mean men couldn't find her

Nineteen times she went back South
To get three hundred others
15 She ran for her freedom nineteen times
To save black sisters and brothers

Harriet Tubman didn't take no stuff
Wasn't scared of nothing neither
Didn't come in this world to be no slave
20 And didn't stay one either

And didn't stay one either

THINK IT THROUGH

1. What qualities did Harriet have? What lines in the poem tell about these qualities?
2. Why was Harriet Tubman a hero?
3. Which lines in each stanza, or section, end with rhyming words?

You can't make a meal out of one grain of rice. Or can you?

One Grain of Rice

of Rice

A Mathematical Folk Tale by **Demi**

Connect to Your Life

Have you ever been tricked? How did you feel? What did you do?

Key to the Folk Tale

A folk tale has a plot. The **plot** is what happens in a story. It usually involves a problem that a character has to solve. This problem is called the **conflict**. As you read this folk tale, pay attention to the conflict and what each character does about it.

Vocabulary Preview

Words to Know
famine
implored
modest

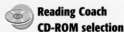

**Reading Coach
CD-ROM selection**

Long ago in India, there lived a $\boxed{\text{raja}}$ who believed that he was wise and fair, as a raja should be.

> **raja**
> (rä′ jə)
> prince or ruler in India

The people in his province were rice farmers. The raja decreed that everyone must give nearly all of their rice to him.

"I will store the rice safely," the raja promised the people, "so that in time of famine, everyone will have rice to eat, and

10 no one will go hungry."

> **famine**
> (făm′ ĭn)
> *n.* shortage of food

Each year, the raja's rice collectors gathered nearly all of the people's rice and carried it away to the royal storehouses.

For many years, the rice grew well. The people gave nearly all of their rice to the raja, and the storehouses were always full. But the people were left with only just enough rice to get by.

Then one year the rice grew badly, and there was famine and hunger. The people had no rice to give to

20 the raja, and they had no rice to eat.

The raja's ministers implored him, "Your Highness, let us open the royal storehouses and give the rice to the people, as you promised."

> **implored**
> (ĭm plôrd′)
> *v.* begged; past tense of *implore*

"No!" cried the raja. "How do I know how long the famine may last? I must have the rice for myself. Promise or no promise, a raja must not go hungry!"

Time went on, and the people grew more and more hungry. But the raja would not give out the rice.

THINK IT THROUGH
The raja believes he is wise and fair. What is he really like?

30   One day, the raja ordered a feast for himself and his court—as, it seemed to him, a raja should now and then, even when there is famine.

A servant led an elephant from a royal storehouse to the palace, carrying two full baskets of rice.

A village girl named Rani saw that a trickle of rice was falling from one of the baskets. Quickly she jumped up and walked along beside the elephant, catching the falling rice in her skirt. She was clever, and she began to make a plan.

40   At the palace, a guard cried, "Halt, thief! Where are you going with that rice?"

"I am not a thief," Rani replied. "This rice fell from one of the baskets, and I am returning it now to the raja."

REREAD
What do you think Rani's plan is?

When the raja heard about Rani's good deed, he asked his ministers to bring her before him.

"I wish to reward you for returning what belongs to me," the raja said to Rani. "Ask me for anything, and you shall have it."

50 "Your Highness," said Rani, "I do not deserve any reward at all. But if you wish, you may give me one grain of rice."

"Only one grain of rice?" exclaimed the raja. "Surely you will allow me to reward you more plentifully, as a raja should."

"Very well," said Rani. "If it pleases Your Highness, you may reward me in this way. Today, you will give me a single grain of rice. Then, each day for thirty days you will give me double the rice you 60 gave me the day before. Thus, tomorrow you will give me two grains of rice, the next day four grains of rice, and so on for thirty days."

"This seems still to be a modest reward," said the raja. "But you shall have it."

And Rani was presented with a single grain of rice.

The next day, Rani was presented with two grains 70 of rice.

And the following day, Rani was presented with four grains of rice.

On the ninth day, Rani was presented with two hundred and fifty-six grains of rice. She had received in all five hundred and eleven grains of rice, only enough for a small handful.

"This girl is honest, but not very clever," thought the raja. "She would have gained more rice by keeping what fell into her skirt!"

THINK IT THROUGH
Why does the raja think the reward is small?

80   On the twelfth day, Rani received two thousand and forty-eight grains of rice, about four handfuls.

On the thirteenth day, she received four thousand and ninety-six grains of rice, enough to fill a bowl.

On the sixteenth day, Rani was presented with a bag containing thirty-two thousand, seven hundred and sixty-eight grains of rice. All together she had enough rice for two full bags.

"This doubling adds up to more rice than I expected!" thought the raja. "But surely her reward
90 won't amount to much more."

On the twentieth day, Rani was presented with sixteen more bags filled with rice.

On the twenty-first day, she received one million, forty-eight thousand, five hundred and seventy-six grains of rice, enough to fill a basket.

On the twenty-fourth day, Rani was presented with eight million, three hundred and eighty-eight thousand, six hundred and eight grains of rice— enough to fill eight baskets, which were carried to her
100 by eight royal deer.

On the twenty-seventh day, thirty-two Brahma bulls were needed to deliver sixty-four baskets of rice.

The raja was deeply troubled. "One grain of rice has grown very great indeed," he thought. "But I shall fulfill the reward to the end, as a raja should."

REREAD

Why does the raja feel he needs to keep giving rice to Rani?

On the twenty-ninth day, Rani was presented with the contents of two royal storehouses.

On the thirtieth and final day, two hundred and fifty-
110 six elephants crossed the province, carrying the contents
of the last four royal storehouses—five
hundred and thirty-six million, eight
hundred and seventy thousand, nine
hundred and twelve grains of rice.

REREAD
Write this amount as a numeral.

All together, Rani had received more
than one billion grains of rice. The raja had no more
rice to give. "And what will you do with this rice,"
said the raja with a sigh, "now that I have none?"

"I shall give it to all the hungry people," said Rani.
120 "And I shall leave a basket of rice for you, too, if you
promise from now on to take only as much rice as
you need."

"I promise," said the raja.

And for the rest of his days, the raja was truly wise
and fair, as a raja should be.

THINK IT THROUGH

1. What lesson do you think the raja learns?
2. What is the conflict between the raja and the farmers? How does Rani solve it?
3. At first the raja doesn't think Rani is clever. How does Rani prove to the raja that she is more clever than he?

Each day, Rani received double the amount of rice as the day before. See how quickly one grain of rice doubles into so much more.

Day 1	Day 2	Day 3	Day 4	Day 5
1	2	4	8	16
grain of rice	grains of rice	grains of rice	grains of rice	grains of rice
Day 6	**Day 7**	**Day 8**	**Day 9**	**Day 10**
32	64	128	256	512
grains of rice	grains of rice	grains of rice	grains of rice	grains of rice
Day 11	**Day 12**	**Day 13**	**Day 14**	**Day 15**
1,024	2,048	4,096	8,192	16,384
grains of rice	grains of rice	grains of rice	grains of rice	grains of rice
Day 16	**Day 17**	**Day 18**	**Day 19**	**Day 20**
32,768	65,536	131,072	262,144	524,288
grains of rice	grains of rice	grains of rice	grains of rice	grains of rice
Day 21	**Day 22**	**Day 23**	**Day 24**	**Day 25**
1,048,576	2,097,152	4,194,304	8,388,608	16,777,216
grains of rice	grains of rice	grains of rice	grains of rice	grains of rice
Day 26	**Day 27**	**Day 28**	**Day 29**	**Day 30**
33,554,432	67,108,864	134,217,728	268,435,456	536,870,912
grains of rice	grains of rice	grains of rice	grains of rice	grains of rice

To count how many grains of rice Rani received in all, add all of these numbers together. The answer: 1,073,741,823 —more than one billion grains of rice!

Mountain Medicine

Imagine you live in Kentucky in the early 1900s. You break your leg. Will you get a cast for your friends to sign?

by Rosemary Wells

Connect to Your Life

Have you, or has anyone you know, ever been injured? Did help come right away? What did you do?

Key to the Article

"Mountain Medicine" is an example of **narrative nonfiction.** The article tells about real people, places, and events. But the writer presents the information as a story. The writer also uses **dialogue** to show how people in Kentucky talked in the early 1900s.

At that time, there were many places in Kentucky that didn't have doctors. People often asked for help from neighbors who didn't know much about medicine. To give better care, one woman started a nursing service.

Vocabulary Preview

Words to Know

splint	intend
raging	sterilizer

 Reading Coach CD-ROM selection

The narrator's father has an accident. Read to find out what kind of help he receives.

When Mamma sees four men carrying Pa home with his leg crushed, she screams. The men try to make Mamma sit down. One of them tells me,

"There's a horse doctor with a bone saw down in Krypton. We'll send him up to take the leg off."

REREAD
What is the plan for Pa's broken leg?

Mamma makes me fetch Biddy, the granny woman who takes care of our mountain people.

Biddy is over a hundred years old but she can still
10 rip the bark off a whole willow tree. She boils the willow bark until it softens up like collard greens. She cools it and packs it over Pa's leg. Then she puts an ax, blade up, under the bed to cut the fever. She leaves Mamma a folded paper of easing powder and goes away down the hollow to somebody else.

easing powder
medicine that is supposed to stop pain

The easing powder doesn't do a speck of good, so Mamma gives Pa drops of turpentine against blood poisoning, and
20 sips of white lightning against the pain.

white lightning
whiskey that was made at home. Making it was against the law.

"They're going to take his leg off, John," Mamma tells me. "Pa is never going to work again, and we have only those dimes in the mason jar."

If Pa can't work, we will have to move in with Mamma's sister Sally and Jip Cox. I'll have to sleep three to a bed with my big cousin Judah Cox and the baby. Supper time means eating their leftovers.

"Wait until the doctor comes," I say. "Wait until he
30 comes." But both of us know the doctor got his license
by sending away five dollars and a matchbook cover.

THINK IT THROUGH
Give at least three examples from the story that show that
the mountain people do not have a real doctor.

FOCUS
Find out who comes to help.

We wait a night and a day and another night and a
day. Then I hear someone. A horse coming up Beech
Fork makes a rushing noise in the deep gravel along
the water's edge.

"Doctor's here!" I tell Mamma. But it isn't the
doctor at all. It is a lady. She rides up the steep
riverbank, shirtfront moon-white against our blue
mountain evening.

40   When she comes to our door, a line of bats skims
over her head but she doesn't pay them any
mind, so I know she isn't a mincy city lady.

Right off she asks me my name, and I tell
her it's John Hawkins.

"Well, my name is Mary Breckinridge.
I'm a nurse," she says back.

Her voice has a softness to it. She takes off her
jacket, and hangs it on a towel hook. Then she goes
to Pa.

50   Shivers of bone show through Pa's leg. I can't look
longer than an eye blink.

"How did this happen?" she asks.

But Mamma can't answer.

> **mincy**
> (mĭn′ sē)
> stuck-up

"I need you to help me," Mary tells my ma. "We're going to try and save this leg. We have to clean it up and splint it, and then in the morning we'll get him down the mountain to a hospital."

splint
(splĭnt)
v. tie sticks to, for support

I run to the cool darkness of the woodshed to tend Mary's horse. That way I don't have
60 to hear my pa cry out, or smell those nursey smells from what's inside Mary's saddlebags.

But I can't keep away. I go back and peek in the window of the cabin. Mary is holding a needle up to the light of the oil lamp. The silvery gleam of the point gives me the all-overs. She jabs it into a rubber-lidded bottle, then *spang* into Pa's arm.

all-overs
(ôl' ō' vərz)
strange feelings

I fall away from the window, sick as if I had soap suds in my belly. Bats circle me
70 like swimming black handkerchiefs. I breathe in the smell of horse sweat and young corn until I get steady.

REREAD
How does John react to Mary's nursing?

When I get back into the cabin, my mamma and my pa are both asleep. On the table I see Mary's saddlebags stuffed with evil-looking scissors and bottles.

"You've got your eye on that needle, haven't you, John?" Mary asks me, her blue eyes on my every move and a smile kicking at the corners of her mouth.
80 She brings out sandwiches and offers me one. I have never tasted anything like chicken salad.

THINK IT THROUGH
Does John trust Mary? How do you know?

I wake up when voices and sunlight fill the house. After breakfast Mary asks me, "How did your pa get hurt, John?"

"Ridin' the tides," I say.

"Tides?" says Mary. "Tell me what that means."

"Well," I say, "you know in the winter there's timber-cutting teams? They clear cut the big trees on the top of the mountain. Then the river men ride the

90 logs down the chutes."

"Chutes?" asks Mary.

"Yes, ma'am. Chutes is where the water froths up mean and wild. Tides is when the water's real high and floody in the springtime. A river man rides a tree all the way from the top to the bottom of the mountain two days without stoppin'. My pa's a river man. He's good. The lumber company pays him extra. He didn't

100 expect no accidents."

froths
(frôths)
foams

REREAD
Try to picture this job in your mind. Why is riding a tree dangerous?

"No one ever does," says Mary.

From up the mountain Jip Cox and his brothers come to help. Two broom handles are run through the sleeves of two old coats and this makes a stretcher for Pa. My mamma's sister Sally is right behind the men, telling them what to do. No matter how I beg, Mamma won't let me go with them.

Four men carry the stretcher ends. They walk herky-jerky, trying not to jiggle Pa,

110 and disappear into the shadows of a deer path alongside of Beech Fork. Pa's face is the color of a tallow candle.

herky-jerky
(hûr' kē jûr' kē)
in an unsteady manner

jiggle
(jĭg' əl)
shake

I slip away after them, telling only Sister Sally, who has stayed to keep Mamma company. Sister Sally tries grabbing me by the wrist. "No, you don't go nowhere, John Hawkins!" she says. "Not nowhere!" But Sister doesn't want to spill the pail of shuck beans in her lap, and I am too quick for her.

I follow them down like a fox, stepping on no 120 twigs, making no sound.

I don't show myself until noon when I get hungry. "Too late to send me back, ain't it?" I say.

Only Mary smiles. She pulls me up on her horse.

"I thought you might would give me a lickin'," I tell her.

"Once I had a little boy like you," says Mary. "I never was angry at him."

"What happened to him?" I ask her.

"I have no doubt he is sitting in God's 130 lap in heaven this very minute, looking right down on us," she tells me.

REREAD

Why do you think Mary is kind to John?

We cross into Middle Fork. "Did you leave a note telling your mamma where you are, so she doesn't worry about you?" Mary asks.

"I told Sister Sally," I answer.

THINK IT THROUGH

Why do you think John is eager to go with his pa and Mary?

FOCUS

Read to discover what Mary and John learn about each other.

"Can you read and write, John?" asks Mary.
"No, ma'am," I answer. "Not a bit."

I feel Mary sigh in and out behind me. "How much does the lumber company pay a man for
140 riding a fifty-foot tree trunk down a
   raging river for two days?" she asks me.

raging
(rā′ jǐng)
adj. wild and powerful

"Real good. Six dollars, Pa says."

Mary takes my hands. "Count out six fingers," she says.

But I only can do two and five. I hang my head. Her arm circles me like Mamma's when I get a bee sting. Down the mountain we go. All the time I feel her arm around me.

"John," she says, "what are you going to be when
150 you grow up?"

"River man like my pa," I say proudly.

I am afraid she'll say back, *Oh, why do you want to get crushed in the river?* She doesn't. She says, "You can be anything you want to be and so can I."

"But . . . but you already are," I say back.

"Not yet," says Mary.

"Well, what then are you going to be more?" I ask.

I feel her thinking behind me.

160 Then she says, "I've been riding all over this mountain country, John. Everybody here is very poor. But poor as they are, they share their bread with me and give me a place to sleep as if I were their own kin. Many of them need help. I **intend** to bring doctors and nurses and good medicine to the mountain people. I intend to build a hospital here if I have to brick and mortar it with my own hands."

intend
(ǐn tĕnd′)
v. plan

REREAD
What is Mary's goal?

Wendover Big House—the cottage hospital Mary Breckinridge built in 1925

Then she doesn't say more. But hearing her I feel
170 the same as I did the night I sat on my pa's lap and
we watched a shooting star from beginning to end
across the sky.

THINK IT THROUGH
Why do you think Mary tells John about her plans? Find details
that support your opinion.

FOCUS ———————————————————————
Find out what happens to Pa.

At the bottom of the mountain Pa is taken to the
Hyden Railway Station in a mule cart. He is bound
for the hospital in Lexington. When he says good-bye,
I kiss his face and hands. He is as hot as a chimney.
We go back to Mary's big house at Wendover.

I don't ask after Pa for days on end. Quiet as a
mouse I hoe weeds in the Wendover garden and

180 collect eggs every morning. Will they fix my pa's leg? Will we have to live with Sister Sally? Big Judah haunts my sleep.

Miss Peacock and Miss Texas are Mary's other nurses. They feed me wonderful victuals. But Nurse Peacock sees me pick at my supper when I worry at night.

victuals
(vĭt' lz)
food

"John," says she one day, "the doctor sent word to say your pa's doing fine. Says he's going to keep his leg."

190 Big Judah goes on home from my dreams.

In the library Nurse Texas shows me how to write my name and read some out of a book. Nurse Peacock teaches me the dominos and I learn to count up all the numbers.

THINK IT THROUGH

What does John do while his father is in the hospital?

FOCUS

Mary shows a drawing to John. Learn what it is.

One evening Mary draws some careful squares on paper at the card table.

"What is that?" I ask.

"It's my plan for an outpost clinic at Beech Fork," she answers. She shows me how the lines on paper

200 really mean rooms with doors and windows. She shows me how twelve inches make a foot. She tells me the clinic will be thirty feet by thirty feet. "There's a closet right here," she explains. "There's a kitchen and a sterilizer and a refrigerator. There's a waiting room for patients and a

sterilizer
(stĕr' ə lī' zər)
n. machine that kills germs

dispensary, where the nurses give out medicine. Morning sunshine comes in all the windows."

Mary gives me the ruler to keep. I study her plan. I put Mary's picture of it, number by number, line by 210 line, into my head.

In August Pa comes back from Lexington walking on both legs. Mary takes us to Camp Creek where Jip Cox and two mules meet us. My pa is not a good talker to women. Staring at the ground, he thanks Mary while he turns his hat in his hands.

I can see Mary in the eye of my memory. She eases out her reins and lets her horse eat from a patch of weeds. "Someday," she says, "I will need your help."

> **REREAD**
> What kind of help do you think Mary will need?

220 When I get home, I choose a flat pasture above Beech Fork. I collect up a barrelful of white stones. Then I lay out the plan for Mary's clinic, placing her ruler end over end in the grass. Thirty feet by thirty feet. Kitchen, waiting room, dispensary. My stones are large as goose eggs. They wait for her in the cornflowers, measured out just right for when she comes to build here.

If you were a hawk flying over, you could see them from the air.

THINK IT THROUGH

1. Do you think John grew up to be a river man? Find details in the story to support your answer.
2. Why was it important that John's pa not lose his leg?
3. When John first saw Mary, he was surprised that "it isn't a doctor at all. It is a lady." Why do you think he thought she wasn't a doctor? Do you think a boy today would have the same thought?

Mary Breckinridge

Bridges to History

Mixed Genres

History is full of amazing stories. In this unit you will learn about events that happened long ago in Troy, Rome, Egypt, and China. See how differently history can be told as you read a **legend,** a **true account,** and two **informative articles.** You'll discover how people long ago had some of the same problems we have today.

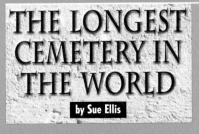

THE TROJAN WAR:

THE WOODEN HORSE

BY TANA REIFF

Not all gifts are good. This story from the past may make you look twice at the next gift you receive.

Connect to Your Life

What do you know about ancient Greece? Work with a partner. Make a list of some things you know.

Key to the Legend

Reading Coach CD-ROM selection

A **legend** is a story that has been told for many years. It is often based on events that really happened. This story tells about a war between the Greeks and the Trojans around 1200 B.C. The Trojans were from Troy, an ancient city in Asia. There really was a war, but many events in the story may not have happened.

Several events led to the start of the Trojan War. Paris, the prince of Troy, was the judge of a contest among three goddesses. A golden apple was the prize. Paris decided that

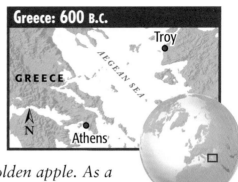

Greece: 600 B.C.

Aphrodite would get the golden apple. As a reward, she promised him that he could have Helen as his wife. Helen was married to a Greek king, but Paris kidnapped her anyway. As a result, a war began that lasted ten years. Midway through the battle, a Greek hero named Achilles was killed. Afterward, Odysseus became the leader of the Greek army.

FOCUS
Read to find out how the Greeks will try to win the war.

After Achilles (uh-KIHL-eez) died, another great hero rose up in the Greek army. His name was Odysseus (oh-DIHS-yoos). He was king of Ithaca, but he fought like everyone else.

> **Ithaca**
> (ĭth′ ə kə)
> island of
> western Greece

"There is only one way we can win over the Trojans," said Odysseus. "We must get past the gate and into the city."

"But how?" the other men wondered. "We can't get in the gate. And we can't break down the wall."

10   Odysseus asked Athena, the goddess of wisdom, what they should do.

Athena told him a poem:
Could is should,
Should is would,
Would is wood, of course.
What began with an apple
Must end with a horse.

What could this mean? Odysseus wondered. He
knew about the golden apple that had started the
20 Trojan War. But what was this about a horse? Then it
came to him. He must build a wooden horse!

Odysseus worked out a plan. He and his men built
a huge wooden horse. It was so big that 20 men could
fit inside it. There was a trap door in the belly of the
horse. There were wheels under its feet.

THINK IT THROUGH

Describe the wooden horse. Then predict how it might help
the Greeks.

FOCUS

Read to find out how the war ends.

The next morning, the Trojans looked over their
wall. There were no Greeks in sight. Where could they
be? The Trojans believed the war must be over. They
believed the Greeks had given up and gone home.
30 Then the Trojans saw the wooden horse outside the
gate. They believed the Greeks were leaving them a
gift of peace.

"Beware of Greeks bearing gifts," King Priam's
helper said. "They could be playing a trick."

But King Priam opened the gate. A group of men
rolled the horse into the city. There it sat as the
Trojans went to sleep. They slept well, believing they
had won the war and peace had come at last.

But in the middle of the night, the trap door in the
40 horse opened. Out came the 20 Greeks.
Among them were Odysseus and Menelaus.
They all ran toward the city gate and
opened it wide.

Menelaus
(mĕn′ ə lā′ əs)
Helen's husband

The rest of the Greek army had not really gone home. They had sailed in their boats, just out of sight of Troy.

During the night they sailed back and waited on land. When the gate opened, the army rushed into Troy.

The Trojans did not have a chance. The Greeks
50 killed everyone in sight. Then they set the city on fire. Soon, there was nothing left of Troy.

THINK IT THROUGH

1. How are the Greeks able to fool the Trojans?
2. What might have happened if King Priam had listened to his helper?
3. Do you think it was necessary for the Greeks to destroy the city? Explain your opinion.
4. Now that you've read the story, explain Athena's poem.

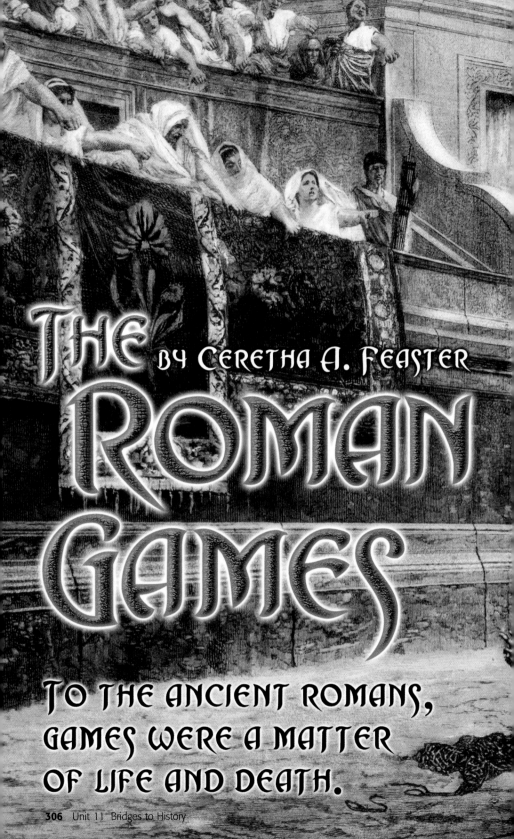

THE

BY CERETHA A. FEASTER

ROMAN GAMES

TO THE ANCIENT ROMANS,
GAMES WERE A MATTER
OF LIFE AND DEATH.

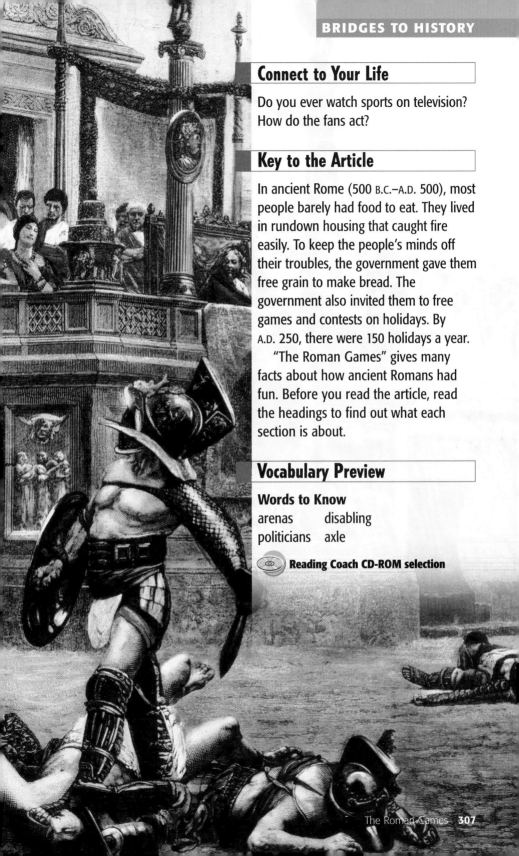

Connect to Your Life

Do you ever watch sports on television? How do the fans act?

Key to the Article

In ancient Rome (500 B.C.–A.D. 500), most people barely had food to eat. They lived in rundown housing that caught fire easily. To keep the people's minds off their troubles, the government gave them free grain to make bread. The government also invited them to free games and contests on holidays. By A.D. 250, there were 150 holidays a year.

"The Roman Games" gives many facts about how ancient Romans had fun. Before you read the article, read the headings to find out what each section is about.

Vocabulary Preview

Words to Know

arenas   disabling
politicians   axle

Reading Coach CD-ROM selection

gladiators fight to honer the dead (handwritten)

FOCUS

Read to find out what Romans did for fun long ago.

How did Romans have fun during 500 B.C.–A.D. 500? They watched games. People piled into big arenas . They were entertained by gladiator fights, wild animal shows, and chariot races.

arenas
(ə rē′ nəz)
n. buildings where people watch sports events or shows

The Gladiators

Gladiator fights had not always been held for fun. They began as a way to honor dead soldiers. When a soldier died in battle, Romans would force two enemy soldiers to fight until one died. The

10 enemy soldier's death was a way to show respect for the fallen Roman soldier.

REREAD
How were fights used to honor dead people?

Rich people continued this tradition. When their loved ones died, they made slaves fight. The slaves fought until one was killed. The slave's blood honored the rich person's dead relative.

Watching people fight to the death became popular. Rich people began to make slaves fight on holidays. They invited their friends to watch. These fights became the first Roman public games. The fighters

20 became known as gladiators.

Soon rich politicians saw the games as a way to gain votes. They put on big ~~fights~~ in big arenas. They invited the common people. They gave the people food. The people loved the food and games. In return, the people voted for these politicians. All the politicians wanted to win votes. So, each politician tried to put on the biggest and best games.

politicians
(pŏl′ ĭ tĭsh′ ənz)
n. people who hold or run for government offices

Thousands of people came to cheer the gladiators.
30 They did not care about the gladiators as people.
They only wanted to see the gladiators fight and die.

THINK IT THROUGH
How did gladiator fighting become popular?

FOCUS
As you read, look for details that show what a gladiator's life was like.

Gladiators were mostly criminals, slaves, and poor people. Most of them did not choose to fight. Many criminals had to fight as part of their punishment. Slaves could fight or be killed. The winners were lucky. They lived, and they won prize money. Gladiators who won many fights could earn or buy their freedom.

Some free men became gladiators because they were poor. They needed the prize money. Others just
40 liked to fight. They liked to hear people cheering for them. People cheered loudly for the fighters they liked. Gladiators were as well-liked as many rock stars are today.

Gladiators
people came to cheer the gladiators

gladiators went to fighting school

As gladiator fighting became more popular, more fighters were needed. Schools were built to train men to be good fighters. Slaves, prisoners of war, and criminals were forced to go to the schools. Free men went to the schools too. They all lived in big, cold, crowded rooms. They lived by rules. If someone broke
50 the rules, he was punished. No weapons were allowed in the rooms. The men trained with wooden swords. Wooden swords would keep them from killing each other or their trainers. The training was long and hard. For hours and hours each day, the men practiced. They learned how to move and strike. They used a fat wooden pole that looked like a person. They practiced fighting the pole. They became good fighters. Some of the best gladiators came from these schools.

REREAD
How did gladiators train?

60   Once in the arena, gladiators had to fight by the rules. If they did not fight hard, they might be beaten or killed. A gladiator won by killing or disabling the other fighter. Sometimes both fighters fought bravely, but neither won. This was called a draw. Both men were allowed to live. When a gladiator lost, an official decided whether he should live or die. If the official gave a thumbs up, he lived. Thumbs down and the loser was killed at once. This made the crowd cheer.

disabling
(dĭs ā′ blĭng)
n. hurting badly

70   Sometimes, women gladiators fought in the arenas. The women's battles were staged just to make people laugh. Women fought male dwarfs or one another. Women gladiators were banned around A.D. 200.

dwarfs
(dwôrfs)
very small people

THINK IT THROUGH
What were the advantages and disadvantages of being a gladiator?

some gladiators were killed and some lived

Animals were tra[ining?] an as show. Animals fought each other (handwritten)

FOCUS

How were animals used in games?

Wild Animal Shows

From 65 to 63 B.C. Julius Caesar, a well-known senator, wanted the people to vote for him. He decided to have the best shows of all times. He had hunters trap monkeys, elephants, lions, tigers, bears, horses, and many other animals. They brought wild
80   animals from all over the world to Rome. Some animals were trained to make the people laugh. Monkeys and elephants were the favorite trained animals. In one show, six elephants marched into the arena. They sat at tables. They ate and drank like humans. The crowd roared. But many animals were not so lucky. They were made to fight each other. Before the fight the animals did not get much food. Two starving animals were pushed into the arena. The animals fought until one killed the other.
90   Of all the animal shows, people liked watching men fight wild animals best. The men used spears, swords, daggers , clubs, and bows and arrows. A man fought until he killed the animal. The crowd cheered. Animal fighting was a big hit. It went on for hundreds of years. Each year thousands of animals were killed.

> **daggers**
> (dăg′ ərz)
> short knives

THINK IT THROUGH

Name three ways animals entertained the Romans.

chariot races were also

FOCUS

Read to find out about chariot racing. *Popular.*

Chariot Racing

Chariot racing was Rome's most popular public game. The races cost a lot of money. So they had races only a few times a year. As many as 24 races were run in a day.

100   Merchants owned the horses, drivers, and chariots. They trained the horses and drivers to race. The merchants rented their horses, drivers, and chariots to government officials. The officials planned the races. The owners who had winning teams grew rich from the rental fees and prize money.

There were four racing groups. Each group had a different color—the Whites, Reds, Blues, and Greens. The Greens and Blues were the most popular groups. Each group had its own fans. Racing fans could
110 get crazy. Sometimes unhappy fans beat and killed one another.

Chariot racing was dangerous. Charioteers, or drivers, risked their lives to beat the other drivers.

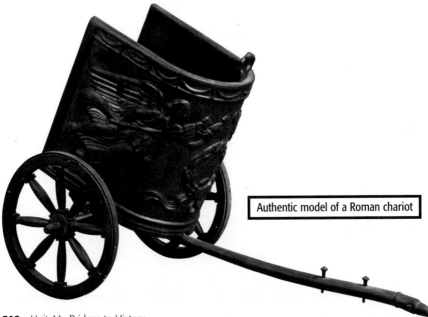

Authentic model of a Roman chariot

Hores Pulled the chariots

The chariot was small and lightweight. It could be pulled by two or four horses. Chariots pulled by four horses were most common. A driver needed great skill. He had to drive fast and control the horses.

When the drivers entered the starting gates, a hush fell over the crowd. An official let the gatekeeper know when to open the gates. Then the race began.

120

Chariot racing scene from the movie *Ben Hur*

IF THE DRIVER WAS LUCKY, HE COULD PULL OUT HIS DAGGER.

The drivers had to go around the track seven times (about two and one-half miles). Getting around the track was not easy. Drivers would sometimes attack each other. Each wanted to gain the lead. The lane on the inside of the track was the shortest distance around the track. All drivers tried to get to the inside lane. Some drivers tried to slow down other drivers. They would try to break a rival's wheels or axle .

130 They tried anything they could think of to get ahead. The speed and meanness made the races exciting. Cheering crowds rose to their feet when their color was winning.

axle
(ăk' səl)
n. rod connecting a pair of wheels

A crash was one of the worst things that could happen. In a crash the driver and horses could get hurt or killed. Sometimes the chariot would break off in a crash. The horses would keep going, dragging the driver along the ground. If the driver was lucky, he could pull out his dagger. Then he could cut the reins that were tied around his waist.

140 Winning drivers won fame and money for their owners. The owners paid the drivers. Winning charioteers made a lot of money. They could become rich and popular. Then they were treated like movie stars are treated today.

Chariots could crash

End of the Games

The games were so popular that they might have gone on forever. But around A.D. 300, the number of Christians began to grow. Christians believed the games were murder. Christian leaders spoke against the games. Many Romans did not want the games to 150 end. But they gave in to the Christians. By A.D. 400, the gladiator schools were closed. About 40 years later all gladiator fights, animal shows, and chariot races had ended.

THINK IT THROUGH

1. Why was chariot racing so dangerous?
2. Why did the games end?
3. Choose one of the games from this article. How is it like a modern sports event such as wrestling or soccer? How is it different?
4. What was good about the Roman games? What was bad about them? Make a list. Then explain why each thing was good or bad.

Chariots ended all

the games

King Tut's Tomb:
A Treasure and a Curse

by Delores Nemo

How do you find

buried treasure?

With a lot of

hard work!

Connect to Your Life

Have you ever made an exciting discovery? How did you feel?

Key to the True Account

Tutankhamen was an Egyptian king who died over 3,000 years ago. Before he was buried, his followers turned his body into a mummy. They dried out his body. Then they wrapped it so that it would last for a long time. The Egyptians believed that King Tut needed food, chairs, jewelry, and even pets after he died. So these things were buried with him.

King Tut was buried in a secret place. His followers did not want his body disturbed. But many scientists wanted to know more about the ancient Egyptians and how they lived. So they spent a lot of time trying to find out where Tut was buried.

Vocabulary Preview

Words to Know

tombs   cabinet
curse   examined

 Reading Coach CD-ROM selection

Read to find out why ancient Egyptians buried so
much treasure with their dead kings.

Gold, silver, jewels—all were buried with the kings of
Egypt from 1570 to 1070 B.C.! Why was so much
treasure beneath the earth?

Egyptians wanted their kings to be happy after
death. They wrapped the kings' bodies to make them
last a long time. Those wrapped bodies were called
mummies. Egyptians placed the mummies
in tombs . They filled the tombs with gold,
jewels, furniture, and even food.

10   Egyptians tried to protect the treasures
from robbers. They built the tombs far
below the ground. Some say the Egyptians
put a curse on the tombs. *Dig up a tomb
and you will die.* But robbers did not believe
in curses. They still found the tombs. They
took as much treasure as they could. But
had they found and robbed all of them? In
1907, one man decided to find out.

tombs
(toomz)
n. rooms where people are buried

curse
(kûrs)
n. magic spell to cause something bad to happen to someone

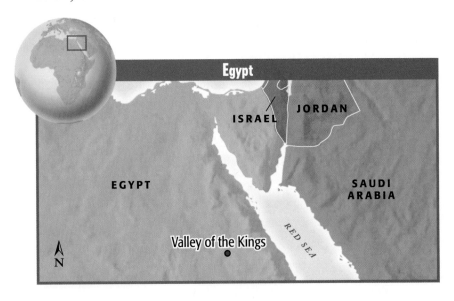

Egypt

JORDAN

ISRAEL

EGYPT

SAUDI
ARABIA

Valley of the Kings

RED SEA

N

That man was Lord Carnarvon, a wealthy
20 Englishman. He wanted to find a tomb that had not
been robbed. He asked Howard Carter to help him.
Carter was an archaeologist (är′ kē ŏl′ ə jĭst′). An
archaeologist is a scientist who digs up the earth to
study the past. Carter looked for old graves and
buried cities. He carefully dug them up to learn about
the people. He thought there was still one tomb that
had not been found—King Tutankhamen (to͞ot′ äng kä′
mən). King Tut became king when he was just nine
years old. He died at age 18. Carter and Carnarvon
30 started working together.

THINK IT THROUGH
Why did Carter and Lord Carnarvon start working together to
find King Tut's tomb?

FOCUS
Find out what happens when Carter starts looking for
the tomb.

Carter went to Egypt and hired many workers. He
soon learned about the curse. This did not stop him.
He and his workers began looking in an area called
the Valley of the Kings. Most of the tombs were there.
The valley was a rocky place with no trees or water.
The heat was sometimes over 100 degrees!
For a number of years, Carter found little. Lord
Carnarvon was ready to give up. The search had
already cost him a lot of money. He wanted to quit. But
40 Carter wanted to keep looking. He asked for one more
try. He wanted to search one more place. He bought a
yellow canary for good luck. Then he and his men
started digging again.

Soon, Carter's men found some stone huts. These huts belonged to workers. The workers had built one of the king's tombs. First the men cleared away the huts. Then, late in 1922, they made an amazing discovery. They found a step cut into the rock.

50   Carter was very excited. He and the men dug carefully. They uncovered 12 steps leading down into the ground. The bottom step led to a door. Maybe this was a royal tomb!

| royal |
| (roi′ əl) |
| belonging to a king or queen |

THINK IT THROUGH

What kind of person was Carter? Use examples from the article to support your answer.

FOCUS ——————————

Read to discover what Carter and Carnarvon find.

Carter was eager to find out what was behind the door. But Lord Carnarvon was at home in England. Carter knew he would want to be there. He decided to wait for Carnarvon. Lord Carnarvon had to travel by train and boat. It took him over two weeks to get back to Egypt.

60   Finally, Carter and Lord Carnarvon stood at the door. They could read a name: Tutankhamen. Had they really discovered King Tut's tomb? They broke down the door. They found a hall. But they still had to wait. It took workers two days to dig out the hall. Then they found another door.

Howard Carter and workers open Tutankhamen's tomb at Luxor, Egypt, in 1922.

70   Carter made a hole in the second door. He poked a candle through the hole. The light revealed amazing treasures. Carter couldn't believe his eyes. How could this be the tomb of a man who had died over 3,000 years ago? The room still smelled like perfume. There were chairs, beds, vases, and golden statues.

Another door awaited them. But this door could not be opened right away. First, all the treasures had to be carefully removed and sorted. This would take at least a few months.

80   That night Carter went home. He found out that a cobra had killed his pet canary. It had happened at the very moment he entered the tomb. Egyptians believed that cobras protected kings from their enemies. Was there really a curse? Had it struck Carter?

> **cobra**
> (kō′ brə)
> kind of snake

THINK IT THROUGH
Tell in your own words what happened after the first door was opened.

FOCUS
Find out what happens when Carter opens the door to the second room.

Several months later, the first room was finally cleared. Carter chipped away the rocks on the third door. Before him was a wall of gold! It was really a cabinet. The cabinet held the
90   coffin. There was also a smaller room beyond the room with the cabinet. In this room was a statue carved with four heads. Each head was the lid of a tiny coffin. Inside each coffin was one of the king's organs. His

> **cabinet**
> (kăb′ ə nĭt)
> n. piece of furniture with shelves or drawers

heart, liver, stomach, and intestines had been kept apart from his body. Carter would have to carefully remove the statue. It would take more time before he could actually see King Tut's mummy.

Lord Carnarvon did not want to wait much
100 longer. He wanted to take some of the treasures back to England. He had spent so much money on the search. The Egyptian government said no. The treasures should stay in Egypt. Carter agreed with the Egyptians. He and Carnarvon had an argument. They stopped working together.

> **REREAD**
> Do you agree with Carter or Carnarvon? Why?

Weeks later, a mosquito bit Lord Carnarvon. The bite became infected, and he died. He never saw King Tut's mummy. At the moment he died, all the lights in
110 the city of Cairo went out. His dog died at his home in England. Had the mummy's curse struck again?

Carter went on with his work. He still had a long way to go. Would he ever be able to open the coffin?

Finally, the moment arrived. Carter slowly raised the lid. There was another gold coffin inside! It was even more beautiful than the first. Its cover was a golden image of Tut. Workers had to pull the second coffin out of the first. Then Carter opened the lid of the second coffin. There was a third coffin! It was
120 made of solid gold.

Finally, Carter opened the third coffin. There lay the mummy of Tut, with a mask on his face. His body was wrapped in linen.

Tut was carefully unwrapped. More jewels were found in the wrappings. Doctors were called to examine the mummy. Unfortunately, one doctor died while on his way to the tomb. Had the curse struck

again? The doctors who examined Tut found no signs of disease. They thought Tut
130 might have been killed.

> **examined**
> (ĭg zăm′ ĭnd)
> v. looked carefully at; past tense of *examine*

Though many strange things happened, Carter never believed that mummies had magic powers. He spent seven more years studying the tomb and its treasures. He lived for many years. Luckily the treasures did not stay in Egypt. They have traveled all over the world for millions of people to enjoy.

THINK IT THROUGH

1. Why was it so hard to get to Tut's mummy after the second door was opened?
2. Do you think there was really a mummy's curse? Explain your opinion using details from the article.
3. Do you think that Carter discovered the tomb because of good luck or hard work? Find examples in the article to support your opinion.

OVER 2,000 YEARS AGO, A CHINESE RULER PROTECTED HIS COUNTRY FROM INVADERS. BUT AT WHAT COST?

THE LONGEST CEMETERY IN THE WORLD

BY SUE ELLIS

Connect to Your Life

What do you know about ancient China? With a partner, make a chart. List some things you already know about China. Later, fill in what you learned as you read.

What I know about China	What I want to find out	What I learned

Key to the Article

Around 200 B.C., ancient China had millions of people. But the country was not united. It was divided into many villages. Invaders from the north often raided the villages. So villages joined together to protect themselves. A man named Qin fought for and won control of all the villages. Then he made a plan to protect these villages from enemies.

Vocabulary Preview

Words to Know

emperor   volunteers   convicts

 Reading Coach CD-ROM selection

Qin became China's emperor in 221 B.C.
He called himself Qin Shi Huangdi (chĭn
shĭ hwäng dē): "the first emperor." Qin had
two goals. One was to bring together the
Chinese people. The other was to protect them from
tribes to the north. These enemy tribes raided villages.
They killed farmers and took their land.

emperor
(ĕm' pər ər)
n. male ruler of a large area

Qin's goals seemed fine. Qin, however, was not a
kind person. He was the emperor. Everyone had to
10 obey him. His armies did what he wanted. His
generals were very loyal. If not, Qin had them killed.

Qin thought of several plans to reach his goals. First,
he had his soldiers destroy walls inside China. Many
short walls divided Chinese provinces from each other.
Getting rid of those walls would help unite the people.

Then Qin got rid of books. Books held new ideas.
Qin decided that burning books would get rid of ideas
that divided people. All the people would think the
way Qin wanted them to think. So most books were
20 burned. This action upset the educated class. But Qin
didn't care about educated men. In fact, he used them
in the third part of his plan.

Qin decided to build a long wall. This wall would
keep out the enemy. China already had some short
walls near its border. Qin's engineers decided to make
those walls part of a new wall. The new wall would
run for almost 1,850 miles. It would begin at Longxi
in the south. It would end at the sea in the north. It
would follow the Yellow River.

THINK IT THROUGH

What were Qin's goals? How did he plan to reach his goals?

FOCUS
How could such a huge wall be built? Read to find out.

30　　First, builders planned watch towers. The watch towers were two bow shots apart. A guard in one tower could see the next tower. If the enemy came, one of the guards could shoot his bow. Workers built 25,000 of these towers. Most were 40 feet high. The wall would run from tower to tower.

Along with the towers, workers built outposts. These outposts housed many soldiers to defend the wall. Fifteen thousand of them were built along the wall.

Now Qin was ready for the wall itself to be built. He
40　needed workers—many workers—to do this huge task. Qin's army rounded up almost a million workers. Who were the workers? They were not volunteers. They were not builders. Many were educated men. These men were not very strong or fit. They were writers, teachers, students, artists, and musicians.

> **volunteers**
> (vŏl′ ən tîrz′)
> *n.* people who choose to work without being paid

Convicts became workers too. They were the most badly treated workers. To mark them, soldiers shaved their heads and made
50　them wear iron collars. When any workers died, their widows had to take their places.

> **convicts**
> (kŏn′ vĭkts′)
> *n.* people found guilty of crimes and sent to jail

Qin's army forced these workers to build the Great Wall. They dug out stone and earth with poor tools. They hauled heavy loads. There was no rest. They lived and slept outdoors in tents of rags. They were naked in the summer. In the winter, they wore rags. They often froze to death.

> **REREAD**
> Why was the work so hard?

THINK IT THROUGH
Whom did Qin get to build the wall? How were these workers treated?

The building depended on the land of the area. The southern part of the wall was built first. Workers built two walls of granite blocks about 25 feet apart. These walls were 6 to 12 feet high. Workers put brick on the outside of the walls. Then they built the walls higher. The sides grew closer together as the wall rose. The sides rose as high as 15 feet. Then workers filled in the area between the sides. They used rocks, earth, and clay to fill in the area. They also used the bodies of dead workers. They packed down the filling. Finally, bricklayers covered the filled area with bricks. This made a road that people could walk on.

REREAD

This section tells about six steps workers used to build the wall. What are they?

In the northern area, the land was different. Here the ground was made up of loess (lō′əs). Loess is a yellow-brown fine soil. The northern workers cut

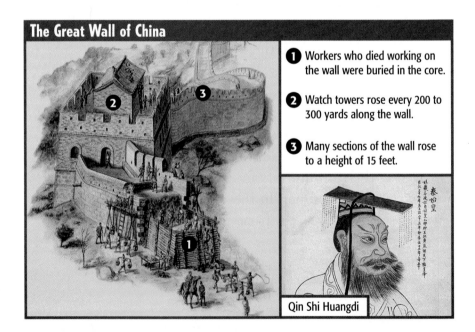

The Great Wall of China

❶ Workers who died working on the wall were buried in the core.

❷ Watch towers rose every 200 to 300 yards along the wall.

❸ Many sections of the wall rose to a height of 15 feet.

Qin Shi Huangdi

huge sections of this loess. Then they covered the sections with a stone face. The northern wall was not as strong as the southern wall.

The wall took only seven years to finish. How could such a big job take so little time? Each pyramid 80 of Egypt took 20 to 40 years to complete. No other wonder of the world was built in such a short time.

The speed of building was due to Qin. His army forced millions of people to work. The people died from the cruel work. If they worked too slowly, they were killed. Many starved to death. They died from harsh weather. Tens of thousands died. When they died, their bodies were dumped into the wall filling. Other workers took their places. That's why the Great Wall is called the Longest Cemetery in the World. 90 Thousands of Chinese workers are buried inside it.

Qin reached his goals. He made China into one country. He had a wall built to keep out enemy tribes. Many parts of the Great Wall still stand today, 2,200 years later. The Great Wall is a Wonder of the World.

But what was the cost of the wall? Most Chinese people hated Qin. His wall cost thousands of lives. The wall kept out people from other countries. It kept out education, art, and new thought. And saddest of all, the wall is filled with the bones of its builders.

THINK IT THROUGH

1. Why was the southern part of the wall stronger than the northern part?
2. Why did it take only seven years to build the Great Wall?
3. What does the author of the article think of Qin? Use examples from the article to support your answer.

Reader's Choice

Longer Selections for Independent Reading

Mixed Genres

What kind of writing do you enjoy most? Do you like fiction? Or do you like to read about real people? Maybe mystery stories are your favorite. You're sure to find something you like in this unit. The stories and articles are longer than the ones you read earlier. And that's the best part! You can spend more time with stories, people, and events that you enjoy.

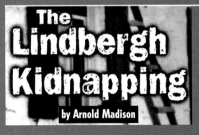

Miles

by Jerry Spinelli

Some people try to run away from a problem. One boy runs straight into one.

Connect to Your Life

Have you ever tried out for a sport only to find out you weren't very good at it? Did you keep playing? Did you enjoy it?

Key to the Story

"Miles" is a novel excerpt. It is part of a book called *Space Station Seventh Grade*. The author, Jerry Spinelli, feels that the main character in the book is more like himself than any other character he's created. In the story, a boy named Jason tries very hard to do something that he feels is expected of him. As you read, decide whether you agree or disagree with the way he behaves.

Vocabulary Preview

Words to Know

lap	backstretch
calisthenics	double-crossed

FOCUS

The narrator tries out for a sport he loves. Read to find out what happens.

I didn't make the baseball team.

The coach said he already had a ninth-grader for shortstop, and an eighth-grade second-stringer, and I wasn't quite good enough to beat them out. I said I'd be willing to play another position. He said he had veteran ninth-graders at all the positions. I told him I wanted to be a major leaguer someday. I told him I hit almost .330 in Little League last year. He looked impressed. He said that's the kind of spirit he likes to see. He said it's not that I don't have the talent, it's just that I need another year to grow. To mature. In the meantime, he said, he wants me to stay in shape. He said he'd like to see me go out for track. It'd be good for me, he said, and nobody gets cut from track.

I tried out for the sprints . I figured that would help me be a better base-stealer. But I was too slow for the sprints.

I tried the half mile. It was too long to run full speed, and too short to run slow. I couldn't figure it out.

sprints
(sprĭnts) races over short distances, in which the runners run very fast

That's how I became a miler.

At first I wasn't too excited about it. I didn't see how running the mile was going to help me be a better shortstop. I was only doing it because the baseball coach was grooming me for next year.

Then I saw a mile race on TV. Some great miler
from England was running, and as he finished each
lap the announcer was screaming: "He's
on a record pace! He's on a record pace!"

30 Each lap the people in the stands went
crazier. On one side of the screen they
showed the world record time, and on the other side
they showed the runner's time. The whole stadium was
standing and screaming, like they were pushing him
with their voices, and even though it was the last lap,
instead of going slower he was going
faster. I couldn't believe it. The stadium
was going bananas, and he was flying and
the world record time and his time were

40 getting closer and closer and he broke the
world record by 3/10 of a second. And
even then he didn't collapse, or even stop. He just kept
jogging another lap around the track, holding his arms
up and smiling and waving to the cheering crowd.

Even though it was Saturday, I went outside and
ran ten times around the block.

> **lap**
> (lăp)
> *n.* one complete
> trip around a
> track

> **REREAD**
> Find examples
> showing that the
> crowd wants the
> runner to break
> a record.

THINK IT THROUGH
Why does the narrator go out for track?

Miles **335**

I turned out to be a pretty rotten miler.
We had our first time trials , and I came in
dead last. My time was 6 minutes and 47
50 seconds. The guy that broke the world
record did it in less than 3 minutes and
50 seconds.

> **time trials**
> practice races in
> which runners
> are timed

To top it off, I threw up afterward.

And to top that off, the place where I threw up
happened to be the long-jump pit. Which didn't make
the long jumpers too happy, but which the coach
thought was just fine. He said now they had a good
reason to jump farther than ever.

But all that, it was nothing. It was all just peaches
60 and cream compared to the worst part, the really,
really bad thing: one of the people that beat me was
named Marceline McAllister. The girl.

"I'm quittin'," I told Peter Kim, who was on the
track team too. A half-miler.

"Why?" he said.

"*Why?* You see who I lost to in the time trials?"

"I wasn't watching."

"The girl."

"Which one?" he said. There're other ones on the
70 team too, but she's the only miler one.

"McAllister," I said.

"Marceline?"

"Yeah. Her."

"The one that plays the trombone?"

"Yeah."

He shrugged. "So?"

"So?" I hollered. "Waddaya mean, so? She's a girl,
man! You ever lose to a girl?"

He said maybe I had a cramp.

80   "I didn't have no cramp."

"Maybe you just had a bad day."

"So what?" I screeched. "How bad could it be? She's still a girl. I got beat by a girl. I'm quittin'."

Then he started talking to me. He reminded me that some of the other girls on the team were doing better than last too. In fact, one of them was the second-fastest sprinter in the one-hundred-pound class. He said he heard that at our age a lot of girls are better than boys, because they

90 mature faster. He said in another couple years I'd probably beat her easy. And he reminded me that the baseball coach had his eye on me.

REREAD

Do you agree with Peter? Why or why not?

"Yeah," I said, "he's really gonna be impressed, watching me lose to a girl."

"He didn't tell you to beat anybody," Peter said. "He just said to keep in shape."

I tried to explain. "Peter, all that stuff doesn't make any difference. The thing is, she's a girl. And a girl's a

100 girl. You know what I'm saying? A *girl*. G-I-R-L. You understand me?"

Peter's expression changed. "No," he said, "I don't understand. I'm Korean, remember? Do what you want." He turned and left.

"Okay," I said. "I won't quit." He kept walking. I called, "Just don't tell Dugan! Peter? Hear? Don't tell anybody!"

THINK IT THROUGH

What is the main reason the narrator wants to quit?

It was a long, long track season.

Every day we started with calisthenics.

110 Then most days we ran around the whole school grounds. *Five* times. Some other days we did intervals. That's where you run real fast as hard as you can for a while, then walk for a while (a littler while), then run fast again. Run-walk-run-walk. You just listen for the whistle to tell your legs when to start or stop. You'll never know how cruel a whistle is until you're walking after your tenth interval, and you hear it blow again.

120 As much as I hated practice, there was one good thing about it: you weren't running *against* anybody. There were no places. No first. No last.

That's why I dreaded the first meet.

> **calisthenics**
> (kăl′ ĭs thĕn′ ĭks)
> *n.* physical exercises such as pushups and sit-ups

> **meet**
> (mēt)
> athletic contest

> **REREAD**
> Why does the narrator dread the first meet?

Ham wanted to know when it was.

"Why?" I asked him.

"Mom and I thought we'd like to come see it."

"See me lose?" I said. I didn't tell them about the girl. "I toldja I'm just running to keep in shape
130 for baseball."

"We just like to come and see you, that's all," he said. "We came to all your Little League games, didn't we?"

"That was different. I'm good at baseball."

"We don't care," he said. "We don't come to see you be a star. Just to play."

"Well, anyway," I said, "the meet's away."

Which was true. It was at Mill Township.

I came in last. By a lot. But the thing was, it didn't really bother me. That's because on the bus over to the meet I all of a sudden realized something: even though I was running, I wasn't really in the *race*. If all I was supposed to be doing was staying in shape for baseball, there was no use getting all uptight about where I finished. I was actually running for the baseball coach, not the track coach. I was a baseball player disguised as a track runner.

REREAD

How does the narrator convince himself that it is OK to be a slow runner?

I didn't really want to break the world's record. I was no miler. I was a shortstop.

It was a big relief when I thought about all that. It still might look to some people like I was losing to a girl. But inside I knew the truth. You can't lose if you're not racing.

After the mile the coach called to me. "Herkimer? You okay?"

"Yeah," I said. I was still jogging. I was hardly puffing. I thought I'd do another couple laps around the grass. Really get in shape.

"Hold it," he said. He came over. "Nothing wrong? Muscle pull? Dizzy?"

"Nah," I told him. "I'm okay."

He looked at me funny. "So why were you taking it so easy?"

I told him the whole thing, which to be fair I probably should have done the first day of practice. I told him about the baseball coach. About being groomed for next year. About wanting to be a major league shortstop.

He was nodding his head while I said these things. When I finished, he still kept nodding, looking at me. Then he stopped. He bent over so his face was right opposite mine. He didn't blink. His voice was hoarse. Almost a whisper.

"What's your first name?"

"Jason."

"Jason? Jason, when you're on my team, you run. And you run as well as you can. I don't care if you're slower than a turtle, you'll try your best when you're on my team. You will run as hard as you can. Every step of the way. Do you understand?"

I nodded.

"And next time I see you dogging it, you are no longer on my team. Understood?"

I understood.

So much for taking it easy.

So I did my calisthenics and ran my five times around the school and did my intervals and I tried harder.

THINK IT THROUGH
What makes Jason try harder?

"And next time I see you dogging it, you are no longer on my team. Understood?"
I understood.
So much for taking it easy.

FOCUS ——————————————————————————

| Look for evidence that Jason is changing.

In the second meet I brought my time down to 6:30. I was still last. McAllister's time was 6:15.

190 In the next couple meets I kept improving. But so did she. Our best miler, Floatmeier, a ninth-grader, only talked to me once. He said, "When you gonna beat that girl?" I tried. But by the middle of the season she was still a good ten seconds faster.

Ham kept asking about the meets. I kept telling him they were away. After a while he got the idea and stopped asking.

Then something happened that made me try even harder. We were racing Shelbourne, and they had a

200 girl miler too—and *she* beat me.

The next day at practice I ran around the school six times. I did my calisthenics perfectly. Even after fifteen intervals I dared that whistle to blow again.

Next meet, for the first time, I didn't come in last. I beat somebody. A kid on the other team.

Peter saw I was trying harder. He started running with me at practice. (He takes track seriously, like I take baseball.) During my races he would stand at the last turn with a stopwatch, and at each lap he would

210 call out my time and yell, "Go, Jason! Go! Go!" And on the last lap, coming off the final turn, he would yell at me, "Sprint! Now! All out! Sprint! Now! Now!" And he would be sprinting along on the grass with me.

My times got better. I broke the six-minute barrier with a 5:58. (In the meantime Floatmeier was running in the 4:50's.) McAllister kept getting better too. I was closing the gap on her, but the closer I got, the harder it got.

220   Then, on the next-to-last meet of the season, going down the backstretch , I got closer to McAllister than ever before. I was so close I could feel little cinder specks that her spikes were flipping back. Her hands were tight fists. Her hair was flapping like mad from side to side and slapping her in the neck. I could hear her breathing. She was kind of wheezing.

backstretch
(băk' strěch')
n. straight part of a track on the opposite side from the finish line

REREAD
Can you feel how hard McAllister is running?

Grunting. And all of a sudden, right there on the
230 backstretch, it came to me: *Marceline McAllister wasn't faster than me.* Not really. She was just trying harder. She was trying so hard it scared me.

    After practice one day, one of the ninth-graders—a slow ninth-grader—grabbed me outside the girls locker room and dragged me inside. He wouldn't let me out till I read what was on the wall: "McAllister sucks trombones."

    "See?" he sneered. "Even the girls don't like her."

THINK IT THROUGH
What does Jason learn? How do you think it will affect him?

FOCUS ———
Read to find out how the last meet begins.

    I practiced hard in the days before the final meet.
240 But not super hard. The problem wasn't in my legs. It was in my head. I knew I could beat her now, but I didn't know if I wanted to pay the price. And the price was pain. I found that out following her down

the backstretch that day. I was really hurting. My legs felt like they were dragging iron hooks through the cinders. My head was flashing and thundering. But the worst part of all was my chest. It felt like somebody opened me up and laid two iron shotputs inside me, one on top

250 of each lung, and each time I breathed out, the shotputs flattened the lungs a little more. By the last one hundred yards there was only about a thimbleful of air to suck from.

shotputs
(shŏt′ pŏŏts′)
heavy metal balls thrown in an athletic event

When I remembered all that pain, and realized it would have to get even worse for me to go faster, I wasn't sure beating her was worth it. I felt like somebody, somewhere, double-crossed me. I couldn't believe I

260 would have to try so hard just to beat a girl.

double-crossed
(dŭb′ əl krôst′)
v. tricked;
past tense of
double-cross

The day before the meet, Floatmeier gave me a little punch in the shoulder. "Last chance," he said.

When they called the milers to the start, me and McAllister, as usual, being seventh-graders and the slowest, lined up at the back of the pack. Only this time somebody else lined up with us. It was

Pain . He was grinning. I swore right there

270 this would be the last race I ever ran in my life.

Pain
Jason thinks of his pain as a person who is running in the race with him.

In all my other races, what I did was stay pretty far behind McAllister for the first two or three laps. That way I could save my energy and sprint after her on the last lap. But this time I stuck with her right from the start. Like a wart.

By the end of the first lap I was already blowing hard. My legs were getting a little heavy. Pain didn't touch me yet, but he was right beside me, still grinning. We were really smoking.

280   We kept it up the second lap. Didn't slow down at all. Her spikes were practically nicking my knees. Our breathings had the same rhythm.

At the half-mile mark things started to get a little scary. Never before, this far into the race, were we this close to the leaders. I was almost as tired already as I usually was at the end of a whole mile. Something had to give. Pain was right there, stride for stride, grinning away. Something was going to happen.

It did. Coming off the first turn into the backstretch

290 of the third lap. The leaders started to go faster. McAllister speeded up too. She was trying to stay with them. *She's crazy!*

I had no choice. I had to go too. I stepped on it, and all of a sudden Pain wasn't alongside me anymore. He was *on* me. He was beating up on my head. He was pulling on my legs. He speared a cramp into my side. He opened up my chest and dumped in those two iron shotputs.

Little by little McAllister

300 pulled away: three yards . . . five yards . . . ten yards. . . . When she leaned into the far turn I got a side view of her. She was running great. Long strides. Arms pumping. Leaning just a little forward. Keeping her form. Everything the coach told us.

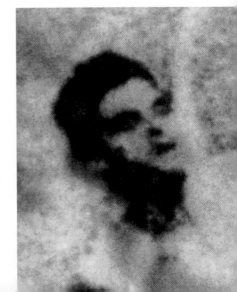

A feeling I never expected in a million years came
over me: I admired her. I was proud of her. I knew she
was hurting too, maybe even as bad as me, but there
she was, gaining on the guy in front of her. I wanted
to be like her.

The gun went off: last lap. Four hundred forty
more yards and my racing career would be over.

THINK IT THROUGH
How is Jason's attitude changing during this race?

FOCUS ———————————————————
Read to find out what happens during the last lap.

I reached out, like my own breath was a twisted
rope, and pulled myself along. My lungs sagged under
the shotputs. I tried to forget that. I shook my arms to
relax. *Stride long. Head steady. Keep your form. . . .*
I don't know whether she slowed down or I got
faster, but the gap between us closed: ten yards . . .
five yards . . . three yards. . . . We were on the final
backstretch, and I was where I started, nipping at her
heels. *Now!* I thought. I pulled alongside her.
Floatmeier and some others were already sprinting for
the tape, but we were in our own private race,
crunching down the cinders, gasping like
asthmatics, side by side. We never turned to
look at each other.

Then, going into the final turn, she started
to edge ahead. A couple inches. A couple
feet. I went after her. My lungs disappeared.
Only the shotputs now. And now they were doing

asthmatics
(ăz´ măt´ ĭks)
people who have
asthma, an illness
that makes
breathing difficult

something. They were getting warm. They were getting hot. They were burning.

I caught her coming off the final turn. Side by side again. There was no form now. No nice fresh strides. With every step we staggered and knocked into each other like cattle coming down a chute. I wished I had the shotputs back, because in my chest now was something worse: two balls of white-hot gas. *Stars!* A pair of stars in my chest. A billion degrees Centigrade. And they were expanding. Exploding. Searing hot star gas scalding into my stomach and arms and legs, into my head. My eyes were star gas. Faces on the side lurched and swayed. The track wobbled under my feet. Elbows, shoulders, hips colliding. If Peter was running with me I didn't know it. I couldn't see. I couldn't hear. I couldn't breathe. I was dying.

REREAD
Which words and phrases help you understand how Jason is feeling?

I don't know when I crossed the finish line. I only know they stopped me and held me up and dragged me around with my arms draped over their shoulders.

Somebody came over and slapped me on the back. "Way to go!"

It was Floatmeier's voice.

"Why?" I gasped.

"You beat her, man!"

I opened my eyes. Floatmeier was grinning and holding out his hand. I was too weak to slap it. I sort of petted it.

Then there were hands coming down from everywhere. I did my best to hit them all. "Way to go, Herk," they kept saying. "Way to gut it . . . Way to run . . . Good race . . . Good race . . . Good race . . ."

Finally I plopped to the ground. Little by little I got my shoes off. My chest was returning to normal. The star gas must have gone out through my eyes: they were burning.

370   Another hand, palm up, in front of me. I slapped it. I looked from the hand to the face. It was McAllister. She looked sick. Her lips were bluish and wet and her mouth was crooked. But then it smiled.

"Good race," she said.

THINK IT THROUGH

1. How do Jason's feelings toward McAllister change?
2. What do you think Jason learns about himself? Use examples from the story to support your answer.
3. How do Peter, the coach, and Floatmeier each encourage Jason? Whose method is most effective? Use examples from the story to support your opinion.

Helen Keller

by Margaret Davidson

Helen lived in a world with no light or sound. How would she learn?

A Strange Fever

The beginning was happy for Helen. She laughed and loved and grew like any other baby. First she crawled, then she walked, and she was learning to talk. Each day was full of adventures.

Then everything stopped. One day Helen laughed and played as usual. The next day she lay tossing and turning in bed. She was very, very sick. The doctor was called. But he could do little to help. A strange fever was burning her up.

10   Probably Helen had scarlet fever. Today there are medicines that would have made her well. But Helen was born over one hundred years ago—before these medicines were discovered.

> **scarlet fever**
> (skär′ lĭt fē′ vər)
> a serious disease producing a high fever and red bumps on the skin

So day after day Helen grew weaker. The doctor could not give her mother and father much hope. Helen Keller was only eighteen months old. The doctor was sure that she could not live much longer.

Then suddenly the fever fell. Helen seemed to be
20 getting better. Mr. and Mrs. Keller sighed with relief. "Everything will be all right now," the doctor said.

But it wasn't.

Helen slept for many hours. When she woke again it was morning. The sun was shining in through the window. Sunlight splashed across her bed.

Mrs. Keller bent over her little girl. She smiled and waved her hand in front of Helen's face. Helen's eyes were wide open, but she didn't blink.

That was strange. Mrs. Keller waved her hand again—
30 closer to Helen's eyes. Helen stared straight ahead.

Now Mrs. Keller grabbed a lamp. She shone its bright light right into Helen's eyes. Helen kept on staring.

Helen's mother began to scream. "Helen's blind! She can't see. My baby's blind!"

One morning soon after, Mrs. Keller dressed Helen and sat her down in the middle of the bedroom floor. Just then a loud bell in the back yard began to ring.

This was the Keller family's signal for meals. And Helen loved to eat. Whenever she heard the bell she trotted to the table as fast as she could. But now she did nothing. Nothing at all.

Mrs. Keller was making Helen's bed. "Helen?" she said. "*Helen?*" But Helen didn't move.

Mrs. Keller picked up a can of stones—one of Helen's toys. She rattled it in Helen's ear. Helen didn't even turn her head.

Then her mother knew. This time she didn't scream. She just bent and gathered Helen in her arms. "My baby's *deaf* too," she whispered.

THINK IT THROUGH
What causes Helen to become deaf and blind?

FOCUS
Read to find out how Helen lives with blindness and deafness.

The Dark Silence

The doctor looked at Helen. He shook his head.

"There is nothing I can do," he said.

But Helen's father and mother refused to give up hope so easily. Tuscumbia, Alabama, was a very small town. And this was the only doctor there. So they took Helen to other doctors in other—bigger—towns. But the answer was always the same. "No hope."

Finally the Kellers understood that Helen would live all her life alone in dark silence.

60 She could not see the brightest light. She could not hear the loudest noise. Soon she forgot the words she had been learning. Then she became *dumb*—she could not speak at all.

Helen's body continued to grow. But how could her mind grow in the dark silence? There was so much she could no longer understand. She cried. But she didn't know she was sad. She screamed and kicked. But she didn't know she was angry. She smiled very seldom. She never laughed at all.

70 She wanted people to understand her, but she could not talk to them. She did not know any words. Helen didn't even know her own name. So now Helen began to make signs.

A nod meant *yes*. A shake of the head meant *no*. A pull meant *come*. A push meant *go away*. When Helen wanted something big she spread her hands wide—as if she were holding a big ball. When she wanted something small she took a tiny pinch of skin between two fingers.

REREAD
With a partner, show how Helen communicates.

80 When Helen wanted her mother she patted her own cheek and made a soft mewing sound.

Helen's father wore glasses. Helen liked to feel them—to take them off and put them on her father's nose. When she wanted her father she pretended to put on a pair of glasses too.

Soon Helen had sixty signs to tell people what she wanted.

THINK IT THROUGH
How does Helen adjust to her loss of sight and hearing? Find three examples.

FOCUS

Read about how Helen tries to learn.

Helen tried to find out about the world by touching everything she could. The Kellers lived on a small farm. Helen loved to pat the horses and cows. Her mother taught her how to feed the chickens. Some grew so tame they ate right out of her hand. Then Helen would run her hands over their plump warm bodies. She liked to touch anything that moved. But there was so much she could not really understand.

Helen put her fingers on her father's face and hands. She felt him holding a book. So Helen too held up a book in front of her face. But she didn't know what books were for.

She felt her mother pulling up weeds in the garden. So Helen tried to pull them up too. But how could she know the difference between a weed and a flower?

Worst of all were lips. Again and again Helen felt other people's lips moving. So she moved her lips too. But she didn't know what the moving lips meant.

What was everyone doing? What was going on? Helen became more and more angry. Sometimes the feeling of anger was more than she could stand. Then she kicked and screamed and tried to smash everything she touched. But this didn't help either. Helen grew even more angry. Soon not a day passed without a terrible temper tantrum.

REREAD
What words and phrases help you understand how angry Helen is?

tantrum
(tăn´ trəm)
n. sudden, violent display of anger

There was so much she could not know! One day Helen spilled some water on her apron. She took it off and laid it down in front of the fireplace—but it did not dry fast enough to please her. She moved it closer and closer. Finally she laid the apron right on top of the flames.

The flames shot up through the apron—then to
120 Helen's dress! Fire! She was on fire!

Helen screamed. Luckily someone was in the next
room. The fire was put out before it did any harm.

"But she could have been killed," Mrs. Keller said.

"Or she could have burned the whole house
down," Helen's father answered, "and us with it."

How much longer could this go on?

When Helen was five years old, her sister Mildred
was born. All Helen knew about this baby was that it
took up too much of her mother's time. Time that up
130 until now had belonged to her!

Too often when Helen wanted to run into her
mother's arms she found that the baby was already
there. One day Helen reached out for her doll's
cradle—and found the baby inside. This was too
much! Helen growled like an animal.
Then she reached out and knocked the
cradle over. The baby fell screaming to
the floor.

REREAD
Should Helen be
blamed for her
behavior?

Luckily Mildred wasn't hurt. But what
140 about next time? Helen was growing bigger and
wilder every day.

"Next time she might really hurt the baby—or
worse," Helen's father said. "No, I'm afraid there is only
one thing we can do. We will have to send Helen away."

"Send her away?" Mrs. Keller cried. "Where would
we send her?"

But she knew the answer herself. There
was only one place that would take a wild
creature like Helen—the State
150 Insane Asylum!

**insane
asylum**
(ĭn sān'
ə sī' ləm)
place where
people with
serious mental
illnesses are
cared for

"Let's wait just a little bit longer," Mrs. Keller begged.

Mr. Keller nodded. But they both knew that this was no real answer. They both knew that sooner or later Helen would have to be sent away.

Then one day Mrs. Keller read about a special school in Boston, Massachusetts, called Perkins Institute. Perkins was a school for the blind. But once, long ago, the teachers there had taught a little girl who was both blind *and* deaf. Somehow they had
160 worked out a way to make her understand the outside world.

"Write to them," Mrs. Keller begged her husband. "Maybe they can help Helen too."

Helen's father shook his head. He had almost run out of hope. But that night he sat down and wrote a letter to Perkins Institute.

Now there was nothing else to do but wait.

THINK IT THROUGH
Why is Helen dangerous to herself and others?

"*Next time she might really hurt the baby—or worse. . . . No, I'm afraid there is only one thing we can do. We will have to send Helen away.*"

Helen needs help. Where will it come from?

The Stranger Comes

What was going on? Helen had known all day that *something* was. The house had been cleaned from top to bottom—even the guest room had been opened and aired. Wonderful smells kept coming from the kitchen. And everyone was busy—much too busy to bother with her.

REREAD
How can Helen tell what is going on?

Late in the afternoon Helen felt her mother put on her hat and her gloves. Helen had learned long ago that this meant her mother was going somewhere. So she held onto her mother's skirt. She wanted to go too. But Mrs. Keller pulled away gently, and drove off in the carriage alone.

Whatever was going on, Helen didn't like it! She was six years old. But she had no words to tell how she felt. Every once in a while she shook her head sadly. And she waited.

For a long time nothing happened. Then suddenly Helen stood very still. She seemed to be listening as hard as she could. In a way she was. Not with her ears, but with her whole body.

Helen couldn't hear the loudest noise in the world. But sometimes she could feel things slam or shake around her. She could feel their *vibrations* coming through the air and the ground.

vibrations
(vī brā′ shənz)
n. shaking movements

Now she felt the thud of horses' hoofs, the vibration of carriage wheels coming back up the drive. The carriage stopped in front of the porch. Now Helen felt footsteps coming toward her across the porch floor. It must be her mother. Her mother was home at last! Helen held out her arms 200 and felt herself being scooped up.

But this wasn't her mother! These were a stranger's arms!

The stranger was Miss Annie Sullivan. She had come all the way from Perkins Institute to try to help Helen. But of course Helen didn't know this. All she knew was that a stranger was holding her close. And Helen didn't like to be held by strangers.

So she kicked, she twisted, she tried to break free. But the stranger's arms only tightened around her! 210 Helen began to growl.

"Let her go, Miss Annie!" Helen's father cried. "Or she will hurt you!" The arms loosened and Helen sprang free.

Helen did not like strangers, but she was curious about them. So now she came back. She patted her hand across Annie Sullivan's face and down over her dusty travelling dress.

Annie laughed. "I can see that she doesn't like to be touched. But she isn't a bit frightened, is she?"

220   Mr. Keller took his time answering. "No, Miss Annie," he finally said. "And I think that you will sometimes find that that's a problem."

THINK IT THROUGH
How do Helen and Annie react to each other?

| Annie tries to teach Helen. Read to find out what happens.

Early the next morning Mrs. Keller led Helen into Annie Sullivan's room. It was time for the first lesson to begin. Helen didn't know this of course. So she just wandered around the room—touching all the new things the stranger had brought with her.

230 One of the first things she found was Annie's suitcase, lying open on the bed. Her curious hands plunged inside. And what was this? Helen's face lit up. She knew right away. It was a doll! She had others in her room. She wanted this one too. Helen snatched it out of the suitcase and hugged it close.

REREAD
What does Helen do when she wants something?

"It's a present for Helen from the little blind girls at Perkins," Annie told Mrs. Keller. "And it's also as good a place to begin as any."

She picked up Helen's hand. Helen started to tug away. But then she stopped. What was the stranger
240 doing with her hand?

"This is called the finger alphabet," Annie explained to Helen's mother. "It's a way of talking to the deaf. I am making the shapes of the letters D-O-L-L into Helen's palm. Then I will take her hand and run it over the real doll in her arms. You see, first the word—and then what the word stands for. The word—and what it stands for again. I am simply trying to connect these two things in her mind."

"Look, Miss Annie!" Mrs. Keller cried. "Helen is
250 making those movements too!"

And she was. Slowly, Helen Keller's fingers were making the shapes of the word D-O-L-L.

"What a quick little monkey you are," Annie murmured—and she bent down to help. Then she saw the look on Mrs. Keller's face.

"No, no! You must not get your hopes up so soon," Annie said quickly. "Helen has learned how to make the shapes of her first word. And very fast too. But she does not know that these shapes stand for all the dolls in the world. She does not know they have *meaning*."

> **REREAD**
> What point is Annie trying to make?

260

Now Annie turned back to Helen. "So come on! Let's go on with the lesson."

Annie pulled the doll out of Helen's arms. She meant to give it back as soon as Helen spelled the word D-O-L-L again. But Helen didn't know this. All she knew was that the stranger was taking her doll away from her. And she wanted it back!

Again and again Helen reached for the doll. But her hand only touched empty air. She began to growl.

270

"Look out, Miss Annie," Mrs. Keller cried. But her warning came too late. Helen came charging. Her fist shot out. And she hit Annie Sullivan right in the mouth.

Helen could not hear her pain-filled cry. But she could feel the stranger jerk away. She smiled.

"Oh, let her have the doll," Mrs. Keller cried. "It's the only way to calm her."

"No," Annie said. "There is another way. Helen must learn self-control."

280

"But Helen doesn't know what self-control is," Mrs. Keller answered. "She doesn't know how to keep her temper."

"Then that is the first lesson I must teach her," Annie Sullivan said. "For I do not think I can teach her anything else until I do."

> **REREAD**
> Why must self-control be the first lesson?

Helen came charging again. But this time Annie was ready for her. She grabbed Helen's arms and hung on as tight as she could.

290 Helen kicked and screamed for quite a while. Then suddenly she went limp. "So, my girl," Annie said. "Have you had enough? Are you ready to go on?"

But it was a trick. As soon as Annie let go, Helen ran from the room. She would not come back all day.

Helen slept as well as ever that night. But Annie Sullivan didn't. She lay in bed and thought about Helen. Annie had been in Tuscumbia for only one day. But already she knew that everyone in this house felt too sorry for Helen. They had let her have her 300 own way for years. Now she was badly spoiled.

"And that must stop," Annie thought. "For how can I reach her mind while she rants and rages like a wild animal? No, I must be loving—but firm. That's the best way to help Helen."

rants
(rănts)
v. speaks in an angry, violent way

THINK IT THROUGH
What are the biggest problems Annie faces in teaching Helen?

FOCUS
Look for details that show how Annie deals with Helen's actions.

The Worst Fight of All

Helen didn't know that Annie had come to help her. All she knew was that a stranger was trying to make her do things she did not understand, things she did *not* want to do. So six-year-old Helen did what she 310 had been doing for years. She fought back.

She ran. She hid. She fought with sly tricks. One day Helen locked Annie in her room and hid the key. Helen's mother tried to get Helen to show where she had hidden the key. Helen just turned away—and smiled. Finally her father had to put a ladder up to the window and carry Annie down like a sack of potatoes.

But most of the time Helen fought with her fists. Day by day those fights grew worse. Helen was strong. But the stranger was stronger. Helen could
320 fight for hours. But this stranger never seemed to tire!

"It's that little bit of strength that's going to save us," Annie Sullivan wrote a friend one day, ". . . if she doesn't kill us both first!"

> **REREAD**
> What does Annie mean?

Annie tried to keep cheerful. It was not always easy. One day Helen's hand brushed against Annie's face—and came away wet. Helen didn't know what tears meant, so she just turned away.

Then came the worst fight of all.
330 Helen had the table manners of a pig. She knew how to use her knife and fork and spoon. But she liked to use her hands instead.

She began each meal in her own chair, but she never stayed there for long. Most of the time she wandered from place to place—grabbing what she wanted from other people's plates.

Annie watched with horror as Helen stuffed other people's food in her mouth. But Annie didn't say anything—so long as
340 Helen stayed away from her.

> **horror**
> (hôr′ ər)
> *n.* great disgust

Then one morning Helen stopped behind Annie's chair. Her nose wriggled to sort out the smells. What was that on the stranger's plate? She sniffed again. Then she knew. It was sausage! And Helen loved sausage.

But did she dare? Helen stood there for a moment. Then she touched her way round the table again. At every chair she stopped and sniffed. Everyone else's sausage was gone. Now here she was, back at the stranger's plate.

350   Once more the delicious smell of sausage came drifting up to her. It was just too much. Out flashed Helen's hand. Down came the stranger's on top of it!

Helen tried to jerk free. The stranger held on tight. And one by one she peeled Helen's fingers away from the sausage.

"Oh, let her have it just this once," Mr. Keller said. "She doesn't know any better."

Annie shook her head. "She must learn that other people have rights too," she answered.

THINK IT THROUGH
What kind of person is Annie? Use examples from the biography to support your answer.

FOCUS
Read to find out what happens next.

360   So the fight began. Helen kicked and screamed. She pounded her fists on the floor. Helen's mother and father hated to see her this upset. They got up and left the room quickly. Annie locked the door behind them. Then she went back to her chair.

For a while Annie sat. Helen rolled and raged on the floor. But Helen was growing hungrier every minute. What was the stranger doing? Was there any sausage left on her plate? Finally Helen got up to find out.

370 She sniffed—and yes! There was some sausage left. Helen's hand crept forward. Annie pushed it back. Helen's hand crept forward again. Annie pushed it away again.

Helen lost her temper. But this time she didn't yell and scream. She just pinched the stranger's arm as hard as she could.

Annie slapped back—hard. Helen shook herself. That hurt! But it didn't stop her. Helen pinched the stranger

380 again. And once more Annie slapped Helen. *Pinch—slap. Pinch—slap.* "I can keep this up as long as you can," Annie Sullivan said.

> **REREAD**
> Could Annie have found another way to make Helen understand? Explain your opinion.

Suddenly Helen wheeled away. She touched her way around the table again. But all the chairs were empty! Everyone else was gone!

Helen raced for the door. She tugged on it as hard as she could. It would not open! Then Helen knew. She was locked in with the stranger. And all the

390 understanding arms were gone!

Helen backed against the wall. She wanted to stay as far away from Annie as she could. But she was growing more and more hungry. Finally Helen edged her way back to the table again and began to eat— with her fingers.

Annie sighed—and put a spoon in Helen's hand. Helen held it for a moment. Then she threw it as hard as she could across the room.

Annie pulled Helen out of her chair and dragged

400 her across the room to pick up the spoon. Then she plunked her back in her seat again.

"Now you're going to eat that oatmeal," Annie said. "And with that spoon!"

Helen kicked. She screamed. She wriggled like an eel. But inch by inch Annie Sullivan forced the spoon up to Helen's mouth. She forced Helen to swallow one spoonful. And then another. Then Annie began to relax.

Too soon! Helen jerked free. She threw the spoon at Annie. Annie ducked. And everything started all 410 over again.

But this time Helen didn't fight so hard. She was so hungry, and so tired. This time, when Annie let go, Helen kept right on eating until finally her bowl was empty, her breakfast all gone.

But so was the morning. The sun was high overhead when Annie finally unlocked the door. Smells of lunch filled the house.

Annie led Helen outside to wander in the garden. She went to her room to think. Things could not go 420 on this way much longer. Something would have to be done—and fast.

But what? Annie paced back and forth across her room. Slowly a plan began to form in her mind. But first she would have to talk to Helen's mother. It was not going to be easy to find the right words.

THINK IT THROUGH

What does Annie do that Helen's family cannot do? Why can Annie do this?

Annie paced back and forth across her room. Slowly a plan began to form in her mind.

FOCUS ————

Read about what Annie plans for Helen.

W-A-T-E-R!

"Miss Kate, I want to take Helen away with me," Annie said.

"What?" gasped Mrs. Keller.

"I must teach Helen to mind me," Annie

430 explained. "But I can't do it here in this house. Every time I try, she turns to you and away from me. More and more she will think of me as an enemy. Then everything will be lost."

mind
(mīnd)
v. obey

Mrs. Keller didn't say *no*. But she didn't say *yes* either.

Annie tried again. "It will just be for a while. Just until Helen learns that I am a part of her life too."

"There is a little garden house near here," Mrs. Keller said slowly. But she still didn't say *yes*.

Annie leaned forward. "I know it is a gamble," she

440 said softly. "It is also our last chance."

Last chance. Mrs. Keller sat very still for a moment. Then she nodded *yes*.

REREAD

Why is this the last chance?

So Helen and Annie went to live in the little house on the other side of the garden. At first Helen kicked and screamed and fought as hard as ever. But slowly there came a change.

Helen still fought, but not as hard. And not as often. Sometimes she would even let the stranger hold her for a moment. Then one day Helen did not fight at all.

450 "The first great step has been taken," Annie wrote a friend. "Helen has learned how to mind!"

THINK IT THROUGH

How does Annie convince Mrs. Keller to go along with her plan?

But Helen still didn't know what words were. Day after day Annie spelled into Helen's hand. And Helen learned to make more and more shapes back. By the end of March—in less than two weeks—she could make twenty-one word-shapes. The next day she learned how to make eight more. But she didn't know what they meant. It was just a game she played with her hands.

April 5, 1887, began like any other day. After 460 breakfast Annie began to spell into Helen's hand. But Helen was restless this morning. The window was open and the smells of spring came pouring in. Besides, Helen was growing very tired of this game with no meaning!

She tugged on Annie's skirt, then pointed to the window. Her meaning was very clear. *Let's go out!*

At first Annie tried to go on with the lesson. But Helen's face darkened. Her hands clenched into fists. She was holding her new doll in her lap. Now she 470 picked it up and threw it as hard as she could. It broke into many small pieces.

Helen didn't care. She didn't love the doll anyway. She felt the stranger sweep up the pieces. Then the stranger handed her her hat. So Helen knew they were going outside after all. She skipped and danced by the stranger's side. No more lessons! She was getting her own way!

Or was she?

Helen and Annie wandered in the garden for a 480 while. Then they came to an old pump house. Helen liked to play in its cool dampness. She ran inside.

In the middle of the floor stood a pump. Annie Sullivan began to move its handle up and down. Soon a steady stream of water came pouring out of its spout. Now she took Helen's hand and held it under the cool flow. W-A-T-E-R, she spelled into Helen's wet palm.

At first Helen pulled away. But then suddenly she stopped. A new light seemed to come to her face.

490   Annie saw the look. W-A-T-E-R, she spelled quickly. W-A-T-E-R!

W-A-T- . . . Helen began to spell back. And with each movement her face grew brighter. For suddenly she knew! The shapes that the stranger was making with her fingers *did* have a meaning! *Everything had a name.* Everything in the whole world had a name! And she could learn them all!

THINK IT THROUGH
What has Helen finally discovered? Why is it important?

FOCUS
Find out what happens after Helen learns the word *water.*

"Oh, yes, Helen," Annie whispered. "That's *it!*" And she bent down to hug the shaking little girl.

500   But Helen pulled away. She didn't have time for *that* now! She dropped to the ground and thumped on it hard. *Name it!* she was demanding. So—laughing, sobbing—Annie did.

Helen paused for a moment. She fluttered off the word on her fingers. She nodded. Then she whirled away again. In the next few minutes she learned six new words. And she knew what they meant!

Then suddenly Helen stopped. She thumped herself across the head. Annie burst out laughing. "Yes, dear," 510 she said. "There's a word for you too." And she bent down and spelled H-E-L-E-N into the little girl's hand.

Helen had a name at last!

Now Helen reached out and patted Annie's arm. At first Annie thought she was just saying "thank you." But Helen wanted something more than that. She patted Annie's arm again.

"Oh," said Annie. "So you want to know that too." And Annie spelled T-E-A-C-H-E-R into Helen's waiting hand.

REREAD
What is Helen asking?

520 A few minutes later two new people came out of the pump house. The wild little girl was gone. And so was the stranger. Now Helen Keller and Teacher walked hand in hand.

So Much to Learn

Helen wanted to know the names for everything she touched. And Teacher gave them to her. Before the first day was over Helen learned how to make thirty word shapes. Before the first month was over she knew how to spell one hundred words.

From early morning until late at night Helen spelled 530 the words she knew. She spelled until her eyelids drooped and her fingers could hardly make the shapes.

"You really should slow her down," a worried friend said, "or she will hurt her brain." Teacher just smiled. She knew that nothing could stop Helen now.

THINK IT THROUGH

1. How did Helen's behavior change after she began to understand the meaning of words? Why?
2. Why do you think Annie didn't give up?
3. How did Helen's strong will and courage help her?
4. What do you think might have happened to Helen if Annie had not been able to help her?

Helen Keller and Annie Sullivan

A baby is kidnapped. Who is the kidnapper? Use the clues to help you decide.

WANTED

INFORMATION AS TO THE WHEREABOUTS OF

CHAS. A. LINDBERGH, JR.

OF HOPEWELL, N. J.

SON OF COL. CHAS. A. LINDBERGH

World-Famous Aviator

This child was kidnaped from his home in Hopewell, N. J., between 8 and 10 p. m. on Tuesday, March 1, 1932.

The Lindbergh Kidnapping

by Arnold Madison

Connect to Your Life

Have you ever read or heard about a kidnapping? Who are often the targets of kidnappers?

Key to the Article

"The Lindbergh Kidnapping" is a **true account**. It tells the facts about a famous crime that happened in 1932. In 1927, Charles Lindbergh was the first person to fly alone over the Atlantic Ocean without stopping. He became famous. People followed the news of his son's kidnapping as closely as people follow the trials of famous people today. The article also tells about the clues the police used to find a suspect. As you read, take notes to help you remember the clues.

Vocabulary Preview

Words to Know

estate	plot
foreigner	receipts
figure	

 Reading Coach CD-ROM selection

The news swept around the world like a tidal wave. The Lindbergh baby had been kidnapped!

In March, 1932, Charles A. Lindbergh was one of the most famous men anywhere. Five years before, he had flown across the Atlantic Ocean. He had been the first to do it nonstop and alone. He was a hero. Almost every country named something after him. Later he married Anne Morrow. Their first son was born in 1930 and was named Charles, Jr.

10   The Lindberghs lived on an estate in New Jersey. On March 1, 1932, Charles came home from work as usual. Anne did not feel well. Charles, Jr. was asleep in his upstairs bedroom. He had a cold. A few minutes after nine, Charles and Anne were in the living room.

estate
(ĭ stāt′)
n. large house surrounded by a lot of land

Suddenly Charles looked around. "What was that?"

Charles had heard a sound like wood breaking. He and Anne listened for a few moments. But there were

20   no more sounds. A little later Anne went to her room. Charles worked in the library.

At ten o'clock, the baby's nurse, Betty Gow, went to see if Charles, Jr. was all right. She did not turn on a light. She did not want to wake the baby. She let her eyes get used to the dark. She felt carefully around the crib. The child was gone.

Betty went to Anne's room. "Mrs. Lindbergh, do you have the baby?"

"Why, no, I don't have the baby."

30   Charles raced upstairs. He checked the crib. Two large pins were still in the blankets. The baby's nurse

had pinned the blankets to the mattress. The pins would have stopped Charles, Jr. from climbing out of the crib. Someone had taken the baby from the crib.

"Anne," Charles said, "they have stolen our baby."

An envelope lay on a radiator by the window. Lindbergh did not touch it. There might be fingerprints.

> radiator
> (rā′ dē ā′ tər)
> device through which steam passes to heat a room

THINK IT THROUGH
What discovery did Betty Gow make? What event did the Lindberghs ignore?

FOCUS
Read to find out what the kidnapper has left.

40   The police were called. While they waited, Anne and the nurse searched the house. They looked in every room. The baby was not in the house. Lindbergh got his rifle. He and the butler drove around the estate. They found nothing.

When the police came, they started their own search. Clues were found under the nursery window. There was a smudged footprint and two holes in the ground. The police found other clues. A ladder lay nearby in the grass. The ladder had been

50   built by hand. One rung was broken.

> rung
> (rŭng)
> step on a ladder

Charles remembered the sound he had heard earlier. The kidnapper must have stepped on that rung while holding the baby. The weight was too much. The rung had snapped.

The envelope was checked for fingerprints. There were none on it or on the note inside. The

| ransom letter | demanded $50,000. The kidnapper would phone in two to four days. The note said Charles must not call the | **ransom letter** letter asking for money in return for freeing a kidnapped person |

60 police. It also said that Charles should not tell the newspapers. It was too late to stop that. The news was out.

There was something odd about the writing in the note. Words were misspelled. *Gut* was written for good, and *anyding* for anything. The police wondered if a foreigner had written the note. There was a sign drawn at the bottom. Two circles overlapped. Where they met, there was an oval. Three holes in a straight
70 line were punched through each part.

foreigner
(fôr′ ə nər)
n. person from another country

THINK IT THROUGH

Which clues do you think were most important? List them on a sheet of paper.

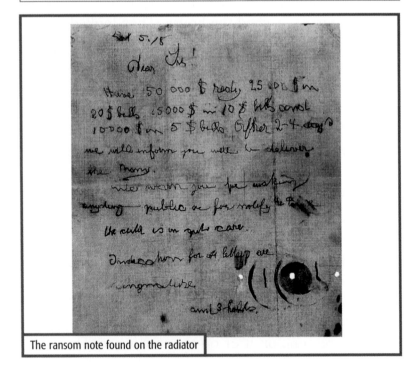

The ransom note found on the radiator

FOCUS ————
Learn what new information the police get.

By the next morning, newspapers across the world carried the news. The police set up headquarters in the estate garage. Hundreds of reporters and onlookers stayed outside the gates. Thousands of phone calls came in on the twenty telephones in the garage.

There were offers of help. One was from the famous gangster Al Capone, who was in prison. He offered $10,000 as a reward. The money would go to anyone who found the baby. Capone secretly tried to

80 make a deal with a New York City newspaper. If the paper could get him free, Capone would help search for the baby. The offer was turned down.

REREAD
Why did Al Capone want to help?

The police began their search. But they did not want to scare the kidnapper. Once the baby was safe, they would work harder. The police did wonder if the kidnapping was an inside job. One clue seemed to show that.

inside job
crime committed by a person who works for the victim

The Lindberghs spent weekends at their

90 estate. But they would stay with Anne's mother during the week. This weekend the baby had caught a cold. So the Lindberghs stayed at their own home all week. How did the kidnapper know they would be there on Tuesday night? How did the kidnapper know how to find the baby's room?

The police questioned the nurse. They also questioned the cook and butler. Charles said these people were innocent. He thought an underworld

100 gang had carried out the kidnapping.

Charles, Jr. was sick and needed special medicine. Charles and Anne were worried about the baby's health. To help them, newspapers across the country printed the diet and the special medicine the baby would need.

A letter arrived on March 4. The envelope had been mailed in Brooklyn, New York. At the bottom of the letter was the strange design. The same one had been on the first ransom note. The kidnapper now wanted 110 $70,000. Again words were misspelled. *Gut* for good. And the word *aus* appeared. Both were German words. Was the kidnapper a German-born person? The note kept saying "we." Was there a gang, as Lindbergh thought?

The letter also said the baby was well. But the kidnapper wanted the police to stop their search. Nothing would be done until the news stopped appearing in the newspapers.

Another letter arrived a few days later. At the 120 bottom of the page was the same design. Only the police, the Lindberghs, and the kidnapper knew about that. The letter repeated the demand for $70,000.

THINK IT THROUGH
The police believed the kidnapper might be a person who worked for the Lindberghs. Charles believed the kidnappers were a gang. What clues supported each belief?

FOCUS _____
The police and the Lindberghs get help with the case. Read to find out who gives them help.

A man unknown to the police and the Lindberghs wanted to help them. His name was Dr. John Condon. He was seventy-four years old and lived in the Bronx, New York. Charles Lindbergh was a hero to him.

Condon read a newspaper called the Bronx *Home News*. He was a friend of the paper's owner. So Condon put a small ad in the Bronx *Home News*. He
130 offered to pay $1,000 of his own money to the kidnappers. He also offered to act as a go-between.

The next night John Condon received a letter. The note told him what to do when Lindbergh had the money. There was another envelope for Charles Lindbergh. Condon called him. Lindbergh asked the man to come to see him.

The second letter said the baby was 150 miles away. When Lindbergh handed over the money, they would give him the address. First, they wanted the
140 money. Eight hours later Lindbergh would get the address. The secret symbol was at the bottom of the letter.

Lindbergh got the money. An ad was put in the New York *American*—MONEY IS READY. On the night of March 11, Condon received a phone call. The deep voice had a strong accent. Condon thought the man was German. The caller spoke with another person in the background. This person answered in Italian. The first man said Dr. Condon would hear from the gang again.

150 Eight-thirty the next night, Condon's doorbell rang. A taxi driver gave him a letter. Condon was to go to a food market in the Bronx. He was to bring the money with him. There would be another note for him at the market. Condon did not have the money yet. But he wanted to meet the kidnapper.

REREAD
Do you think it was dangerous for Condon not to have the money? Explain your opinion.

The directions brought him to Woodlawn Cemetery in the Bronx. The place was cold and dark.
160 Someone waved a white handkerchief through the

bars of the fence. Condon saw a dim
figure . A cloth hid most of the man's face.

"Did you get the money?" the man asked.

Condon knew the voice. That was the
German-sounding man he had talked
to earlier.

"No. I couldn't bring the money until I saw the
package." *Package* meant the kidnapped baby.

They both heard footsteps. The man leaped over
170 the high fence. He thought Condon had brought the
police. He raced along the street and into a park.
Condon ran after him, catching up to the man.

figure
(fĭg′ yər)
n. shape of a person

THINK IT THROUGH
What instructions did the kidnapper give Lindbergh? What did
Condon plan to do instead?

FOCUS
Read to find out what happens when Condon meets the
kidnapper.

The stranger was scared. "Would I
burn if the baby is dead?"

Dead? thought Condon. What did the
kidnapper mean? The masked stranger
told him the baby was fine. No one should worry.

"You know my name," Condon said. "What
is yours?"

180 "John."

"Are you a German?"

"No, Scandinavian."

Condon again said he would give the man $1,000
of his own money. But the man said, "We don't want

REREAD
Why do you
think the
stranger asks this
question?

your money." Condon wondered how many others were part of the plot.

plot
(plŏt)
n. secret plan

John said there were six people. He was afraid of them. They would get him if he left. The kidnapping had been planned for
190 a year.

Condon told him a newspaper notice would be printed when the money was ready. John said he would send the baby's sleeping suit to Condon. That would prove that Condon was dealing with the right person.

Four days passed before the sleeping suit arrived. Lindbergh checked it carefully. He was sure it was the suit his son had been wearing. At least they now knew they were in touch with the true kidnapper.

THINK IT THROUGH
Identify three details that the kidnapper revealed to Condon.

FOCUS
What do you think will happen when Lindbergh pays the money? Read to see if you are right.

200   A week went by. More letters came from the kidnapper. But no firm deal was set. The money was ready. Each serial number had been noted. By doing this, the police could learn where the money was spent.

Finally, April 2 was agreed on as the date to hand over the money. Lindbergh went to Condon's house. The hours passed slowly. At eight o'clock, a cab driver brought a letter. The kidnapper said everything was ready. St. Raymond's Cemetery in the Bronx was to be the meeting place.

210 Condon and Lindbergh drove there. Charles remained in the car. Condon walked along the street.

A voice called from the dark cemetery. "Here, Doctor."

It was John, who demanded the money. Condon told him that Lindbergh could get only $50,000 and not $70,000.

John thought about this. Then he said, "Well, all right. I suppose if we can't get seventy, we get fifty."

But Condon wanted a note telling how to find the
220 baby. Finally, John said he would go to get the note. Condon would return to the car and get the money.

Condon told Lindbergh what had happened. They removed $20,000 from the box of money, leaving only $50,000. Taking the money, Condon went to the cemetery. The kidnapper returned in thirteen minutes. This might mean that his home was nearby. John gave Condon a note. Then Condon handed over the ransom money.

> **REREAD**
> What steps did Condon take to try to find where the baby was?

230 The note said the baby was on a 28-foot boat named *Nelly*. The boat was near Gay Head, Massachusetts. Lindbergh flew to Massachusetts.

For a day and a half, he searched for the boat. No boat named *Nelly* could be found. Condon put ads in the newspaper, asking better directions. Nine more days passed. There was no further word from the kidnapper.

Lindbergh asked the federal government for help. The Treasury Department had a list of the ransom bills' serial numbers. The list was sent to stores and banks.

240 In Newark, New Jersey, a bank teller saw the list. The money added up to $50,000. He knew the Lindbergh kidnapper had demanded that much money. He told a friend who was a reporter for the

Newark *News*. The reporter decided Lindbergh must have paid the money. But the baby was still missing. A story appeared in the *News*. Other newspapers printed the story. Lindbergh was angry. He was afraid the kidnappers might harm the baby.

250   Everything changed on May 12. A man walking in the woods near the Lindbergh home found a baby's body. The baby's clothing matched Charles, Jr.'s clothes. The baby had been dead for more than two months. He might even have died the night of the kidnapping. Death was caused by a fractured skull.

REREAD
Why had the kidnappers pretended that the baby was still alive?

THINK IT THROUGH
Compare your prediction with what happened after Lindbergh paid the ransom money. What were you right about? What was different?

The note said the baby was on a 28-foot boat named *Nelly*. The boat was near Gay Head, Massachusetts. Lindbergh flew to Massachusetts.

Now nothing stopped the police in their search. Only three clues would help them: the ransom notes, the ladder, and the numbers on the ransom money.

260 The handwriting on the notes was probably disguised. But the spelling was by a foreign-born person. Condon had thought John was German. A large population of German people lived in the Bronx. John read the Bronx *Home News*. This paper was sold mainly in the Bronx.

The ladder was sent to a wood expert. The broken rung gave the police more clues. The police tested the ladder. Charles, Jr. weighed about 33 pounds. A man of 150 to 179 pounds carrying the baby would have broken the ladder rung. The police decided

270 the kidnapper was carrying Charles, Jr. down the ladder. The rung broke. They fell forward. The baby's head hit the wall of the house. This caused the child's death.

REREAD

In your own words, tell what might have happened to the baby.

Also, the ladder had been made by a carpenter. Was the kidnapper a carpenter? One part of the ladder was special. The piece of wood had four clean nail holes. The board had been used for something else. Then it had been removed and put

280 into the ladder. The wood had been inside a building. The nails would have rusted if the board had been outside. But no rust showed in the four holes.

The news about the baby's death and Condon's help appeared in the papers. Many people began to think that Condon was the kidnapper or part of the gang. Condon received angry letters. Some people said they would kill him.

Lindbergh wrote a letter to Condon. He thanked Condon for all his help. The letter was printed in
290 many newspapers. Then people changed their thinking about Condon.

Meanwhile the ransom money was turning up in stores. New Jersey and New York City police questioned hundreds of people. But they were all innocent.

The New York Police Department used a special map of New York City. Wherever a bill from the ransom money was found, a colored pin was pushed into the map. Months and, finally, a year passed. More and more pins dotted the map.
300 The pins formed a spider web, with the Bronx in the middle. Police were now certain the kidnapper lived there. But the detectives could do nothing yet.

THINK IT THROUGH
How did the ransom money help the police?

FOCUS
As you read, look for details that may help solve the case.

A year and a half went by.

During all this time, a wood expert named Arthur Koehler was working with the ladder. He knew that most of the ladder was pine wood. That type of pine grows in North Carolina and nearby states. There were marks in the wood made by a sawmill's knives. The knives were not working correctly.
310 They made grooves. Koehler wrote 1,598 letters to southern sawmills. Had they repaired their knives lately?

REREAD
Why did Koehler ask about the knives?

Finally, one mill answered yes. Koehler tested some of their boards. The boards had the same grooves. Koehler got the names of all the wood supply companies in the New York City area. He visited each one that had bought wood from that mill. One company in the Bronx had bought southern pine from the mill. Koehler

320 searched through thousands of receipts from that company. But he found no clues. The kidnapper may not have bought the wood there.

receipts
(rĭ sēts′)
n. proofs of purchase or money received

After months of work, Arthur Koehler was discouraged. His search only proved one fact. The kidnapper *could* have bought the wood from a company in the Bronx.

Policemen, detectives, and crime experts were working full time on the case. Every clue was

330 checked. Newspapers said the police had messed up the case. But this was not true. Perhaps if they had worked harder at the beginning, they might have captured John. But Lindbergh had asked them to keep away until his son was safe.

REREAD
Do you think the police should have gotten involved sooner? Explain your answer.

Then good luck came their way. On September 15, 1934, a green car pulled into a New York City filling station. The driver paid his bill with a ten-dollar gold

filling station
gas station

340 certificate. The clerk didn't see many of those any more. The government was changing to new money. He didn't want to be cheated with a fake bill. So he wrote the car's number on the bill. The bill was put in a bank.

A few days later, a bank teller was checking some money. The serial number showed that this bill was part of the ransom money. A note had been written on the bill. U-12-41, NY. Detectives found out that the bill had come from a filling station. The police
350 went there and learned about the man in the green car. They checked with the Motor Vehicle Bureau. The car was owned by Bruno Richard Hauptmann, 1279 East 222nd Street, Bronx, New York. They learned that Hauptmann was a German. He was also a carpenter.

THINK IT THROUGH

Which clues were the most helpful in finding a suspect? Use details from the article to support your answer.

FOCUS

Read to find out what happened to Bruno Hauptmann.

The police arrested Hauptmann. They found maps of New Jersey and Massachusetts in his house. Also, more than $14,000 of the ransom money had been hidden in Hauptmann's house and garage.
360 Hauptmann said a friend had given him the money. This friend had then gone back to Germany and had died there. There was no way Hauptmann could prove a friend had given him the money.

Charles Lindbergh came to the police station. The police had him wait outside a room. The door was slightly open. Lindbergh could not see into the room. Inside were a group of men. Each man would call out, "Here, Doctor." These were the words John had yelled the night he was given the ransom money.

370 Lindbergh would never forget the voice of his son's kidnapper.

First, one man called, "Here, Doctor." Lindbergh shook his head no. Then another shouted. Again Lindbergh said that was not the voice. Suddenly Lindbergh heard the same voice he had heard before. That was the man. That was John. The suspect who had shouted was Bruno Richard Hauptmann.

More clues were found inside the Hauptmann house. Someone had written a telephone number on 380 one of the inner walls. The number belonged to Condon. Also, Hauptmann read the Bronx *Home News*. The paper was delivered each day to his house.

The police found another important clue in Hauptmann's attic. A board had been removed from the floor. The wood matched a rung in the ladder. The rung fit into the floor. There were nail holes in the rung and the floor. They matched.

> **REREAD**
> Do you think there were enough clues to prove that Hauptmann kidnapped the baby? Why or why not?

390 Bruno Hauptmann's trial was held in New Jersey. Thousands crowded into the small town.

Charles Lindbergh was at the trial. Anne Lindbergh was too upset to be there. She came only to testify. At times, the people inside the court could not hear what was being said. Outside, the mob was screaming, "Kill Hauptmann, kill Hauptmann."

The trial lasted six weeks. Hauptmann was found guilty of murder. He was put to death on April 3, 1936. This was a little more than four years after 400 the kidnapping.

Anna Hauptmann says her husband did not kidnap the baby. Bruno Hauptmann never confessed to the crime. But the evidence was strong against him.

There are questions which have never been answered. How did Hauptmann know which room the baby was in? Did someone help Hauptmann? What about the Italian voice Condon heard on the phone when speaking to John? Why did Hauptmann keep saying and writing "we"?

410   Bruno Richard Hauptmann knew the answers to those questions. But he is dead. Perhaps we will never learn all the truth about the Lindbergh kidnapping.

Known Signature of Hauptmann	
Composite Signature – Individual letters from the Ransom Notes	

Top line: Hauptmann's signature from his auto registration card; *bottom line*: the same letters reconstructed from ransom notes

THINK IT THROUGH

1. Do you think Bruno Hauptmann was guilty? Find evidence in the article to support your opinion.
2. What questions have never been answered? Do you think the answers to these questions might have helped Hauptmann prove he was innocent? Explain your opinion.
3. In what ways did Lindbergh's fame affect the case?

Student Resources

Active Reading Strategies

Good readers think while they read. Every so often they stop and check their understanding. They predict what might happen next. They question what they're reading. After they finish, they think about what they read. Each strategy below happens in a good reader's mind while he or she is reading.

CONNECT
Think about your own life when you read something. Think of something similar that you have gone through, seen, or heard.

VISUALIZE
Make a picture in your mind of what the text says. Imagine you are looking at what is described.

PREDICT
Try to guess what will happen next in the story or article. Then read on to find out if your guess was correct.

QUESTION
Let questions come to your mind when you read. If something doesn't make sense, don't pass it by. Ask or write a question to yourself. Look for answers as you read.

CLARIFY
Slow down and make sure you understand what you're reading. Reread something to make sure you understood what it meant. As you read farther, expect to understand or to find out more.
These are ways you can clarify your understanding:
- Sum up what happened in your own words, or summarize.
- Identify the main idea of the paragraph, especially in nonfiction.
- Make inferences about what the author meant but didn't say. Read between the lines and use your own experience to figure it out.

EVALUATE
Form opinions about what you read as you read it. Evaluate again after you read it.

The examples on the pages that follow show how each strategy works. The examples are from "Phoenix Farm," by Jane Yolen. In this story, a girl and her family move to their grandmother's house after their apartment burns down. The father of the family had left before the fire. The girl takes only one thing with her—a nest with an egg in it.

CONNECT

Think about your own life when you read something. Think of something similar that you have gone through, seen, or heard.

> Neighbors of Grandma's had collected clothes for us. It made us feel like refugees, which is an awkward feeling that makes you prickly and cranky most of the time.

READER CONNECTS: I know that feeling—wearing someone else's leftovers. I hate that—they never fit right, and they're usually out of style. I feel like everybody knows they're secondhand clothes.

VISUALIZE

Make a picture in your mind of what the text says. Imagine you are looking at what is described.

> On the thirteenth step up from the bottom, tucked against the riser, was a nest. It was unburnt, unmarked, the straw that held it the rubbed-off gold of a wheat field. A piece of red string ran through it, almost as if it had been woven on a loom. In the nest was a single egg.

READER VISUALIZES: In my mind I see a dried straw nest in the corner of the step, protected from the wind. The nest has a red thread running through it. I wonder how the red thread got there. The egg is sitting in the nest.

Try to guess what will happen next in the story or article.

> Ann Marie suddenly said, "Look! Your egg is cracking open!"
> I looked up and she was right. We hadn't noticed anything before, because the crack had run along the red line. When I put my finger on the crack, it seemed to pulse.

READER PREDICTS: I think the egg is finally going to hatch. It will be a baby bird.

> How such a large bird got into such a tiny shell, I'll never know. But that's magic for you. It rose slowly out of the egg . . .

READER CHECKS PREDICTION: I was right! It was a baby bird. But it is surprising that it was so large.

QUESTION

Let questions come to your mind when you read. If something doesn't make sense, don't pass it by. Ask or write a question to yourself.

> I reached over and freed it, and it seared my fingers—the touch of the feather, not the shell. The bird's scarlet body and scaly golden feet pulsed with some kind of heat.

READER QUESTIONS: Why does a newborn bird give off heat? This is really strange. I've never heard of a bird being hot before. What's up with this bird? Maybe it will be explained later.

CLARIFY

Slow down and make sure you understand what you're reading. Reread something to make sure you understood what it meant. As you read farther, expect to understand or to find out more.

> It's been that way since Daddy died.
> Ran off. That's what Nicky says. A week before the fire. Couldn't take it. The recession and all. No job. No hope.
> Mama says it won't be forever, but I say he died. I can deal with it that way.

READER CLARIFIES: I don't understand—is her dad dead or not? She says he died, but Nicky says he ran away. The mom says it's temporary. Oh, I guess that last line explains it—she can only deal with him being gone by pretending he's dead.

EVALUATE

Form opinions about what you read as you read it. Evaluate again after you read it.

> Being thankful to someone doesn't make you like them.

READER EVALUATES: I agree—that's true. Somebody can try to buy your love but it doesn't work. You have to like the person, not their gifts.

Fiction

A work of fiction is a story that the writer made up. It could be based on a real event, or it could be totally imagined. The **elements of fiction** are the most important parts of fiction. They are the **characters, setting, plot,** and **theme.** These elements make up the skeleton of the story.

PLOT AT A GLANCE

The plot is the sequence of events in the story. Remember that the plot is about a problem that characters must solve. Most plots have the following parts.

Climax

Turning point of story; moment of most suspense. Brings a change to the main character

Rising Action

Problem (conflict) is introduced and developed; suspense builds

Introduction

Introduces characters and setting

Falling Action and Conclusion

Ties up loose ends; may resolve the conflict

The **Stranger**

by Sue Baugh

If you saw someone standing by the road on a cold, rainy night, would you stop to help?

One young man does and gets in real danger

FOCUS

A young man decides to help a stranger. Read to find out what he learns about her.

Late one Saturday night, a young man was driving home on a deserted stretch of road. He could hear the rain beating against the roof of his car. His headlights cut through a cold mist that clung to the trees on either side of the road. In the flashes of lightning, tree branches seemed like ghostly hands grasping for his car. He could feel the steady drumroll of thunder. What a night to be out! He

10 shivered and wished he were safe at home.

Suddenly, as he rounded a curve, his headlights lit up a young woman standing by the side of the road. Her hair and white dress were soaked from the rain. She

clung

(klŭng)
v. held on to something; past tense of cling

TERMS IN FICTION

- **Characters:** the people or animals in the story
- **Setting:** where and when the story happens
- **Plot:** what happens. The plot grows around a problem, or conflict. The story is about how the characters deal with this problem.
- **Conflict:** the struggle between two forces. **External conflict** happens between a character and an animal, nature, or person. **Internal conflict** happens in a character's mind, such as a hard choice or a guilty conscience.
- **Theme:** the message the writer wants to share with the reader
- **Narrator:** the voice telling the story to the reader
- **Point of view:** the way the narrator is telling the story

  First person point of view: The narrator is part of the story.

  Third person point of view: The narrator is not part of the story, but is reporting it.
- **Suspense:** the feeling of growing tension and excitement

TYPES OF FICTION

- **Short story:** a short work of fiction that can be read at one sitting. It has a few main characters and a single conflict.
- **Folk tale:** a story that was told over and over by word of mouth. The characters may be animals or people.
- **Historical fiction:** a story set in the past. It may refer to real people or events. The dialogue is usually made up.
- **Myth:** a very old story that was told by ancient people to explain to unknown. The characters often include gods or heroes.
- **Novel:** a long story that cannot be read at one sitting. A novel usually has many characters. The plot is complicated. A novel excerpt is one part of the novel.
- **Legend:** a story about a hero that has been told over and over. Most legends are based on a real person or event.
- **Horror story:** a short story that is meant to scare the reader

Nonfiction

Nonfiction is writing about real people, places, and events. It is mostly based on facts.

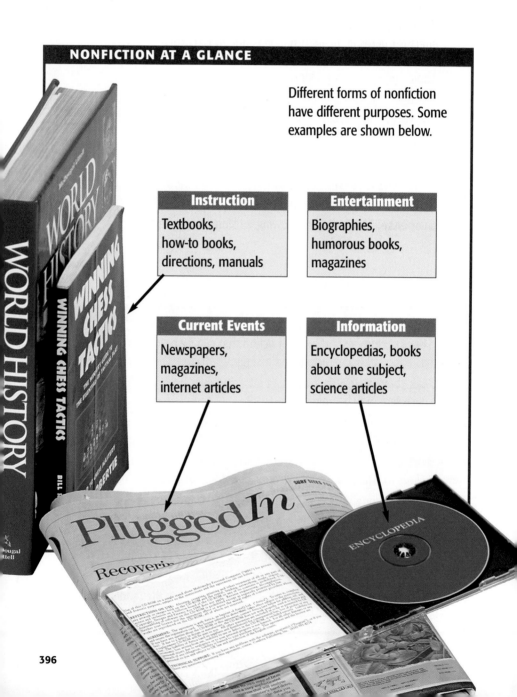

NONFICTION AT A GLANCE

Different forms of nonfiction have different purposes. Some examples are shown below.

Instruction	Entertainment
Textbooks, how-to books, directions, manuals	Biographies, humorous books, magazines

Current Events	Information
Newspapers, magazines, internet articles	Encyclopedias, books about one subject, science articles

TERMS IN NONFICTION

- **Facts:** statements that can be proved to be true
- **Opinions:** statements of personal belief that cannot be proved
- **Chronological order:** the order or sequence in which events happen in time
- **Cause and Effect:** The cause is the reason something happens. The effect is the result, or what happens due to the cause.
- **Visuals:** diagrams, maps, charts, photos, and pictures that are part of an article. They give facts using pictures and sketches with just a few words.

TYPES OF NONFICTION

- **Biography:** a true story about someone's life, written by someone else. It can cover the whole life or just one part.
- **Autobiography:** the true story of a person's life, written by that person.
- **Feature Article:** an article that gives facts about a current subject. It is often found in a newspaper or a magazine. Most include visuals.
- **Informative Article:** an article that gives facts about a subject. The article might be from an encyclopedia, textbook, or book.
- **Interview:** a conversation between two people. One asks the other questions. The answers are written in the form of an interview.
- **Essay:** a piece of writing about one subject. The writer might share an opinion or make a point.
- **True Account:** an article about a real event that is told as a story
- **Narrative Nonfiction:** an article about a real event told in chronological order. It is often historical.
- **Anecdote:** the true story of a small event, usually from the teller's life. An anecdote might be funny, to entertain, or a story that makes a point.

Drama

A drama, or play, is a story that is meant to be acted out. Actors present the play on stage. They act out the story for an audience.

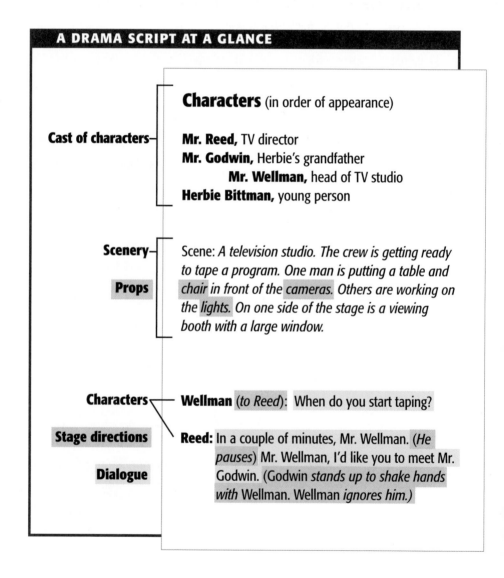

A DRAMA SCRIPT AT A GLANCE

Cast of characters—

Characters (in order of appearance)

Mr. Reed, TV director
Mr. Godwin, Herbie's grandfather
Mr. Wellman, head of TV studio
Herbie Bittman, young person

Scenery—
Props

Scene: *A television studio. The crew is getting ready to tape a program. One man is putting a table and chair in front of the cameras. Others are working on the lights. On one side of the stage is a viewing booth with a large window.*

Characters—
Stage directions
Dialogue

Wellman *(to Reed):* When do you start taping?

Reed: In a couple of minutes, Mr. Wellman. *(He pauses)* Mr. Wellman, I'd like you to meet Mr. Godwin. (Godwin *stands up to shake hands with* Wellman. Wellman *ignores him.)*

TERMS IN DRAMA

- **Stage:** the platform on which the actors perform
- **Script:** the written words for the play. This is the plan that everyone reads in order to perform the play.
- **Cast of Characters:** the list of people who play a part in the story
- **Dialogue:** the words the characters say
- **Stage Directions:** the directions to the actors and stage crew. These words tell how people should move and speak. They describe the scenery—the decoration on stage.
- **Acts and Scenes:** the parts of a play. These usually change when the time or the place changes.
- **Props:** the objects used on stage in the play, such as a telephone
- **Scenery:** the background art or structures on stage to help show the setting

A Stage

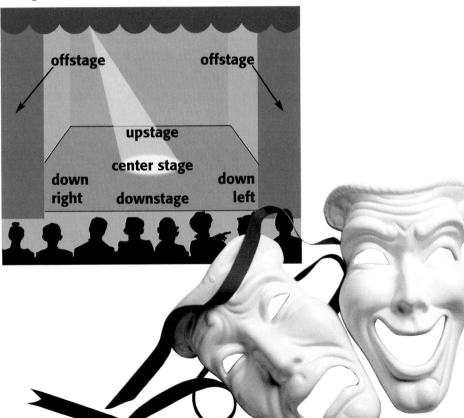

Poetry

Poetry is literature that uses a few words to tell about ideas, feelings, and images. The poet crafts the look of the poem and chooses words for their sound and meaning. Most poems are meant to be read aloud. Poems may or may not rhyme.

POETRY AT A GLANCE

Some People
By Rachel Field

Isn't it strange some people make   **line**
    You feel so tired inside,   **stanza**
Your thoughts begin to shrivel up
    Like leaves all brown and dried!   **rhyming words**

But when you're with some other ones,
    It's stranger still to find
Your thoughts as thick as fireflies   **simile**
   All shiny in your mind!   **visual imagery**

Some People
By Rachel Field

By Rachel Field

Some people make you feel good and some people don't. Do you know someone who belongs in this poem?

Isn't it strange some people make
    You feel so tired inside,
Your thoughts begin to shrivel up
    Like leaves all brown and dried!

5   But when you're with some other ones,
    It's stranger still to find
Your thoughts as thick as fireflies
    All shiny in your mind!

TERMS IN POETRY

- **Form:** the way a poem looks on the page; its shape
- **Lines:** Poets arrange words into lines. The lines may or may not be sentences.
- **Stanzas:** groups of lines in traditional poetry
- **Free verse:** poems without stanzas. They are written like conversation.
- **Rhyme:** sounds that are alike at the end of words, such as *make* and *rake.* Some poems have rhyming words at the end of lines. Some poems have rhymes in the middle of lines too.
- **Rhythm:** the beat of the poem. Patterns of strong (´) and weak (˘) syllables make up the beat.
- **Repetition:** the repeating of sounds, words, phrases, or lines in a poem.
- **Imagery:** words and phrases that appeal to the five senses—sight, hearing, smell, taste, and touch. Poets often use imagery to create pictures, tastes, or feelings in the reader's mind. For example, "The smell of sizzling bacon filled the air."
- **Figurative language:** words and phrases that help readers picture things in new ways. For example, "Snow crystals displayed a rainbow of colors in the sun."

   Simile: a comparison of two things using the words *like* or *as.* For example, "Confetti fell like rain."

   Metaphor: a comparison of two things without the words *like* or *as.* For example, "His face is a puzzle."

   Personification: a description of an animal or an object as if it were human or had human qualities. For example, "The dog smiled joyfully."
- **Speaker:** the voice that talks to the reader
- **Theme:** the message the poet gives the reader through the poem

Vocabulary Strategies

To learn the meaning of a new word, you can look it up in a dictionary. However, you're already an expert at learning new words without a dictionary. In fact, you probably learned most of the words you know one of these ways:

- from clues in the word's context—that is, the words and sentences surrounding it
- by breaking the words into parts
- by thinking about the meanings of similar words you already know

Using Context Clues

You can find clues to a word's meaning in its context, the words and sentences surrounding it. Often these clues can help you to infer, or figure out, the meaning of a word.

Definitions and Restatements. Sometimes the words near an unfamiliar word define the word or restate its meaning. Definitions and restatements may be set off by commas, dashes, parentheses, or a semicolon. They may also be signaled by words such as these:

Signal Words: Definition and Restatement			
which	in other words	that is	or
this means	is/are	is/are called	is/are defined as

Can you spot the words that tell you that *condiments* is being defined in this sentence?

The sauces and relishes used to flavor foods are called condiments.

If you picked the words *are called*, you are correct.

Below, the meaning of *condiments* is made clear in a restatement. What clues help you spot this restatement?

The **condiments**—that is, the sauces and relishes used to flavor foods—are on the side table.

Here both dashes and the words *that is* serve as signals.

Examples. Writers sometimes provide examples that reveal a word's meaning. For instance, look at the example of *stringent* here.

We have **stringent time limits**, including a 14-minute lunch period and three minutes between classes.

The examples of short amounts of time suggest that *stringent* means "strict, or tightly controlled."

These words often introduce examples.

Signal Words: Examples		
such as	like	for example
especially	for instance	including

Not all examples are signaled by clue words, however. Here, the examples of *amphibians* are introduced by a colon.

We have three **amphibians** in our science classroom: a toad, a frog, and a salamander.

Comparisons and Contrasts. Sometimes a sentence compares or contrasts a familiar word or phrase with a less familiar one. If you know one part in the pair, you can often figure out the other. The following words often signal comparison and contrast.

Signal Words: Comparison and Contrast			
like	as	in contrast to	on the other hand
likewise	similarly	instead of	not
		but	unlike

In the first sentence below, *like* signals the comparison between *shy* and *timid*. In the second sentence, *instead of* points out that *withdrawn* is the opposite of *talkative* and *pushy*.

> Like my shy friend, Anna, I am timid in large groups.

> With just Anna, I tend to be talkative and pushy instead of withdrawn.

Cause and Effect. In a cause-and-effect relationship, one event makes another one happen. Knowing this can help you figure out an unfamiliar word.

> Because the weeds in the garden are so profuse, the flowers can't grow.

The effect is that the flowers can't grow. So the cause must be that there are too many weeds. This tells you that profuse means "many in number."

Signal Words: Cause and Effect		
because	consequently	so
since	therefore	as a result

General Context. Sometimes the general context that a word appears in provides clues to a word's meaning. Photos, charts, signs, or even a whole paragraph can serve as the general context. Notice how the details in this passage help you understand the word *seared*.

> Another shudder, and the bird stood free of the egg entirely, though a piece of shell still clung to the tip of one wing. I reached over and freed it, and it seared my fingers—the touch of the feather, not the shell. The bird's scarlet body and scaly golden feet pulsed with some kind of heat.
>
> "What are you," I whispered, then stuck my burnt fingers in my mouth to soothe them.
>
> – Jane Yolen, *Phoenix Farm*

The details about touch, heat, and burnt fingers help you understand that the word seared means "burned," or "scorched."

Analyzing Word Parts

Words can be made up of various kinds of parts: base words, word roots, prefixes, and suffixes. You can often figure out the meaning of an unfamiliar word from the meanings of its parts.

Base Words. A **base word** is a complete word that can stand alone. However, other words or word parts may be added to base words to form new words.

fear + less = fearless

art + ist = artist

You can form a **compound word** by connecting two base words. The meaning of the new compound word is often, but not always, related to the meanings of the base words.

BASE + BASE = COMPOUND WORD

skate + board = skateboard

sand + paper = sandpaper

Prefixes and Suffixes. A **prefix** is a word part attached to the beginning of a word or a word part. Prefixes change the meanings of words.

Common Prefixes		
Prefix	**Meaning**	**Examples**
co-, com-, con-	together	coworker, compound, contribute
de-	remove, reverse	depart, defrost
in-, il-	not	incorrect, illogical
mis-	bad, wrong	mistake, misuse
re-	back, again	replace, rethink
un-	the opposite of	untie, undrinkable

A **suffix** is a word attached to the end of the word or a word part. The suffix usually determines the word's part of speech—that is, whether the word is a noun, verb, adjective, or adverb.

Common Suffixes			
	Suffix	**Meaning**	**Examples**
Nouns	-er, -ist, -or	doer, performer	runner, columnist
	-ation, -ment	action, process	admiration, astonishment
	-ism	idea, theory	patriotism
	-ity, -ness	condition, quality, state	agility, shyness
Verbs	-ate	to act upon	irritate
	-en	to become	tighten
	-ize	to cause to be	terrorize
Adjectives	-able, -ible	able, inclined to	reasonable, horrible
	-ant	to act in a certain way	important
	-ful	full of, resembling	wonderful
Adverbs	-ily, -ly	in the manner of, like	craftily, slowly

Notice how the base words below take on different meanings as prefixes and suffixes are added to them.

PREFIX +	BASE +	SUFFIX =	NEW WORD
un	fair	ness	unfairness
in	excuse	able	inexcusable
dis	appear	ance	disappearance
re	mind	er	reminder

You may need to change the spelling of some base words when adding suffixes: **excuse + able = excusable**.

Word Roots. Word roots, like base words, provide the basic meaning of a word. Unlike base words, however, word roots cannot stand alone. A prefix, a suffix, a base word, or another root must be added to make a word.

Many root words in English come from ancient Greek or Latin. Becoming familiar with the meanings of common root words can help you figure out the meanings of unfamiliar words.

Common Greek Roots		
Root	**Meaning**	**Examples**
auto	self, same	automobile, autograph
geo	earth	geography, geometry
gram	something written	diagram, grammar
log	word, study	dialogue, biology
meter, metr	measure	thermometer, metric
scop	see	microscope, telescope
tele	far, distant	telephone, telegraph
zo	animal	zoology, zookeeper

Common Latin Roots		
Root	**Meaning**	**Examples**
cent	hundred	centipede, century
circ	ring	circle, circus
dic, dict	speak, say	dictate, dictionary
ject	throw, hurl	project, reject
oper	work	operate, cooperate
pass	step	passage, trespass
port	carry	portable, support
scrib, script	write	prescription, inscribe

If you don't know what a word part means, you can look it up. Most dictionaries include entries for word roots, prefixes, and suffixes.

Understanding Related Words

Sometimes groups of words are similar in structure or meaning. Knowing this can help you understand and use them.

Word Families. A **word family** is a group of words that share the same root. This word family shares the Latin root *fin*, from *finis*, meaning "end," "limit," or "boundary."

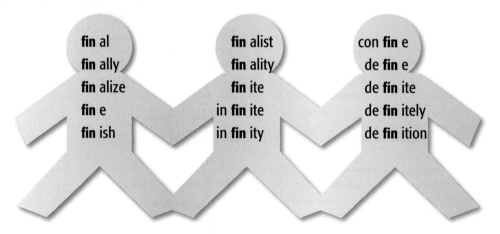

fin al
fin ally
fin alize
fin e
fin ish

fin alist
fin ality
fin ite
in fin ite
in fin ity

con fin e
de fin e
de fin ite
de fin itely
de fin ition

You can use the meanings of familiar words from a word family to figure out what their root means. You can also use their meanings to understand unfamiliar words that share that root.

Here's How **Using Word Families**

- To figure out the meaning of the word *infinite*, first look for the root: **finis or fin**

- Think of other words with the same root, such as *final, finish,* and *finally.*

- Figure out the meaning they share: **"end"**

- Think about prefixes and suffixes that may change meaning: *in-* = "not," *-ite* = "from"

- From these clues, you can make a guess that *infinite* means **"something that has no end."**

Synonyms. Synonyms are words that have similar meanings. For example, all of the words following the sentence below are synonyms for *ran*. However, since their meanings are slightly different, replacing *ran* with any one of them changes the meaning of the sentence. Try it and see.

I <u>ran</u> up the beach.

jogged   hurried   dashed   raced

As you learn new words, pay attention to the slight differences in their meanings. Being aware of these differences can help you choose the words more precisely. For example, *handsome* and *attractive* are both synonyms for *beautiful,* but which of the three would you use to decribe a perfect summer day?

Denotations and Connotations. It's not enough to be aware of a word's dictionary definition, or **denotation.** You also have to be aware of its **connotations,** or the feelings it's meant to create in a person's mind. For example, would you rather be called skinny or slim? Would you describe your new jacket as inexpensive or cheap?

Here are two examples of how related words can send very different messages.

When You Read...	You Think...
Marcie is thrifty.	Marcie is careful about how she spends her money.
Marcie is cheap.	Marcie hates to spend money, even for a good reason.
That plan is daring.	The plan is risky, but bold.
That plan is reckless.	The plan is dangerous, and it's wrong to go ahead.

Using References

What do you do if you come across a new word whose meaning you can't figure out from context clues or word parts? You could ask someone what it means—or you could look up the word in a dictionary.

Dictionaries You probably know that **dictionaries** are available in print or online. They can tell you more that just what words mean. Look at the following dictionary entries to see some of the many details a dictionary can provide about a word.

curable | currency

cu·ri·ous (kyŏŏr' ē əs) *adj.* **1.** Eager to learn more: *curious detectives.* **2.** Arousing interest because of strangeness: *We found a curious shell at the beach.* [First written down about 1340 in Middle English and spelled *curiouse,* from Latin *cūriōsus,* careful, inquisitive, from *cūra,* care.] **–cu'ri·ous·ly** *adv.* **–cu'ri·ous·ness** *n.*

Synonyms: curious, inquisitive, snoopy, nosy. Antonym: indifferent.

curl (kûrl) *v.* **curled, curl·ing, curls.** *–tr.* **1.** To twist or form into coils or ringlets: *curl one's hair.* **2.** To make curved or twisted: *I curled the string around a pencil.* *–intr.* **1.** To form ringlets or curls: *Her hair curls when it dries.* **2.** To move in a curve or spiral: *Smoke curled from the chimney.* *–n.* **1.** A coil or ringlet of hair. **2.** Something with a spiral or coiled shape: *a curl of smoke.* **3.** A weightlifting exercise in which a barbell is raised to the chest or shoulder and lowered without moving the upper arms, shoulders, or back. *–idiom.* **curl up.** To sit or lie down with the legs drawn up: *He curled up on the sofa to read.*

GUIDE WORDS: First and Last Entry Words on Page

ENTRY WORD DIVIDED INTO SYLLABLES

PRONUNCIATION GUIDE

PART OF SPEECH

WORD ORIGINS

OTHER FORMS OF THE WORD

SYNONYMS

ANTONYM

DEFINITION

SAMPLE SENTENCE

IDIOM

—adapted from *The American Heritage Student Dictionary*

Often, a word has more than one meaning. How do you choose the right one from the dictionary?

| **Here's How** | **Choosing the Right Definition** |

1. Rule out definitions that don't make sense. If you're reading about a girl getting ready for a party, for instance, you could rule out the third definition of curl.

2. Check the part of speech. In "Sasha wants to wear her hair in curls," the word curls is a noun, so you would only look for definitions of the noun form.

Thesauruses A **thesaurus** is a dictionary of synonyms. Some thesauruses also include definitions, sample sentences, and **antonyms**. These are words that have opposite meanings to that of the entry word.

When you need to find a replacement for a word, look up the word in a thesaurus. Entries are often listed in alphabetical order.

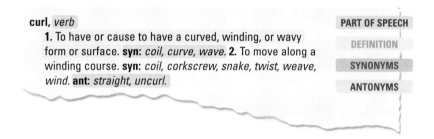

curl, *verb*
1. To have or cause to have a curved, winding, or wavy form or surface. **syn:** *coil, curve, wave.* **2.** To move along a winding course. **syn:** *coil, corkscrew, snake, twist, weave, wind.* **ant:** *straight, uncurl.*

PART OF SPEECH

DEFINITION

SYNONYMS

ANTONYMS

Synonym Finders. A **synonym finder** is a tool that's often in word-processing software. It enables you to display synonyms for a highlighted word—but does not tell you as much as a thesaurus does.

Glossaries. A **glossary** is a list of specialized terms and their definitions. Many books, especially textboooks and nonfiction books, contain glossaries—usually at the back of the book.

A

admiration (ăd' mə rā' shən) *n.* wonder
admiración *s.* maravilla

apology (ə pŏl' ə jē) *n.* act of saying one is sorry for doing something wrong
disculpa *s.* acción de pedir excusas por algo mal hecho

arenas (ə rē' nəz) *n.* buildings where people watch sports events or shows
arenas *s.* edificios donde se realizan competencias deportivas

astronomy (ə strŏn' ə mē) *n.* the study of planets and stars
astronomía *s.* estudio de los planetas y las estrellas

awkward (ôk' wərd) *adj.* clumsy
torpe *adj.* desmañado

axle (ăk' səl) *n.* rod connecting a pair of wheels
eje *s.* barra que une un par de ruedas

B

backstretch (băk'strĕch') *n.* straight part of the track, on the opposite side from the finish line
largada *s.* pista opuesta a la recta final

C

cabinet (kăb' ə nĭt) *n.* piece of furniture with shelves or drawers
gabinete *s.* mueble con cajones o estantes

calisthenics (kăl'ĭs thĕn'ĭks) *n.* physical exercises such as pushups and sit-ups
calistenia *s.* ejercicios físicos como sentadillas y lagartijas

clamping (klăm' pĭng) *adj.* holding
sujetando *adj.* agarrando

cocky (kŏk' ē) *adj.* too sure of oneself
presumido *adj.* engreído

comical (kŏm' ĭ kəl) *adj.* funny
cómico *adj.* divertido

conceal (kən sēl') *v.* hide
ocultar *v.* esconder

contract (kŏn' trăkt') *n.* legal agreement
contrato *s.* acuerdo legal

convicts (kŏn' vĭkts') *n.* people found guilty of crimes and sent to jail
convictos *s.* sentenciados a la cárcel por un delito

courage (kûr' ĭj) *n.* ability to face danger
valor *s.* capacidad de responder al peligro

courses (kôr' sĭz) *n.* tracks on which races are held
pistas *s.* superficies para carreras

crossly (krôs' lē) *adv.* in an angry way
malhumoradamente *adv.* con enfado

curse (kûrs) *n.* magic spell to cause something bad to happen to someone
maldición *s.* hechizo que causa algo malo

D

dazed (dāzd) *adj.* confused or shocked because of a heavy blow
aturdido *adj.* confundido por un golpe fuerte

dejectedly (dĭ jĕk' tĭd lē) *adv.* sadly
desanimadamente *adv.* tristemente

depressed (dĭ prĕst') *adj.* unhappy, sad
deprimido *adj.* triste

determined (dĭ tûr' mĭnd) *adj.* firm in pursuing a goal
resuelto *adj.* firme en perseverar una meta

disabling (dĭs ā' blĭng) *n.* hurting badly
incapacitando *s.* hiriendo

distracted (dǐ străk' tǐd) *adj.* having one's attention turned to
something else
distraído *adj.* que aparta la atención del objeto a que la aplicaba

distress (dǐ strěs') *n.* trouble
apuro *s.* peligro

doom (dōōm) *n.* very bad ending
fracaso *s.* mal final

double-crossed (dŭb'əl krôst') *v.* tricked; past tense of *double-cross*
traicionado *v.* engañado; pasado de *double-cross/traicionar*

dreading (drěd' ǐng) *v.* afraid of
temiendo *v.* sintiendo miedo

drills (drǐlz) *n.* practices
ejercicios *s.* prácticas

E

emperor (ĕm' pər ər) *n.* male ruler of a large area
emperador *s.* gobernante de un imperio

erupted (ǐ rŭp' tǐd) *v.* exploded; past tense of *erupt*
hizo erupción *v.* explotó; pasado de *erupt/hacer erupción*

estate (ǐ stāt') *n.* large house surrounded by a lot of land
finca *s.* casa grande rodeada de tierras

examined (ǐg zăm' ǐnd) *v.* looked carefully at; past tense of *examine*
examinó *v.* miró con atención; pasado de *examine/examinar*

expression (ǐk sprěsh' ən) *n.* look
expresión *s.* mirada

F

falsehoods (fâls' hōōdz') *n.* lies
falsedades *s.* mentiras

famine (făm′ ĭn) *n.* shortage of food
hambruna *s.* escasez de comida

fiery (fīr′ ē) *adj.* full of fire
ardiente *adj.* lleno de fuego

figure (fĭg′ yər) *n.* shape of a person
figura *s.* figura de una persona

foreigner (fôr′ ə nər) *n.* person from another country or place
extranjero *s.* persona de otro país o de otro lugar

fussy (fŭs′ ē) *adj.* hard to please
exigente *adj.* difícil de complacer

G

gaining (gā′ nĭng) *v.* getting closer
alcanzando *v.* acercándose

glared (glârd) *v.* looked in an angry way; past tense of *glare*
miró ferozmente *v.* miró con furia; pasado de *glare/mirar ferozmente*

H

hardware (härd′ wâr′) *n.* tools
quincalla *s.* herramientas

horror (hôr′ ər) *n.* great disgust
horror *s.* espanto

I

iceberg (īs′ bûrg′) *n.* large body of floating ice. Most of the ice is below the water.
iceberg *s.* gran masa de hielo flotante, en su mayoría bajo el agua

immigrant (ĭm′ ĭ grənt) *n.* person who moves to another country to live
inmigrante *s.* persona que llega a vivir a un país distinto al suyo

impatiently (ĭm pā′ shənt lē) *adv.* in an irritated manner
impacientemente *adv.* de una forma irritada

implored (ĭm plôrd′) *v.* begged; past tense of *implore*
imploró *v.* suplicó; pasado de *implore/implorar*

impress (ĭm prĕs′) *v.* make people have a good opinion of you
impresionar *v.* causar una buena opinión

intend (ĭn tĕnd′) *v.* plan
proponerse *v.* planear

intrigued (ĭn trēgd′) *adj.* interested; past tense of *intrigue*
intrigado *adj.* interesado; pasado de *intrigue/intrigar*

irritated (ĭr′ ĭ tā′ tĭd) *adj.* angry
irritado *adj.* molesto

J

jabbering (jăb′ ər ĭng) *v.* talking very fast
farfullando *v.* hablando muy rápidamente

L

lap (lăp) *n.* one complete trip around a track
vuelta *s.* recorrido completo de una pista

M

meters (mē′ tərz) *n.* units of measure; each one is equal to 39.37 inches
metros *s.* unidades de medida equivalentes a 100 cm

mind (mīnd) *v.* obey
hacer caso *v.* obedecer

misfortune (mĭs fôr′ chən) *n.* bad luck
desgracia *s.* mala suerte

modest (mŏd′ ĭst) *adj.* small
modesto *adj.* pequeño

N

navigator (năv′ ĭ gā′ tər) *n.* person who plans and records where an airplane flies
navegante *s.* persona que planea y toma notas del vuelo de un avión

P

parachutes (păr′ ə sho͞ots′) *n.* equipment that slows a person's fall from an airplane
paracaídas *s.* equipo que reduce la velocidad de la caída desde un avión

patrol (pə trōl′) *n.* group assigned to keep watch over an area
patrulla *s.* grupo que vigila

personal (pûr′ sə nəl) *adj.* used by one person only
personal *adj.* que lo usa una sola persona

peso (pā′ sō) *n.* Mexican money that is similar to a dollar in the United States
peso *s.* moneda mexicana

petition (pə tĭsh′ ən) *n.* written request to the government from a person or group
petición *s.* solicitud escrita de un individuo o un grupo al gobierno

physics (fĭz′ ĭks) *n.* science of how matter and energy act together. Sir Isaac Newton developed many physics concepts.
física *s.* ciencia que estudia el comportamiento de la materia y la energía. Sir Isaac Newton propuso muchos conceptos de física.

plot (plŏt) *n.* secret plan
complot *s.* plan secreto

politicians (pŏl′ ĭ tĭsh′ ənz) *n.* people who hold or run for government offices
políticos *s.* personas que se presentan y ocupan cargos públicos

predictions (prĭ dĭk' shənz) *n.* statements about what is going to happen
predicciones *s.* declaraciones sobre lo que puede suceder

preference (prĕf' ər əns) *n.* choice of one thing over another
preferencia *s.* selección de una cosa por encima de otra

presumed (prĭ zo͞omd') *v.* thought something was true; past tense of *presume*
asumido *v.* dado por cierto; pasado de *presume/asumir*

profit (prŏf' ĭt) *n.* money left after spending for supplies and equipment
ganancia *s.* dinero que queda después de pagar equipo y gastos

pulse (pŭls) *v.* beat regularly
pulsar *v.* latir

pushy (po͝osh' ē) *adj.* too bold
atrevido *adj.* descarado

R

raging (rā' jĭng) *adj.* wild and powerful
violento *adj.* furioso, desbocado

rants (rănts) *v.* speaks in an angry, violent way
despotrica *v.* habla en una manera violenta y rabiosa

reassure (rē' ə sho͝or') *v.* make someone feel sure
tranquilizar *v.* alentar

receipts (rĭ sēts') *n.* proofs of purchase or money received
recibos *s.* comprobantes de haber recibido dinero o artículos

recession (rĭ sĕsh' ən) *n.* period of time when businesses lose money
recesión *s.* época de pocas ganancias para los negocios

recognize (rĕk' əg nīz) *v.* know
reconocer *v.* saber

reconciliation (rĕk' ən sĭl' ē ā' shən) *n.* act of getting back together after a fight or argument
reconciliación *s.* reunión de personas que estaban disgustados

refugees (rĕf′ yŏŏ jēz′) *n.* people who must leave home to find protection or shelter somewhere else
refugiado *s.* quienes se van forzados de su hogar a otra parte en busca de protección

responsible (rĭ spŏn′ sə bəl) *adj.* able to be trusted to do the right thing
responsable *adj.* que cumple

retire (rĭ tīr′) *v.* stop working
jubilarse *v.* dejar de trabajar a cierta edad

rookie (rŏŏk′ ē) *n.* first year player
novato *s.* jugador de primer año

S

satellite (săt′ l īt′) *n.* man-made object that circles the earth
satélite *s.* objeto construido por el ser humano que da vueltas alrededor de la Tierra

seared (sîrd) *v.* burned; past tense of *sear*
chamuscado *v.* quemado; pasado de *sear/chamuscar*

serious (sîr′ ē əs) *adj.* important
serio *adj.* importante

shortage (shôr′ tĭj) *n.* not enough of something
escasez *s.* falta

smuggle (smŭg′ əl) *v.* take secretly
contrabandear *v.* transportar en secreto

snorted (snôr′ tĭd) *v.* breathed through the nose in a noisy way like a pig or horse; past tense of snort
roncó *v.* respiró con ruido; pasado de snort/roncar

spleen (splēn) *n.* organ in the human body. The spleen helps to clean the blood and also produces white blood cells.
bazo *s.* órgano del cuerpo humano que limpia la sangre y produce glóbulos blancos

splint (splĭnt) *v.* tie sticks to, for support
entablillar *v.* inmovilizar para dar apogo

sterilizer (stĕr′ ə lī′ zər) *n.* machine that kills germs
esterilizador *s.* aparato que mata los microbios

stirred (stûrd) *v.* caused something to happen; past tense of *stir*
provocó *v.* causó; pasado de *stir/provocar*

stoop (sto͞op) *n.* small porch
pórtico *s.* porche pequeño

strokes (strōkz) *v.* moves the arms and legs to swim
da brazadas *v.* mueve los brazos para nadar

suitable (soo̅′ tə bəl) *adj.* right for the purpose
adecuado *adj.* útil para un fin

suits (soo̅ts) *v.* pleases
agrada *v.* gusta

T

tantrum (tăn′ trəm) *n.* sudden, violent display of anger
pataleta *s.* ataque de furia repentina

tombs (too̅mz) *n.* rooms where people are buried
tumbas *s.* sepulcros o sepulturas

torture (tôr′ chər) *v.* make someone suffer a lot of pain
torturar *v.* hacer sufrir mucho

U

unemployed (ŭn′ ĕm ploid′) *adj.* without a job
desempleado *adj.* que no tiene trabajo

V

vanity (văn′ ĭ tē) *n.* something that one takes great pride in
vanidad *s.* orgullo exagerado

vibrations (vī brā′ shəns) *n.* shaking movements
vibraciones *s.* movimientos rápidos de un lado a otro

volunteers (vŏl´ ən tîrz´) *n.* people who choose to work without being paid
  voluntarios *s.* quienes trabajan sin esperar pago

W

whirled (hwûrld) *v.* spun around very fast; past tense of whirl
  giró *v.* dio una vuelta muy rápido; pasado de whirl/girar

wicked (wĭk´ ĭd) *adj.* bad; evil
  malvado *adj.* malo; perverso

Index of Authors and Titles

K

L

M

N, O, P

R

S

T

V, W

Acknowledgments

Literature

UNIT ONE

New Readers Press: "Midas and the Golden Touch," from *Timeless Tales: Myths* by Tana Reiff. Copyright © 1991 by Tana Reiff. Used by permission of New Readers Press, U.S. Publishing Division of Laubach Literacy International.

HarperCollins Publishers: "The Green Ribbon," from *In a Dark, Dark Room and Other Scary Stories* by Alvin Schwartz. Text copyright © 1984 by Alvin Schwartz. Used by permission of HarperCollins Publishers.

Scholastic: "The Fish Story" by Mary Lou Brooks in *Scholastic Action,* May 6, 1983. Copyright © 1983 by Scholastic Inc. Reprinted by permission.

Robert Scott: "The Turtle and the Swans," from *The Oxford Book of Animal Stories,* edited by Dennis Pepper. Copyright © 1994 by Robert Scott. Reprinted by permission of the author.

UNIT TWO

Scholastic: "River Moon" from *This Big Sky* by Pat Mora. Published by Scholastic Press, a division of Scholastic, Inc. Copyright © 1998 by Pat Mora. Reprinted by permission.

Marian Reiner, Literary Agent: "Winter Dark," from *I Thought I Heard the City* by Lilian Moore. Copyright © 1969 by Lilian Moore. Copyright renewed 1977 by Lilian Moore Reavin. Used by permission of Marian Reiner for the author.

Scribner: "The Falling Star," from *The Collected Poems of Sara Teasdale.* Copyright © 1930 by Sara Teasdale Filsinger; copyright renewed © 1958 by Morgan Guaranty Trust Company of New York. Reprinted with the permission of Scribner, a division of Simon & Schuster.

Dial Books for Young Readers: "Genius," from *A Dime a Dozen* by Nikki Grimes. Copyright © 1998 by Nikki Grimes. Used by permission of Dial Books for Young Readers, a division of Penguin Group (USA) Inc.

Alfred A. Knopf: "Dreams," from *Collected Poems* by Langston Hughes. Copyright © 1994 by the Estate of Langston Hughes. Reprinted by permission of Alfred A. Knopf, a division of Random House Inc.

UNIT THREE

Random House Children's Books: From *The Titanic: Lost . . . and Found* by Judy Donnelly. Text copyright © 1987 by Judy Donnelly Gross. Reprinted by permission of Random House Children's Books, a division of Random House, Inc.

Grosset & Dunlap: From *Volcanoes: Mountains That Blow Their Tops* by Nicholas Nirgiotis. Copyright © 1996 by Nicholas Nirgiotis. Used by permission of Grosset & Dunlap, an imprint of Penguin Books for Young Readers, a division of Penguin Group (USA) Inc.

Ashley Bryan: "The Hurricane," from *Sing to the Sun* by Ashley Bryan. Text and illustrations copyright © 1992 by Ashley Bryan. Reprinted by permission of the author.

Grosset & Dunlap: "Water Woman," from *Wonder Women of Sports* by S. A. Kramer. Text copyright © 1997 by S. A. Kramer. Used by permission of Grosset & Dunlap, Inc., an imprint of Penguin Books for Young Readers, a division of Penguin Group (USA) Inc.

Marian Reiner, Literary Agent: "The Swimmer," from *A Tree Place and Other Poems* by Constance Levy. Copyright © 1994 by Constance Kling Levy. Used by permission of Marian Reiner for the author.

Enslow Publishers: *Satchel Paige: The Best Arm in Baseball* by Patricia and Fredrick McKissack. Copyright © 1992 by Enslow Publishers, Inc., Berkeley Heights, N.J.

Samuel W. Allen: "To Satch" by Samuel W. Allen. Copyright © by Samuel W. Allen. Reprinted by permission of the author.

UNIT EIGHT

HarperCollins Publishers: *City Green* by DyAnne DiSalvo-Ryan. Copyright © 1994 by DyAnne DiSalvo-Ryan. Reprinted by permission of HarperCollins Publishers.

Dial Books for Young Readers: "I Am Rosa Parks," from *I Am Rosa Parks* by Rosa Parks with Jim Haskins. Copyright © 1997 by Rosa Parks. Used by permission of Dial Books for Young Readers, an imprint of Penguin Putnam Books for Young Readers, a division of Penguin Group (USA) Inc.

Franklin Watts: "You Dirty Rat," from *True Spy Stories* by James B. Sweeney. Copyright © 1981 by James B. Sweeney. All rights reserved. Reprinted by permission of Franklin Watts, an imprint of Scholastic Library Publishing, Inc.

UNIT NINE

Atheneum Books for Young Readers: "Before the Game," from *That Sweet Diamond: Baseball Poems* by Paul B. Janeczko. Copyright © 1998 Paul B. Janeczko. Reprinted with the permission of Atheneum Books for Young Readers, an imprint of Simon & Schuster Children's Publishing Division.

Curtis Brown Ltd.: "Karate Kid" by Jane Yolen. Copyright © 1996 by Jane Yolen. First appeared in *Opening Days: Sports Poems,* edited by Lee Bennett Hopkins. Published by Harcourt Brace and Company. Reprinted by permission of Curtis Brown Ltd. All rights reserved.

"Final Score" by Lee Bennett Hopkins. Copyright © 1996 by Lee Bennett Hopkins. First appeared in *Opening Days: Sports Poems* edited by Lee Bennett Hopkins. Published by Harcourt Brace and Company. Reprinted by permission of Curtis Brown Ltd. All rights reserved.

Simon & Schuster Books for Young Readers: "This Team the Silver Spokes," from *The Basket Counts* by Arnold Adoff. Copyright © 2000 by Arnold Adoff. Reprinted with the permission of Simon & Schuster Books for Young Readers, an imprint of Simon & Schuster Children's Publishing Division.

Marian Reiner, Literary Agent: "The Sidewalk Racer," from *The Sidewalk Racer: And Other Poems of Sports and Motion* by Lillian Morrison. Copyright © 1965, 1967, 1968, 1977 by Lillian Morrison. Used by permission of Marian Reiner for the author.

UNIT TEN

Carolrhoda Books: *Allen Jay and the Underground Railroad* by Marlene Targ Brill. Copyright © 1993 by Marlene Targ Brill. Published by Carolrhoda Books Inc., a division of the Lerner Publishing Group. Used by permission of the publisher. All rights reserved.

Prentice-Hall: "The Gift of the Magi," adapted for *Great American Stories* I by C. G. Draper. Copyright © 1985 by Prentice-Hall, Inc. All rights reserved to Pearson Education.

HarperCollins Publishers: "Harriet Tubman," from *Honey, I Love* by Eloise Greenfield. Text copyright © 1978 by Eloise Greenfield. Used by permission of HarperCollins Publishers.

Scholastic: *One Grain of Rice: A Mathematical Folktale* by Demi. Copyright © 1997 by Demi. Published by Scholastic Press, a division of Scholastic Inc. Reprinted by permission.

Dial Books for Young Readers: "Mountain Medicine," from *Mary on Horseback* by Rosemary Wells. Copyright © 1998 by Rosemary Wells. Used by permission of Dial Books for Young Readers, an imprint of Penguin Books for Young Readers, a division of Penguin Group (USA) Inc.

UNIT ELEVEN

New Readers Press: "The Trojan War," from *Timeless Tales: Myths,* retold by Tana Reiff. Copyright © 1991 New Readers Press, U.S. Publishing Division of Laubach Literacy International. Used by permission.

UNIT TWELVE

Little, Brown and Company: "Miles," from *Space Station Seventh* Grade by Jerry Spinelli. Copyright © 1982 by Jerry Spinelli. Reprinted by permission of Little, Brown and Company, Inc.

Scholastic: "Helen Keller," from *Helen Keller* by Margaret Davidson. Text copyright © 1969 by Margaret Davidson. Reprinted by permission of Scholastic Inc.

Franklin Watts: "The Lindbergh Kidnapping," from *Great Unsolved Cases* by Arnold Madison. Text copyright © 1978 by Arnold Madison. All rights reserved. Reprinted by permission of Franklin Watts, an imprint of Scholastic Library Publishing, Inc.

Art Credits

COVER

Boy Copyright © David Waldorf/FPG International/Getty Images; *volcano* Copyright © Schafer & Hill/Getty Images; *plane* Copyright © George Hall/Corbis; *face* Copyright © Julia Smith/Getty Images; *pagoda* Copyright © Keren Su/FPG International/Getty Images; *Trojan Horse* © Bettmann/CORBIS; *swimming* Copyright © AP Photo/Dennis Paquin; *baseball* Digital Imagery copyright © 2001 PhotoDisc, Inc.; *sunflower* Digital Imagery copyright © 2001 PhotoDisc, Inc.; *baseball* Copyright © David Madison/Getty Images; *karate* Digital Imagery copyright © 2001 PhotoDisc, Inc.; *skateboarders* Copyright © Michael Wong/Getty Images; *Book background* Photo by Sharon Hoogstraten.

UNIT ONE

2 Copyright © David Waldorf/FPG International/Getty Images; **4** Copyright © Olney Vasan/Getty Images; **4** *background,* **6-7** *background, foreground,* **8, 11** Digital Imagery copyright © 2001 PhotoDisc, Inc.; **11** Illustration by Jericho Hernandez; **11, 12** *background* Digital Imagery copyright © 2001 PhotoDisc, Inc.; **12** Copyright © David Waldorf/FPG International/Getty Images; **14-15** Copyright © David Waldorf/FPG International/Getty Images; **18** Illustration by Jericho Hernandez.

UNIT TWO

25 *top* Copyright © Phil Banko/Getty Images; *bottom* Copyright © James Henry/Getty Images; **26** Copyright © Anne-Marie Weber/FPG International/Getty Images; **27, 28** *foreground* Digital Imagery copyright © 2001 PhotoDisc, Inc.; **28** *background* Copyright © James Henry/Getty Images; **29** Copyright © James Henry/Getty Images; **29** *background* Digital Imagery copyright © 2001 PhotoDisc, Inc.; **30** Illustration by Jericho Hernandez; **32** Copyright © Phil Banko/Getty Images; **33** *top* Illustration by Jericho Hernandez; *bottom,* **34, 36** Digital Imagery copyright © 2001 PhotoDisc, Inc.

UNIT THREE

39 Digital Imagery copyright © 2001 PhotoDisc, Inc.; **40** Copyright © Ralph White/Corbis; **41, 43** The Granger Collection, New York; **47** Copyright © Ralph White/Corbis; **48** Copyright © Schafer & Hill/Getty Images; **53** Copyright © Vince Streano/Corbis; **54** Copyright © Roger Ressmeyer/Corbis; **56** Digital Imagery copyright © 2001 PhotoDisc, Inc.; **57, 59** National Oceanic and Atmospheric Administration/Department of Commerce; **60** Copyright © George Hall/Corbis; **62** Courtesy of the Hurricane Hunters; **64** "The Hurricane", from *Sing to the Sun* by Ashley Bryan. Illustration copyright © 1992 by Ashley Bryan. Reprinted by permission of the author.

UNIT FOUR

67 Photo by Sharon Hoogstraten; **68** Copyright © Todd Eckelman/FPG International/Getty Images; **69** Jeff Greenberg/PhotoEdit; **73, 74, 77, 79** Photo by Sharon Hoogstraten; **78** Copyright © Todd Eckelman/FPG International/Getty Images; **80** *left* Copyright © Julia Smith/Getty Images; *right* Digital Imagery copyright © 2001 PhotoDisc, Inc.; **81, 84, 89** Digital Imagery copyright © 2001 PhotoDisc, Inc.; **93** Copyright © Julia Smith/Getty Images; **95** Digital Imagery copyright © 2001 PhotoDisc, Inc.

UNIT FIVE

97 *top* Copyright © Keren Su/FPG International/Getty Images; *second to bottom* Copyright © Lonnie Duka/Getty Images; *bottom* Copyright © Roger Tidman/Corbis; **98** Copyright © Keren Su/FPG International/Getty Images; **99** Copyright © Nicholas Devore III/Photographers/ Aspen/PictureQuest; **100, 104, 105** *bottom* Copyright © Keren Su/FPG International/Getty Images; **105** *top* Photo courtesy of Kimiko Sakai; **106** Photo by Sharon Hoogstraten; **106-107** Copyright © Digital Vision; **107, 109, 115** Photo by Sharon Hoogstraten; **115** Boondocks copyright © 2000 Aaron McGruder. Distributed by Universal Press Syndicate. Reprinted with permission. All rights reserved; **116** *background* Copyright © Richard Hamilton Smith/Corbis; *foreground* Copyright © Roger Tidman/Corbis; **117** Copyright © Martyn Vickery / Alamy; **122-123** *top* Copyright © Martyn Vickery / Alamy; *bottom* Copyright © Felicia Martinez/PhotoEdit/PictureQuest; **124** Copyright © Martyn Vickery / Alamy; **126** Copyright © Martyn Vickery / Alamy; **127** *background* Copyright © Richard Hamilton Smith/Corbis; *foreground* Copyright © Roger Tidman/Corbis; **128** Copyright © Lonnie Duka/Getty Images; **129** *top, bottom* Copyright © Lonnie Duka/Getty Images; **130** Digital Imagery copyright © 2001 PhotoDisc, Inc.; **133** Illustration by Jericho Hernandez; **134** Copyright © Sunset Avenue Productions/ Artville/PictureQuest; **140** Digital Imagery copyright © 2001 PhotoDisc, Inc.; **141** Copyright © Michael Llewellyn/Getty Images.

UNIT SIX

143, 144, 146, 149 Illustration copyright © 1989 by Barry Moser. Used by permission of HarperCollins Publishers; **152** *foreground* Copyright © Bruce Forster/Getty Images; *background* Copyright © Owen Franken/Getty Images; **153** Copyright © Owen Franken/Getty Images; **154-155** Digital Imagery copyright © 2001 PhotoDisc, Inc.; **155** Copyright © Owen Franken/Getty Images; **156** Illustration by Jericho Hernandez; **162, 163** Digital Imagery copyright © 2001 PhotoDisc, Inc.; **167** Copyright © Burke & Triolo/Artville/ PictureQuest; **171** Digital Imagery copyright © 2001 PhotoDisc, Inc.; **173** Copyright © Burke & Triolo/Artville/PictureQuest.

UNIT SEVEN

178-179 Digital Imagery copyright © 2001 PhotoDisc, Inc.; **179** Copyright © Robert Stark/Getty Images; **183** Copyright © Don Morley/Getty Images; **188** © AP Photo/David Longstreath; **189** Digital Imagery copyright © 2001 PhotoDisc, Inc.; **189** Copyright © Al Bello/Staff/Getty Images North

top, bottom Copyright © Peggy Fox/Getty Images; **196** Copyright © Bettmann/Corbis; **197** ® Officially licensed by The Negro Leagues Baseball Museum, Inc., Kansas City, MO; **200** Copyright © Joseph Schwartz Collection/Corbis; **205** Digital Imagery copyright © 2001 PhotoDisc, Inc.

UNIT EIGHT

207 Alabama Department of Archives and History, Montgomery, Alabama; **208** Copyright © John Lund/Getty Images; **209** Illustration by Jericho Hernandez; **212** Digital Imagery copyright © 2001 PhotoDisc, Inc.; **215** Copyright © Steve Taylor/Getty Images; **216** Digital Imagery copyright © 2001 PhotoDisc, Inc.; **217** Copyright © Chet Phillips/Photodisc Green/Getty Images; **218** Copyright © Bettmann/Corbis; **219** Alabama Department of Archives and History, Montgomery, Alabama; **221** ©AP Photo/Gene Herrick; **223** Digital Imagery copyright © 2001 PhotoDisc, Inc.; **227** Copyright © Bettmann/Corbis; **228** Copyright © Terry Whittaker, Frank Lane Picture Agency/Corbis; **235** Copyright © Stockbyte/PictureQuest.

UNIT NINE

241 *second from top* Digital Imagery copyright © 2001 PhotoDisc, Inc.; **241** *second from bottom* Copyright © Michael Wong/Getty Images; **242** Copyright © David Madison/Getty Images; **243** Digital Imagery copyright © 2001 PhotoDisc, Inc.; **245** Copyright © David Madison/Getty Images; **247** Digital Imagery copyright © 2001 PhotoDisc, Inc.; **248** Illustration by Jericho Hernandez; **249** Digital Imagery copyright © 2001 PhotoDisc, Inc.; **250** Copyright © Zigy Kaluzny/Getty Images; **251** Digital Imagery copyright © 2001 PhotoDisc, Inc.; **252** Copyright © Michael Wong/Getty Images; **253** Digital Imagery copyright © 2001 PhotoDisc, Inc.; **254** Digital Imagery copyright © 2001 PhotoDisc, Inc.; **254** Illustration by Jericho Hernandez.

UNIT TEN

259 detail of *Autumn Heritage.* Copyright © Jim Gray/www.jimgraygallery.com; **260** *background Woman Brushing Her Hair by Edgar Degas* Copyright © Archivo Iconografico, S.A./CORBIS; **260** Copyright © Corbis; **261, 263** Photo by Sharon Hoogstraten; **268** *background* Copyright © Sunset Avenue Productions/Artville/PictureQuest; **268** *foreground* Illustration Copyright © Bill Cigliano; **278** Digital Imagery copyright © 2001 PhotoDisc, Inc.; **280, 281, 283, 287** from *One Grain of Rice: A Mathematical Folktale* by Demi. Published by Scholastic Press, a division of Scholastic Inc. Copyright © 1997 by Demi. Reprinted by permission; **288** *Autumn Heritage* copyright © Jim Gray/www.jimgraygallery.com; **289, 296, 298, 299** Photo courtesy of Frontier Nursing Service, Inc.

UNIT ELEVEN

301 *center* Copyright © Gian Berto Vanni/Corbis; *bottom* Digital Imagery copyright © 2001 PhotoDisc, Inc.; **302, 305, 306, 309** Copyright © Bettmann/Corbis; **311** Copyright © Archivo Iconografico, S.A./Corbis; **312** Copyright © Araldo de Luca/Corbis; **313** Photofest; **314** Digital Imagery copyright © 2001 PhotoDisc, Inc.; **316** *background* Copyright © Gian Berto Vanni/Corbis; *foreground* Copyright © Roger Wood/Corbis; **320** Copyright © Hulton-Deutsch Collection/Corbis; **323** *top;* Digital Imagery copyright © 2001 PhotoDisc, Inc.; *bottom* Copyright © Roger Wood/Corbis; **324** Copyright © Todd Gipstein/Corbis; **328** *left* Illustration by Patrick Whelan; *right* By Permission of the British Library.

UNIT TWELVE

331 Courtesy of the New Jersey State Police Archives; **333** Copyright © Brandtner & Staedeli/Getty Images; **335** Digital Imagery copyright © 2001 PhotoDisc, Inc.; **344** Copyright © Brandtner & Staedeli/Getty Images ; **347, 348** *background* Digital Imagery copyright © 2001 PhotoDisc, Inc.;